VICTORIES AT SEA

COLIN M. BARRON

Other Books by Colin M. Barron

Running Your Own Private Residential or Nursing Home

The Craft of Public Speaking

Planes on Film: Ten Favourite Aviation Films

Dying Harder: Action Movies of the 1980s

Battles on Screen: World War II Action Movies

A Life by Misadventure

Practical Hypnotherapy

VICTORIES AT SEA

In Films and TV

Colin M. Barron

Victories at Sea: In Films and TV by Colin M. Barron.

First published in Great Britain in 2018 by Extremis Publishing Ltd.,
Suite 218, Castle House, 1 Baker Street, Stirling, FK8 1AL, United Kingdom.
www.extremispublishing.com

Extremis Publishing is a Private Limited Company registered in Scotland (SC509983) whose Registered Office is Suite 218, Castle House, 1 Baker Street, Stirling, FK8 1AL, United Kingdom.

Copyright © Colin M. Barron, 2018.

Colin M. Barron has asserted the moral right under the Copyright, Designs and Patents Act 1988 to be identified as the author of this work.

The views expressed in this work are solely those of the author, and do not necessarily reflect those of the publisher. The publisher hereby disclaims any responsibility for them.

This book is a work of non-fiction. Unless otherwise noted, the author and the publisher make no explicit guarantees as to the accuracy of the information included in this book. All hyperlinks indicated in the text were considered to be live and accurately detailed at time of publication.

This book may include references to organisations, feature films, television programmes, popular songs, musical bands, novels, reference books, and other creative works, the titles of which are trademarks and/or registered trademarks, and which are the intellectual properties of their respective copyright holders.

All rights reserved. No part of this publication may be reproduced, stored in a retrieval system, or transmitted, in any form or by any means, electronic, mechanical, photocopying, recording or otherwise, without the prior permission in writing of the publisher.

This book is sold subject to the condition that it shall not, by way of trade or otherwise, be lent, re-sold or hired out, or otherwise circulated without the publisher's prior consent in any form of binding or cover other than that in which it is published and without a similar condition including this condition being imposed on the subsequent purchaser.

A CIP catalogue record for this book is available from the British Library.

ISBN: 978-0-9955897-4-2

Typeset in Goudy Bookletter 1911, designed by The League of Moveable Type.

Printed and bound in Great Britain by IngramSpark, Chapter House, Pitfield, Kiln Farm, Milton Keynes, MK11 3LW, United Kingdom.

Cover artwork is Copyright ©2018 James Culver, all rights reserved.
Incidental interior images are Copyright © Pixabay.
Book design is Copyright © Thomas A. Christie.
Author image is Copyright © Thomas A. Christie.

The copyrights of third parties are reserved. All third party imagery is used under the provision of Fair Use for the purposes of commentary and criticism.

While every reasonable effort has been made to contact copyright holders and secure permission for all images reproduced in this work, we offer apologies for any instances in which this was not possible and for any inadvertent omissions.

CONTENTS

Acknowledgements .... Page 1

Introduction .... Page 3

1. Battleships: Warships in Action .... Page 9
2. Raids from the Sea .... Page 43
3. Operation Dynamo .... Page 67
4. Beneath the Waves .... Page 87
5. Underwater Sabotage .... Page 125
6. Carrier Warfare .... Page 141
7. Amphibious Operations .... Page 175
8. Cold War Operations .... Page 209
9. Action in the South Atlantic .... Page 239
10. Other Genres .... Page 265

References .... Page 299

Appendix I: List of aircraft used in *Midway* (1976) .... Page 305
Appendix II: List of aircraft used in *War and Remembrance* (1988) .... Page 307

Index .... Page 309

Illustrations .... Page 345

About the Author .... Page 371

VICTORIES AT SEA

In Films and TV

Colin M. Barron

ACKNOWLEDGEMENTS

The author wishes to thank Simon D. Beck and Bruce Orriss for the information about aircraft used in *War and Remembrance*.

Thanks are also due to Simon for the photo of one of the Douglas SBD Dauntlesses used in this production.

INTRODUCTION

THIS book may be considered the third in a trilogy about films covering different aspects of warfare. *Planes on Film* (2016) concerned my ten favourite aviation films, while *Battles on Screen* (2017) was largely about movies dealing with conflict on land. This new tome focuses on the war at sea, with an emphasis on the Second World War.

The book features some changes in structure, though. My previous two military books contained an in-depth analysis of ten films, plus some bonus chapters. In this new volume I have studied a much larger number of films, and have also included a few notable TV movies and TV series. I have also covered time periods other than the Second World War. So I have included discussion of TV series such as *War and Remembrance* (1988), which features a spectacular and realistic recreation of the Battle of Midway. I have also discussed a number of naval movies from the Cold War era, and even included a chapter on the 1982 Falklands War and the various TV movies and proposed films that the conflict has inspired.

As with *Planes on Film* and *Battles on Screen*, though, the book is largely concerned with the Second World War and the impact that naval operations had on the outcome. It is often said that the first major setback suffered by Hitler was the Battle of Britain, when the Luftwaffe failed to destroy the RAF. Yet the first indication that Hitler might lose the war came even earlier than this, in June 1940, when the Allies successfully evacuated 340,000 soldiers from the beaches at Dunkirk. Had the Germans successfully prevented this naval operation and captured or killed the surviving members of the British Expeditionary Force, then it is likely that Churchill would have been forced to accept a peace agreement on Hitler's terms. As things happened, these 340,000 soldiers formed the nucleus of the force which invaded France four years later.

The subsequent Battle of Britain in the summer of 1940 was clearly won by the RAF, but this would not have been possible without supplies of the latest 100 octane petrol from the USA, which was shipped across the Atlantic in tankers. This high-octane fuel (which was not available to the Germans) boosted the performance of the Rolls-Royce Merlin engines used in the RAF's Spitfires and Hurricanes, and was thus a decisive factor in the battle.

The failure of the Luftwaffe to secure air superiority over southern England was a key factor in Hitler's decision to cancel Operation Sealion, the invasion of Britain. Yet, as many writers and historians have pointed out in the last few decades, the Germans were simply not equipped to carry out an invasion of the south of England in 1940 as they had very few landing craft and were dependent on converted river barges and other makeshift craft. They also had very few surface ships. The German Navy (the *Kriegsmarine*) had 16 destroyers in March 1940. Half of them were sunk by the Royal Navy in the Norwegian campaign, leaving them with just eight vessels, which was insufficient to escort an invasion force.

By comparison, the Royal Navy had hundreds of ships which could have decimated an invasion fleet, including many capital ships with thick armour and heavy guns. At this point in the war (1940) the Luftwaffe had no modern torpedo bombers and also lacked bombs large enough to sink battleships. Even the wake of British capital ships would have been enough to sink many of the Germans' makeshift landing craft.

In addition, the Mark I Spitfires and Hurricane fighters the RAF possessed in 1940 had little capability against ships and troops on the ground. Their armament consisted of just eight 0.303 inch Browning machine guns with only 15 seconds firing time and at that point in the war they could not carry bombs or rockets, which would have been more effective weapons to use against a landing force. The Bristol Blenheim and Fairey Battle light bombers of RAF Bomber Command had proven ineffective in France as they were slow, lightly armed and appallingly vulnerable to fighter attack and anti-aircraft fire. Thus it was the threat posed by the Royal Navy, not the RAF, which really deterred Hitler from invading Britain in 1940.

In other theatres of war, naval actions proved decisive in ensuring an Allied victory. The three turning points of the war (all in 1942) were the battles of Midway, El Alamein, and Stalingrad. Midway was a decisive victory for the US Navy, while El Alamein was the beginning of the end for the Axis forces in North Africa. Though it was a land and air battle, it succeeded largely because the Allies had built up a huge superiority in men and equipment as a result of supply convoys. Another factor in Allied success in North Africa was the tiny island of Malta, which was used as a base for attacks by RAF aircraft and Royal Navy submarines on Axis ships supplying Rommel's troops in North Africa. Malta came close to surrender in mid-1942, and was only held after a massive Allied effort to resupply the island with food, fuel and weapons, with the Operation Pedestal convoy in August

1942 being the most heavily defended convoy of the war up to that point.

The success of Soviet forces at Stalingrad (and subsequent battles on the Eastern Front) was also helped by large quantities of supplies – including tanks, aircraft, guns, trucks and food – which were shipped to Russia in the Arctic convoys.

The subsequent invasion of Europe by Allied forces in June 1944 was only possible because the Allies were able to ship huge quantities of men and equipment across the Atlantic as a result of them winning the battle against Hitler's U-Boats.

In the Pacific theatre, naval actions were decisive in Allied victory. Though WW2 was finally ended by the dropping of two atomic bombs on Hiroshima and Nagasaki in August 1945, Japan was already on its knees by that time as most of its navy was lying at the bottom of the Pacific and US submarines had decimated its merchant fleet.

Thus, I would argue that the war at sea – which lasted from the first to the last day of WW2 and involved every theatre of war – was really the most decisive conflict which swung the war in favour of the Allies. Curiously, relatively few films and TV series have covered this aspect of WW2. For example, only a handful of films have been made about the Battle of the Atlantic, with *The Cruel Sea* (1952) being the best-known. Alistair MacLean's 1955 debut novel *HMS Ulysses* was based on his personal experiences as a torpedo tube operator aboard a cruiser involved in escorting Arctic convoys. Though the film rights were acquired not long after publication of the book, no movie was ever produced (though there has been a BBC radio adaptation). MacLean himself thought the reason was that it would be too difficult and expensive to obtain a suitable vessel for filming. This is probably also one reason why a feature film about the Falklands War has never been made, a subject which I will discuss in greater detail in a later chapter.

In summary, then, the war at sea is an aspect of WW2 which hasn't received as much attention from film-makers as one might expect, and I hope you find my own analysis of various naval battles and their depiction on the small and large screen to be of interest.

Colin Barron
April 2018

1
BATTLESHIPS: WARSHIPS IN ACTION

UNTIL the invention of nuclear bombs, battleships were the most destructive weapons known to man. With thick armour plating and guns of up to 18 inches in calibre, they could deliver a colossal weight of fire on any enemy ship or ground target and were hard to sink.

After the First World War there was great concern about the huge cost of these leviathans and the threat they posed to peace. In effect, battleships were the nuclear weapons of that era, and talks were held between the greatest maritime powers in an effort to reduce the number and size of these vessels. This particularly affected Britain, Japan and the USA. Germany was not involved in these talks as she was already constrained by the provisions of the Armistice agreed at Versailles in 1918 which prohibited her from building heavy warships. Germany had, in any case, scuttled much of her fleet at Scapa Flow in 1919 after WW1 had ended.

The talks culminated in the Washington Treaty of 1922, which reduced the total battleship and aircraft carrier tonnage which the USA, Britain, France, Japan and Italy could have, and also limited the size of new vessels to 35,000 tons. This had great implications for Britain, as it meant that only two new battleships – HMS *Rodney* and HMS *Nelson* – were built between the two wars. Both were designed according to the provisions of the Washington Treaty, and the main effect was that the aft half of the vessel was shortened drastically and the main armament of nine 16-inch guns was mounted in three triple turrets ahead of the bridge with the superstructure mounted aft of them. This gave the vessels an odd appearance as they resembled oil tankers, and led to them sometimes being referred to as the 'cherry tree' class as they had been 'cut down by Washington' (a reference to the well-known incident in which the young George Washington attacked his father's cherry tree with an axe).

The shortened hull also resulted in a lower speed, as it is a basic principle in naval architecture that a long, narrow ship goes faster than a short, wide one. In theory, the *Rodney* and *Nelson* could manage 23 knots flat out, but in practice they were pushed to reach even 20 knots. This meant that they couldn't keep up with the modern, fast battleships which appeared in WW2 and could attain about 30 knots, and the Royal Navy had to adjust its tactics accordingly. In addition, the peculiar layout of the main turrets – in which the middle one was higher than the forward and aft ones – meant that the rearmost turret could not fire directly forward. They were also expensive. In today's money they cost £1.6 billion each, which is comparable to the £1.95 billion cost of the Royal Navy's latest acquisitions, the new carriers HMS *Queen Elizabeth* and HMS *Prince of Wales*.

On the credit side, the *Nelson* and *Rodney* had a devastating armament of nine 16-inch guns each, more than any other Royal Navy warship before or since (HMS *Furious* at one point had a turret containing a single 18-inch gun, but this was removed in WW1 when she was converted to an aircraft carrier). The new *King George V* class of battleships which entered service from 1940 onwards only had 14-inch guns, while the last battleship ever built for the Royal Navy, HMS *Vanguard* – which was launched in 1944 – had 15-inch guns that had been originally fitted to HMS *Furious* and HMS *Glorious* and were removed when these vessels had been converted to aircraft carriers some decades earlier. (In the Royal Navy, there is a longstanding tradition that weapons removed from old ships which are being scrapped can be fitted to new ones. That is the reason that many of the ships in the 1982 Falklands Task Force were fitted with WW2-vintage 20mm Oerlikon and 40mm Bofors guns.)

Thus the *Nelson* and *Rodney* had unparalleled firepower which was only matched by the new American *Iowa*-class battleships, which first entered service with the US Navy in 1943 and also had nine 16-inch guns. During WW2, the Imperial Japanese Navy possessed two huge battleships – the *Yamato* and *Musashi* – with 18.1 inch guns, but these vessels achieved little during the war, largely because of shortages of fuel oil. Both of these vessels were sunk by American carrier-based aircraft in 1944.

When WW2 began on 3 September 1939, the Royal Navy was the largest in the world, but – although it had a lot of ships – many of them were old and obsolete. The most modern battleships in service were the *Nelson* and *Rodney*, but these were first launched in the mid-1920s. All the other battleships were of WW1 vintage, which meant that they were slow and lacked modern anti-aircraft armament.

The Royal Navy also possessed a few battlecruisers; vessels with the same armament as a battleship, but with thinner armour to give them a higher speed. Foremost amongst these was HMS *Hood* – regarded as one of the most handsome warships ever built – which had a number of design flaws which would lead to its demise during the battle of the Denmark Strait on 24 May 1941. In particular, it had very thin deck armour which made it especially vulnerable to plunging fire (the very thing which led to its loss) but, although there were plans to remedy this, this never happened before it encountered the *Bismarck* in May 1941.

One of the earliest naval engagements in WW2 took place on 13 December 1939 and became known as the 'Battle of the River Plate'. At that point in the war, Germany was using heavy cruisers with thick armour and 11-inch guns (known as 'pocket battleships') to attack merchant shipping in the South Atlantic and Indian Ocean. These vessels had a displacement of 10,000 tons and were designed around the limitations imposed by the Versailles Treaty, which forbade Germany to build ships larger than this – although the Germans later ignored the treaty altogether, building leviathans like the *Bismarck* and *Tirpitz*.

Under the command of Captain Hans Langsdorff, one of these 'pocket battleships' – the *Graf Spee* – attacked a number of unescorted Allied merchant vessels in the South Atlantic and the Indian Ocean. On 30 September she sank the *Clement*. On 5 October she captured the *Newton Beach* and then sank it two days later. The *Ashlea* was sunk on 7 October. The *Huntsman* was captured on 10 October and sunk on 17 October. Over the next few weeks the *Trevanion*, *Africa Shell*, *Doric Star*, *Tairoa* and *Streonshalh* all fell victim to *Graf Spee's* guns. Captain Langsdorff was a humane and honourable man who always rescued the crews of merchant vessels he was intending to sink.

The Royal Navy responded to these developments by sending a force of cruisers to hunt down and sink the German vessel and, on 13 December, British Naval Force G (based in the Falkland Islands) caught up with the *Graf Spee* near the mouth of the River Plate off the coast of Uruguay.

The Royal Navy's force consisted of three cruisers – HMS *Ajax* and HMS *Exeter* plus HMNZS *Achilles*. Though each of these vessels had smaller guns than the *Graf Spee*, they managed to inflict crucial damage on the German vessel's fuel system, forcing it to seek sanctuary in the neutral harbour of Montevideo in Uruguay for urgent repairs.

What happened next was a triumph of diplomacy and counter-intelligence. The British put pressure on Uruguay to force it to ask the *Graf Spee* to leave as soon as possible or else face internment. In addition, British Intelligence fostered the impression that a huge force of British vessels, including an aircraft carrier, had been assembled just over the horizon to sink the German cruiser. The ruse worked and, on 17 December, the *Graf Spee* weighed anchor, sailed down the River Plate and was then scuttled by its crew. Captain Langsdorff shot himself. At a stroke, one of Germany's greatest maritime assets had been neutralized without the British firing a shot.

These dramatic events in the South Atlantic became the subject of a film, *The Battle of the River Plate* (1956), which was the penultimate contribution between writer-producer-directors Emeric Pressburger and Michael Powell, whose previous films included *A Matter of Life and Death* (1945) which had starred David Niven. The source material for the screenplay was Powell's 1956 book, *Graf Spee*, and a second book – *I Was Graf Spee's Prisoner* – by Patrick Dove, who also acted as a technical advisor on the film.

Several real naval vessels were used in the production. HMS *Exeter* was played by HMS *Jamaica*, HMS *Ajax* was portrayed by *HMS Sheffield*, HMS *Cumberland* depicted herself, and the Indian Navy's INS *Delhi* was HMS *Achilles*. The part of the *Graf Spee* was played by the US Navy's heavy cruiser USS *Salem*.

Some filming was carried out in Montevideo itself while many scenes were shot in the Grand Harbour at Valetta in Malta. Shots set on ships' bridges were filmed at Pinewood Studios, but lacked the realism of those in the later production *Sink the Bismarck!* (1960).

The cast included Peter Finch as Captain Langsdorff, Anthony Quayle as Commodore Harwood aboard his flagship HMS *Ajax*, while John Gregson was Captain Bell of HMS *Exeter*. Patrick MacNee (who later starred as John Steed in the popular TV series *The Avengers*) was Lieutenant Commander Medley, and there were also appearances by Jack Watson, John Le Mesurier and Barry Foster. One of the captured merchant seamen was played by Anthony Newley, who in the 1950s had appeared in small roles in a large number of British war films. Newley later married Joan Collins and had a successful career as a singer and songwriter, even penning the title song to the James Bond movie *Goldfinger* (1964) in collaboration with Leslie Bricusse and John Barry. The film ends with the British fleet sailing into the sunset, something that looks splendid in colour and VistaVision, and Captain Langsdorff's tragic demise was not featured.

The greatest film about the Royal Navy in WW2, though, would probably be *Sink the Bismarck!* (1960), which described the maiden voyage of this vessel in May 1941, its encounter with HMS *Hood* and HMS *Prince of Wales* in what would later become known as the 'Battle of the Denmark Strait', its crippling by Fleet Air Arm Swordfish torpedo bombers, and its eventual sinking by Royal Navy warships.

The screenplay by Edmund H. North was based on the 1958 book *The Last Nine Days of the Bismarck* by C.S. Forester, a prolific British novelist who was responsible for the series of 12 *Hornblower* books published from 1937 onwards and which formed the basis of both the 1950 movie *Captain Horatio Hornblower*, starring Gregory Peck, and the ITV series *Hornblower* (1998-2003) with Welsh actor Ioan Gruffudd in the title role.

One problem facing the makers of *Sink the Bismarck!* was how to depict ships which no longer existed, as most of the ships which participated in the sea battles in the film had either been scrapped or sunk many years before. One exception was HMS *Victorious*, which was a brand-new aircraft carrier in May 1941 and remained in service until the late 1960s. In the film *Victorious* plays herself, plus HMS *Ark Royal* in some scenes. The producers were also fortunate that Britain's last battleship, HMS *Vanguard*, was still in service in 1959. Although she couldn't double for the *Bismarck* (or any of the British warships) in long shot as she looked so different from them, many deck scenes and shots of gun turrets (both interior and exterior) were filmed on this vessel. In fact, taking part in this film was probably the most important thing this ship did in her entire service career as, by the time she was launched, the era of the battleship was already over.

The filmmakers also shot some scenes aboard HMS *Belfast*, a *Town*-class cruiser which was still in active service in 1959 (and is now preserved as a tourist attraction near Tower Bridge, London by the Imperial War Museum). Director Lewis Gilbert also had access to some decommissioned Royal Navy ships which were laid up at Portsmouth awaiting scrapping, and scenes of fires and explosions were shot on those vessels.

Although as much footage as possible was shot aboard real warships, it was clear that extensive miniature work would be required to recreate various sea battles. At that time it was thought that the world's greatest experts in miniature work were to be found in the USA, rather than the UK, so the first person the producers contacted was L.B. Abbott (who later created the excellent model ship scenes in *Tora, Tora, Tora* in 1969). As things turned out, Abbott didn't take part in the production, and the job was given to Howard Lydecker, a Hollywood special effects expert. Along with his brother Theodore, he had created many excellent model shots in various Republic serials in the 1940s. The Lydeckers had invented a system for flying model aircraft along invisible wires which involved three filaments – two along which the model flew, and a third to pull it along. They also realised the importance of making miniatures as large as possible, and of using forced perspective and natural lighting to achieve realism. A few years later Howard Lydecker collaborated with L.B. Abbott on the miniature effects for the Irwin Allen TV series *Voyage to the Bottom of the Sea* and *Lost in Space*.

The miniatures themselves – consisting of several warships and a number of Fairey Swordfish biplane torpedo bombers – were built by John Stears of Shawcraft Models in Uxbridge. Stears had previously built the numerous miniature aircraft used in *Reach for the Sky* (1956). He also worked on an uncredited basis on a number of 1950s war films including *Carve Her Name with Pride* (1958), which was also directed by Lewis Gilbert. He later achieved fame for creating the models and special effects for the first five James Bond films and some of the special effects for the first *Star Wars* film in 1977.

Up to that point, the usual way of depicting moving ship models in British films involved using bottomless craft which ran on rails on the floor of the studio water tank, but the ships in *Sink the Bismarck!* were cast in fibreglass and actually floated, being pulled along by underwater cables. The huge outdoor water tank at Pinewood Studios – the size of a football pitch – was used, and incorporated an enormous painted backdrop. At the time this water tank was the largest in any UK film studio.

The film was shot in monochrome Cinemascope using an anamorphic lens, but as this was not ideal for model shots where a large depth of field was required, these sections were filmed in standard 35mm stock which was then cropped top and bottom to achieve the correct picture ratio. As a result the miniature shots had a somewhat lower resolution than the rest of the movie and were slightly grainy, something which actually added to the realism.

Edmund H. North's screenplay was fairly accurate, though in many cases the actual names of individuals were not mentioned. For example the character played by Laurence Naismith was described as the 'First Sea Lord' and never as 'Dudley Pound'. Similarly, the real names of the captains of these British vessels never appeared in the screenplay. At the time this was common practice in film scripts to avoid litigation, but it is hard to see why this was always necessary as many of the characters depicted were dead. Kenneth More played the part of Captain Shepherd, who is in charge of the hunt for the *Bismarck*. In reality this would have been Captain R.A.B. Edwards, chief of naval operations, but More's character was made fictional to allow the introduction of additional plot elements for dramatic effect, such as his grief over his wife's death, his fears for his son's safety (his son is an air gunner on a Fairey Swordfish) and his implied future romance with Wren officer Anne Davis (Dana Wynter).

The film features a fairly accurate recreation of the battle of the Denmark Strait when the *Bismarck* – in company with the heavy cruiser *Prince Eugen* – was attacked by HMS *Hood* and HMS *Prince of Wales*. HMS *Hood* carried the same main armament as the *Bismarck* in the form of eight 15-inch guns, but – being a battlecruiser rather than a battleship – she was quite thinly armoured. In addition, she was an old vessel which was built during the First World War. HMS *Prince of Wales* was a brand-new ship with good armour but only carried 14-inch guns, something which was a great concern to Winston Churchill who felt that new Royal Navy battleships should have 16-inch guns.

The battle of the Denmark Strait ended with the sinking of HMS *Hood*, while HMS *Prince of Wales* had to retreat with severe damage. However, HMS *Prince of Wales* had managed to hit *Bismarck* three times with her 14-inch guns, and it was this battle damage which led to the *Bismarck* eventually seeking sanctuary in Brest on the French coast, a tactical move which led to her destruction.

Attacks by Fleet Air Arm Fairey Swordfish from the carriers *Victorious* and *Ark Royal* caused further damage to the *Bismarck*. In particular, one torpedo hit *Bismarck's* rudders, causing them to jam and forcing the ship to circle. It was this crippling of the *Bismarck* by aircraft which enabled the Royal Navy to finish her off. One inaccuracy in the film, though, was that it was implied that it was the battleship HMS *King George V* that destroyed the German battleship.

In fact it was HMS *Rodney*, armed with 16-inch guns, which delivered the killer blows which sunk the vessel.

One of the lessons of this whole episode was that any battleship was vulnerable to air attack even if it had very thick armour and the latest defensive armament. This lesson was rammed home a few months later, on 10 December 1941, when the battleship HMS *Prince of Wales* and the battle-cruiser HMS *Repulse* were sunk by Japanese torpedo bombers off the coast of Malaya.

Luck was most definitely not on the side of the Royal Navy that day. Originally Force Z (as it was known) was to be accompanied by an aircraft carrier, HMS *Indomitable*, which could have provided fighter cover. Unfortunately, *Indomitable* had run aground in the Caribbean and was not available. Having said that, even if that mishap had not occurred the carrier would not have arrived in the Far East until late December. The WW1 vintage battlecruiser *Repulse* had not been modernised, and thus lacked effective anti-aircraft weapons. Despite this, she successfully evaded 15 torpedoes by careful manoeuvring but was eventually overwhelmed by the sheer scale of the air attack, which comprised nearly 100 aircraft made up of twin-engine Mitsubishi G4M 'Betty' and G3M 'Nell' bombers.

HMS *Prince of Wales* had modern anti-aircraft weapons, and for this reason her Captain didn't attempt to 'comb' the incoming torpedoes. Unfortunately, a lucky hit by an air-launched torpedo early in the battle knocked out her electric power, rendering most of her anti-aircraft weapons useless – particularly the eight-barrelled two-pounder pom-poms which equipped most British capital ships. Eventually, both vessels were hit by bombs and torpedoes and sank. During the battle, the *Repulse* shot down two aircraft and *Prince of Wales* downed one, while a fourth Japanese bomber crashed on returning to base.

Many lessons were learned from this tragedy, which contributed to the fall of Singapore two months later. One was that capital ships required fighter cover to survive – due to a misunderstanding, a flight of RAF Brewster Buffalo fighters of 453 Squadron – which could have defended the warships – arrived overhead after the battle was over. Also, multiple emergency generators had to be fitted in warships to prevent a single hit from causing a failure of anti-aircraft capability. Also, the two-pounder pom-pom AA gun needed to be phased out in favour of the 40mm Bofors, which had greater range and accuracy. The *Prince of Wales* had a single Bofors gun which had been fitted during a stopover in South Africa, and the subsequent Naval Board of Inquiry into her sinking concluded that this had contributed more to her air defence than her multiple pom-poms.

The pom-pom had another major snag, which was that it lacked a tracer round. There are two main advantages to a tracer round. Firstly, it lets the gunners know where their shells are going, allowing their aim to be corrected. Also, a fiery tracer round heading towards an enemy aircraft can scare the pilot, spoiling his aim. One reason that the Royal Navy was so keen to adopt the 'pom-pom' was that it could use up a large stock of two-pounder ammunition which was left over from WW1.

In reality, the Royal Navy didn't replace all its pom-pom guns with 40mm Bofors weapons until after WW2, but it is interesting that many of the lessons from the sinking of the *Prince of Wales* and *Repulse* had to be re-learned during the Falklands War of 1982 when Royal Navy ships were once again sent into battle without adequate air cover or effective anti-aircraft systems.

Another lesson of this tragic episode was that more 20mm Oerlikon guns needed to be fitted to ships. One of the advantages of the single Oerlikon mount was that it did not require a power supply, being a manually-operated weapon which could be fitted anywhere that there was space. Later in the war, both the Royal Navy and US Navy fitted large numbers of Oerlikons to both merchant vessels and warships.

By mid-1942, it was realised that the era of the battleship was over as the aircraft carrier was the new capital ship and whole fleets of enemy vessels could be destroyed by dive-bombers and torpedo bombers. Battleships were still of considerable value, though, in providing shore bombardment – and the larger the calibre of gun, the better. HMS *Rodney*, for example, provided crucial gunfire support during the Allied landings at Salerno in Italy in 1943 and also thwarted many German counter-attacks in the days following D-Day in 1944. Indeed, the bloodbath and near-failure at Omaha Beach could probably have been prevented if the US troops ashore had been supported by a battleship with large-calibre guns lying offshore all day.

Several battleships were in fact assigned to shore bombardment duties on D-Day, and for some weeks afterwards with the most modern vessel being HMS *Rodney*. It was considered that relatively elderly battleships were suitable for this purpose as the most modern, fast US battleships were needed in the Pacific War.

Although the aircraft carrier became the new capital ship in the Pacific War, the US Navy found that battleships still had an important role to play. As well as providing crucial naval gunfire support (NGS) which was a necessary prelude to any amphibious landing, the latest vessels had formidable anti-aircraft firepower, thanks to steadily increasing numbers of 40mm Bofors and 20mm Oerlikon guns. The Americans produced huge numbers of Bofors and Oerlikon guns under licence, and eventually developed twin and quad mounts for the Bofors, giving them awesome hitting power.

The anti-aircraft power of a modern battleship was demonstrated on 26 October 1942 at the Battle of Santa Cruz when the USS *South Dakota* – which had 68 x 40mm guns and 76 x 20mm weapons – shot down 26 Japanese aircraft in one day. Thereafter, the US Navy used its battleships as floating anti-aircraft platforms. Typically they would sail astern of carriers which were thus protected by their own guns, their supporting battleship's weaponry, and also those in surrounding cruisers and destroyers. Eventually this near-impenetrable anti-aircraft screen forced the Japanese to adopt *kamikaze* tactics.

Another factor which increased the effectiveness of the larger 5 inch anti-aircraft guns fitted to US ships was the development of so-called VT (variable timing) fuses, which are nowadays referred to as radar proximity fuses. These were effectively tiny radar sets fitted in the nose cones of anti-aircraft shells which made them explode when they came within 50 feet of an enemy aircraft, bringing down the target with blast and shrapnel. As the transistor had not yet been invented, the VT fuses used miniature vacuum tubes (valves in UK parlance) which had to be specially designed to survive the shock of being fired from a gun. VT fuses increased the effectiveness of anti-aircraft fire by a factor of four, and they were eventually made available for the Royal Navy's 4.7 inch AA guns.

Although battleships got much of the media attention during the war, it was the humble destroyer which did a lot of the work. One film which dealt with destroyer warfare was *In Which We Serve* (1942) – produced, written and directed by Noel Coward – which described the life of the destroyer HMS *Torrance* from its building and launching in 1938 to its eventual sinking off Crete in May 1941.

The film was based on the wartime exploits of the destroyer HMS *Kelly* – commanded by Lord Louis Mountbatten – which was sunk off Crete by German dive bombers on 23 May 1941. At that point in the war, Germany had captured Greece and followed this up with a combined parachute and sea attack on the island of Crete, which was known as Operation Mercury.

The British, Greek and New Zealand forces defending the island should really have won the battle, because they knew the enemy's plans through Ultra decrypts. In addition, the Royal Navy had a strong presence in the area. On the other hand, the Germans had 1,500 tactical aircraft in that theatre while the RAF had only a handful of planes that could be deployed to the island and lacked long-range fighters. In addition the Allied troops only had a few tanks and artillery pieces.

They also had the misfortune to be commanded by New Zealand General Bernard Freyburg, a WW1 hero who really had no concept of modern warfare and made a number of blunders – the worst of which was that he allowed the German paratroopers to capture a key hill overlooking Maleme airfield. Up to this point the Germans were on the point of losing the battle, as most of their paratroopers had been killed or captured and many of their Junkers Ju-52 transport planes had been destroyed by anti-aircraft and ground fire.

Once Maleme airfield had been taken, the Germans were able to fly in reinforcements in Junkers Ju-52/3m transport aircraft. Although many of these planes were destroyed by anti-aircraft, artillery and mortar fire, the Germans eventually won the battle of attrition and forced the Allies to conduct a Dunkirk-style evacuation.

Earlier in the battle, the Germans had attempted to send large forces by sea to Crete at night using a motley collection of captured barges, steamers and caiques – as the Germans lacked purpose-built landing craft – but this attempted invasion was thwarted by Royal Navy destroyers who sank most of the German fleet. The Luftwaffe could not operate at night, but they struck at Royal Navy vessels as they were retreating towards Alexandria as dawn broke. As a result, several British warships were sunk by dive-bombers, one of them being HMS *Kelly* (F01) commanded by Lord Louis Mountbatten, and the *Kelly*'s WW2 exploits were recounted in *In Which We Serve*.

For the film, HMS *Kelly* became HMS *Torrin*, and Lord Mountbatten was replaced by the character of Captain K.V. Kinross. At the time there was surprise at this casting, as Coward's public image was more of a 'lounge lizard' and certainly not one of an action hero.

This movie can be considered the first of a trilogy of wartime propaganda films. *In Which We Serve* was a tribute to the Royal Navy, *The Way Ahead* (1944) was about the Army, and *Journey to the Stars* (1945) was set on an RAF base. *Journey to the Stars* was the weakest of the three films, largely because it was scripted by Terence Rattigan who seemed to like writing about characters' emotional issues at the expense of action scenes. It felt like *Coronation Street* set on an RAF base.

In Which We Serve, though, had its fair share of action. After a brief prologue which depicts the launching of the fictional HMS *Torrin* in 1938, the action moves to the early morning of 23 May 1941 when the *Torrin* – working as part of a Royal Navy battlegroup – destroys a large German invasion fleet sailing for Crete using its six turret-mounted 4.7 inch guns, and torpedoes.

The German force is decimated but – when the *Torrin* steams for the safety of Alexandria as dawn breaks – a force of Junkers Ju-88 bombers attack the retreating British destroyers. This is one of the most realistic sequences in the film, and employed both a real Ju-88 – which had been captured by the RAF earlier in the war – and a large radio-controlled model.

The Junkers used in the film was a Ju-88 A-5 model, Werke Number 6073, which landed in error at RAF Chivenor in North Devon on 26 November 1941 after a navigational error caused by British electronic countermeasures. Repainted in British markings, it became part of the RAF's Enemy Aircraft Flight based at Duxford. For the film, Luftwaffe markings were re-applied and it was given the codes M2+MK.

Other shots of the Junkers Ju-88 attacking the *Torrin* were achieved using a large radio-controlled model of a Junkers Ju-88 constructed by Woodason Aircraft Models at Heston, which also built many aircraft recognition models used by RAF squadrons. This is believed to be the first time a radio-controlled model aircraft was used in a feature film. At that point, the usual method for 'flying' model aircraft was to suspend them on thin wires and film them in the studio or outdoors. This was the means by which all the miniature flying scenes in *633 Squadron* (1964) and *Mosquito Squadron* (1968) were achieved. About 100 radio-controlled aircraft were used in *Battle of Britain* (1969), though some scenes were still shot in the studio using miniature aircraft suspended on wires.

The radio-controlled Ju-88 sequences were shot on the backlot at Denham Studios, with a mock-up ship's mast in the foreground which could be moved to simulate the violent manoeuvres of the *Torrin*. The model Ju-88 even dropped a couple of bombs at one point, and this footage was intercut with shots of a real (but inert) 250lb bomb falling from an RAF Curtiss P-40B Tomahawk followed by a shot of a depth charge exploding in the water.

All shots of HMS *Torrin* at sea were filmed using the Australian destroyer HMAS *Nepal* (G25), and the scenes of the crew repelling the German air attack used real weapons firing live ammunition. Exploding flak bursts were simulated by fireworks known as 'maroons' (the same method was used in *633 Squadron* and the 1979 film *Hanover Street*).

These scenes show the main air defence weapons used by the Royal Navy in 1941, namely the 4.7 inch main guns, 20mm Oerlikon cannons, two-pounder 40mm four barrelled pom-poms, and quad 0.50 inch Vickers machine guns. Interestingly, the real HMS *Kelly* was never fitted with 20mm Oerlikons, which was rather ironic as Lord Louis Mountbatten had led a personal campaign since 1937 to have this weapon fitted in large numbers to Royal Navy vessels since he believed it be the best gun for shooting down dive-bombers. The 0.50 inch Vickers and the two-pounder pom-pom were considered to be inadequate anti-aircraft weapons and, as mentioned earlier, the ineffectiveness of the pom-pom (particularly the lack of a tracer round) was thought to be a factor in the loss of HMS *Prince of Wales*.

Despite the sailors' valiant efforts, the *Torrin* is hit by a bomb and sinks. Kinross and his surviving crew take to Carley floats (life-rafts) and, as they await rescue, the rest of the film is told as a series of flashbacks depicting different events in the history of the vessel – particularly the battles off Norway and the Dunkirk evacuation in 1940.

As well as being the star, Noel Coward was also the producer and screenwriter of the film. Additionally, he wrote the theme music. Coward was also nominally the director, though much of it was actually directed by David Lean who later found fame with Oscar-winning productions such as *Lawrence of Arabia* (1962), *Doctor Zhivago* (1965) and *Ryan's Daughter* (1971).

John Mills – who appeared in a large number of military roles from the forties through to the sixties – plays the courageous seaman 'Shorty' Blake, while a young Richard Attenborough (in his first film role) is an unnamed stoker who panics under fire but eventually dies a hero, thus establishing an 'Attenborough archetype' which featured in many of his films.

Albert Fosdike ('Shorty' Blake's brother-in-law) was originally to have been played by William Hartnell – who, in his pre-*Doctor Who* days, specialized in military roles – but he turned up late for his first day of shooting and was promptly sacked by Noel Coward. His part was then played by the film's assistant director, Michael Anderson (credited as 'Micky' Anderson), who later became famous for directing *The Dambusters* (1955), *The Yangtse Incident* (1957), and *Operation Crossbow* (1965).

Filming took place in 1942 at Plymouth naval dockyard and the naval station on the Isle of Portland. Smeaton's Tower on the seafront at Plymouth Hoe was used for the leave ashore scenes between 'Shorty' Blake and his wife Freda (Kay Walsh). Their baby was played by Mills' real-life daughter, future actress Juliet Mills.

The film ends with Kinross and his surviving crew being picked up and taken to Alexandria, where they are told that they will all be posted to different Royal Navy ships which have suffered casualties. Before they all leave to their new postings, Kinross addresses them and gives them an inspiring speech.

In Which We Serve proved to be the second most popular film at the British box office in 1943 and even did well in the USA, where it earned $1.8 million in rentals. In 1943 it was nominated for two Academy Awards for Best Picture and Best Original Screenplay (it lost to *Casablanca* and *Princess O'Rourke* respectively), but Coward was presented with an Academy Honorary Award for his outstanding production achievement.

Another class of vessel which performed a vital role in WW2 was the cruiser. With a displacement of 8,000 to 10,000 tons and main guns with a calibre of 6 to 11 inches, these vessels provided effective naval gunfire support and even attacked larger vessels with their guns and torpedoes.

One of the most vital missions carried out by a cruiser in WW2 was the delivery of atom bomb parts and enriched uranium by the cruiser USS *Indianapolis* to the Pacific island of Tinian in July 1945. These were used to assemble the very first atom bomb to be used in combat, *Little Boy*, which was dropped on the Japanese city of Hiroshima on 6 July 1945 by an American Boeing B-29 Superfortress bomber.

The *Portland*-class cruiser USS *Indianapolis* left San Francisco on 16 July and arrived safely at Tinian on 26 July, where it landed its cargo. Two days later it departed Tinian heading for Guam, but at 0.15 hrs on 30 July it was torpedoed by the Japanese submarine *I-58* – captained by Commander Mochitsura Hashimoto – using two Type 95 torpedoes which struck the starboard side of the cruiser forward and amidships. Within minutes the cruiser had sunk, with 300 of the 1,196 crew perishing immediately. The remainder of the ship's complement found themselves in the water and discovered there were insufficient life-rafts and lifejackets to go round. A distress call had been sent by the radio operator immediately prior to the sinking, but was ignored by three different listening stations for various reasons – one officer was drunk, one was asleep, and another thought it was a Japanese trap.

For the next five days many of the survivors died from salt poisoning, sunstroke and shark attacks. Eventually they were spotted by a Lockheed PV-1 Harpoon patrol aircraft which initiated a rescue mission but by the time US Navy ships and flying boats arrived, only 317 out of nearly 900 sailors who had survived the sinking were still alive.

The commander of the USS *Indianapolis*, Captain Charles B. McVay, was subsequently court-martialled for hazarding his ship. The main charge brought against him was that he had not zig-zagged the ship, which would have made it much more difficult for a submarine to carry out a successful torpedo attack. However, the commander of the Japanese submarine *I-58*, Commander Mochitsura Hashimoto, was summoned as a witness for the defence and testified that in this particular case, zig-zagging would have made no difference. Eventually, the court-martial concluded that Captain McVay had not done anything wrong, and he was subsequently promoted to Rear Admiral.

However, the relatives of the deceased sailors (and the media) thought differently, and continued to blame McVay for the tragedy. In 1968 – at the age of 70 – he committed suicide. After reviewing all the evidence, President Bill Clinton exonerated Captain McVay of all charges on 30 October 2000.

In all probability, it was the US Navy high command which was really to blame for the tragedy. A cruiser like the USS *Indianapolis* was well-protected against air and surface vessel attack, but had virtually no anti-submarine capability as it lacked sonar and depth charges. The only way the *Indianapolis* could have destroyed the *I-58* would have been if it had caught it on the surface and hit it with its guns or rammed it. Bearing in mind the importance of the mission – and the huge size of the US Navy in 1945 – it is astonishing that no anti-submarine destroyer escort was provided for both legs of the journey. Had the Japanese sank the *Indianapolis* before it had delivered its cargo then the Second World War might have lasted a few more months.

The fate of the survivors of the *Indianapolis* was mentioned in one scene in *Jaws* (1975), when shark hunter Quint (Robert Shaw) described how many of them were eaten by Great White Sharks. Two films have been made about this sad episode in US Navy history, namely *Mission of the Shark: The Saga of the USS Indianapolis* (1991) with Stacy Keach as Captain McVay, and the more recent movie *USS Indianapolis: Men of Courage* (2016), this time starring Nicolas Cage as the ill-fated commanding officer.

As there were no WW2 cruisers or Japanese submarines in working order in 1991 or 2016, both productions made use of the preserved *South Dakota*-class battleship USS *Alabama* and the submarine USS *Drum*, which lies alongside the *Alabama*, with both being museum ships which are open to the public. Both vessels have been used in a number of film and TV productions including *War and Remembrance* (1988) and *Under Siege* (1992).

Personally I prefer the earlier movie, which has a more realistic feel, as the more recent production relies heavily on rather unconvincing CGI. *Mission of the Shark* also uses some cruiser footage from *War and Remembrance* plus some scenes of the B-29 *Enola Gay* from the TV movie *Enola Gay: The Men and the Mission* (1980) which starred Patrick Duffy as Lieutenant Colonel Paul Tibbs.

One inaccuracy in the earlier movie is that the flying boat which rescues the US Navy sailors is a Grumman HU-16 Albatross, a type which did not enter service till 1949. The more recent production used a genuine Consolidated PBY-6A Catalina for this scene, but unfortunately this rare and valuable aircraft was accidentally destroyed during filming. What happened was that the aircraft suffered some damage to the underside of the nose on 29 June 2015 while executing a sea landing at Orange Beach, California, allowing water ingress into the front fuselage which caused the flying boat's nose to sink into the ocean. Filming of crucial scenes continued and, if you look at the finished film, you can see that the Catalina has a distinctly 'nose down' look as the front end is partially sunken.

After filming was completed, an attempt was made to salvage the aircraft using a floating crane, but this resulted in the aircraft breaking up. It was subsequently scrapped, causing some negative reactions from the historic aviation community who were aghast that such a priceless and irreplaceable airframe should be lost while making a movie. In the past, real aircraft have been wrecked during the making of films. For example, three Mosquitoes were destroyed during the making of *633 Squadron* in 1963, and five Catalinas went up in flames during the filming of *Tora, Tora, Tora* in 1969. But nowadays historic airframes are regarded as priceless artefacts which should be kept out of harm's way.

The film premiered in the Philippines on 24 June 2016, but received generally negative reviews from critics with many commenting on the CGI special effects which they felt were 'garish and unconvincing'. Rather curiously, in the 'Making Of' documentary in the Special Features section of the DVD release it was implied that this was the first film to be made about this incident. No mention was made of the previous film made 26 years earlier, or the numerous documentaries that have been made about the event. This is reminiscent of the claims made by the makers of *Anthropoid* (2015) – about the assassination of SS Officer Reinhard Heydrich in Prague in 1942 – who suggested that their film was the first movie about a little-known incident when in fact several films, including the superior *Operation Daybreak* (1975), had already been made about this historical event.

Small patrol craft also played a key role in various naval actions in WW2, and many were produced by shipyards in Britain, Germany, the USA and Italy. The most powerful armament carried by these vessels was torpedoes with either two or four being carried, giving them the potential to punch above their weight.

Britain produced two main classes of attack boats, the Motor Torpedo Boat (MTB) and the Motor Gun Boat (MGB). Compared with large warships, they could be built quickly and cheaply, required only small crews, and possessed tremendous performance.

The Germans built vessels called S-Boats (known to the Allies as 'E-Boats') with the 'S' standing for 'schnell' which is German for 'rapid' or 'speedy'. These were larger than British

MTBs and were also well-armed with a typical armament being two torpedo tubes (with four torpedoes), three twin 20mm cannon, a 37mm gun and two 7.9 mm machine guns, plus a rack of depth charges at the rear of the vessel. The American equivalent was the PT (Patrol Torpedo) Boat made by Elco, which was armed with torpedo tubes and four fifty-calibre Browning M2 machine guns. Later vessels carried even heavier weapons such as a 40mm Bofors gun or a 37mm cannon.

One excellent film which depicted PT Boat operations in the Pacific Theatre in WW2 was *They Were Expendable* (1945) which was directed by John Ford and starred John Wayne, Robert Montgomery and Donna Reed. Despite his macho image, Wayne never served in the armed forces in WW2 but made a series of patriotic films to boost morale. Over his long career, which lasted well into the seventies, Wayne worked with director John Ford on many occasions with one of their best-known collaborations being the original version of *Stagecoach* (1939).

Ford was well-known as a director of Westerns, but during the war years he helmed a number of patriotic war movies and documentaries including the 18 minute colour documentary *The Battle of Midway* (1942) which provided considerable footage for *Midway* (1976). The voiceover for the 1942 documentary was by actor Henry Fonda, who played Admiral Nimitz in the 1976 film.

They Were Expendable was based on a book by William L. White and told the story of Motor Torpedo Boat Squadron Three, a PT boat detachment defending the Philippines against attack in late 1941 and early 1942. Both the book and the film were fictional, though based on real events. Robert Montgomery's character, John Brickley, was based on

Medal of Honor recipient John D. Bulkeley, while Rusty Ryan (John Wayne) was inspired by the real-life Robert Kelly.

The film begins in early December 1941, when a squadron of PT Boats under the command of Lieutenant John 'Brick' Brickley is sent to the Philippines to help defend the islands against a likely Japanese invasion. Instead of being welcomed by local military commanders, they are subjected to ridicule. Lieutenant 'Rusty' Ryan is perturbed by the attitude of his superior naval officers, who are apparently unconvinced that the plywood-hulled PT Boats could be viable naval craft. Ryan is so disturbed by this that he drafts a request to be transferred to destroyers. But news then comes through that the Japanese have attacked Pearl Harbour, making such a transfer impossible.

Initially the PT Boats are used as messenger vessels, but after a surprise air attack by the Japanese, they are used in combat. Eventually local commanders recognise their effectiveness and use them for attacking large Japanese warships, including a cruiser. Brick misses out on the successful attack on the cruiser as he is admitted to hospital with blood poisoning. While he is thus incapacitated, he begins a romance with Army nurse Sandy Davyss (Donna Reed).

Despite the efforts of the crews of the PT Boats, the Philippines are eventually overrun by the numerically superior Japanese. American garrisons remain on the islands of Bataan and Corregidor, but it is only a matter of time before they are defeated and one of the few remaining PT Boats is used to evacuate General Douglas MacArthur, who vows to return to liberate the islands in the future. Soon all the PT Boats have been lost and the crews are forced to fight as infantry.

Before the islands fall, Brickley and Ryan are airlifted back to the USA as they are needed to train new PT Boat crews.

The film was made with the cooperation of the US Navy and was filmed on location in the Florida Keys and Key Biscayne. Real 80-foot Elco PT boats were used in the production, with 1941/42 hull numbers applied. US aircraft from the naval air stations at Miami, Fort Lauderdale and Key West were painted to represent Japanese warplanes.

Director John Ford fell off some scaffolding and broke a leg during the shooting and so some scenes were directed by Robert Montgomery, who later became a director himself. The film won two Academy Award nominations for Best Sound Recording and Best Visual Effects.

The Ship That Died of Shame (1955) was a black-and-white Ealing Studios film directed by Basil Dearden which starred Richard Attenborough, George Baker and Bill Owen. The screenplay was by Basil Dearden, Michael Relph and John Whiting, and was based on a short story by Nicholas Monsarrat who had written the novel *The Cruel Sea*, which was adapted for the screen in 1952.

The film begins during the early years of WW2 as the Motor Gun Boat (MGB) 1087 and its crew takes part in a series of daring raids on the French coast. Returning from one of these missions, the 1087 is approaching its home port when its crew spot a lone German Junkers Ju-88 returning from a bombing mission against the town. Smoke can be seen on the horizon.

The crew of the 1087 go to action stations and pepper the German bomber with shells from their machine guns and their single 2-pounder pom-pom. The Ju-88 disappears over the horizon, trailing smoke from one engine. Seaman George Hoskins (Richard Attenborough) wants to claim the bomber as a 'kill' as he is sure it won't get back to France, but his Captain – Bill Randall (George Baker) – insists they can only claim the aircraft as 'damaged'.

After the boat docks at the naval base, Captain Randall discovers that his wife Helen (Virginia McKenna) has been killed in the bombing raid. The Ju-88 was attempting to bomb the naval dockyard but hit the Randalls' home instead. Randall is left in a state of shock, and this great trauma affects him for the rest of his life. The 1087 takes part in many dangerous missions for the rest of the war, but she and her crew survive.

In 1948, after the war is over, Hoskins persuades Randall to buy his old boat which has now been stripped of its weaponry and can be used for pleasure cruises. Soon, though, the boat is being used for smuggling. Initially this is for relatively harmless products such as wine, but eventually the 1087 is being used to transport weapons and fake currency.

The normally-reliable 1087 keeps breaking down, almost as though it is ashamed of its current occupation. Then one day the crew are asked to help a wanted person, Raines (John Chandon), escape from Britain. It is implied that he is a wanted murderer and a paedophile. The 1087 really has become 'The Ship That Died of Shame'. The mission ends in disaster with the 1087 wrecked on some rocks, and the film ends with a shot of the 1087 in its prime in its war years, proud of what it is doing. In the US the film was re-titled *PT Raiders*. Although it was not a financial success, it has become a 'cult classic'.

PT-109 (1963) was a biographical film about the wartime exploits of the then-current US President John F. Kennedy, who commanded the torpedo boat PT-109 during the Pacific War. The film was based on the book *PT-109: John F.*

Kennedy in World War II by Robert J. Donovan, which was adapted for the screen by Robert L. Breen.

At the time the Kennedy family was very keen that the latest President should be presented in a positive light and one driving force behind the making of the film was his father, the former wartime US Ambassador to Britain, Joseph Kennedy. The elder Kennedy was by all accounts a nasty piece of work, and no friend of Britain during WW2. He was sympathetic to the Nazi regime and once advised Roosevelt not to support Britain as it was a lost cause. He had also been a former Hollywood producer and head of the RKO Studios at one point, and he used his influence to negotiate the film rights.

Many actors were considered for the role of the young Lieutenant John Kennedy including Warren Beatty, Jeffrey Hunter, Edd Byrnes, Peter Brown and Chad Everett. In the end the role went to Cliff Robertson, who was 39 at the time the film was made, but was portraying a 27-year-old. This follows the common practice in British and American war movies of casting relatively old actors in leading roles. Examples might include Gregory Peck, David Niven, Anthony Quinn and Anthony Quayle in *The Guns of Navarone* (1962), Richard Todd in *The Dambusters* (1955) and *The Longest Day* (1962), and Kenneth More in *Reach for the Sky* (1956). In some scenes in the latter movie a 44-year-old More is playing a 19-year-old. Robertson's casting in *PT-109* was personally approved by John F. Kennedy, and the following year Robertson played probably his most famous role, that of Wing Commander Roy Grant in *633 Squadron*.

Kennedy apparently also had a say in the choice of director, as he vetoed Raoul Walsh after seeing his previous film *Marines Let's Go* (1961). The next candidate to direct the film was Lewis Milestone, who had helmed *All Quiet on the*

Western Front (1930), but he left the project and was replaced by Leslie Martinson – a TV director with little film experience.

The exteriors were filmed at Little Palm Island, which is now a resort in the Florida Keys. Water and Electricity supplies were brought to the island for the production, allowing the construction of the holiday resort some years later.

No wartime PT boats existed in working order at the time the film was made as they had all been destroyed at the end of the war, so several WW2-vintage USAAF 85-foot crash boats were modified to resemble the 80-foot Elco PT boats used in the conflict. Japanese Zeroes were represented by North American AT-6 Texan trainers. Other vessels supplied by the US Navy for use in the film included a Landing Ship Tank (LST), the destroyer USS *Saufley*, plus several small landing craft and whalers from the US Navy station at Key West.

The film opens in August 1942 at a time when American forces are fighting in Guadalcanal. US Navy Lieutenant John F. Kennedy is given command of *PT-109*, a worn-out torpedo boat which is badly in need of repair and refurbishment. His Commander, C.R. Ritchie (James Gregory), is impressed by the young Lieutenant's keenness to get the *PT-109* into running order again.

Kennedy's crew includes Ensign Leonard G. Thom (Ty Hardin) and sailors 'Bucky' Harris (Robert Blake) and Edmund Drewitch (Norman Fell). One of the boat's missions involves rescuing some Marines who have engaged in a raid on Choiseul. After carrying out the evacuation, Kennedy's boat runs out of fuel and is rescued in the nick of time by another PT boat which gives them a tow.

Eventually Kennedy's luck runs out, and one night in August 1943 his boat is sliced in two by a Japanese destroyer. Two members of the crew – Marney (Joseph Gallison) and Kirksey (Sammy Reese) – are killed, but the other eleven survive and Kennedy and the others are forced to swim to a nearby island. The crew are marooned on the island for several days, and Kennedy swims out into the channel every night hoping to attract the attention of a passing PT boat. Kennedy's efforts are unsuccessful, but eventually he hits on the idea of carving a message on a coconut and giving it to two natives who take it to the nearest Allied coast-watchers. Eventually the message gets through; Kennedy and his crew are rescued, and he is given command of another patrol boat, the gunboat *PT-59*.

The film received lukewarm reviews, and even President Kennedy had his doubts about it. One of his main gripes was that it was at overlong at two hours and twenty minutes. It made $3.5 million at US box-office against a budget of $4 million, and the American plastic kit manufacturer Revell made a model of the PT-109 to tie in with the movie. It is of great historical interest, though, as it is the only Panavision colour film about PT boat operations in the Pacific Theatre.

Another movie about torpedo boat operations – this time British Motor Torpedo Boats (MTBs) – was *Hell Boats* (1970) directed by Paul Wendkos, one of six war films made by Oakmont Productions, a low-budget subsidiary of Mirisch Films, which was shot entirely in Malta in 1968.

Oakmont Productions' war movies usually featured an American in the cast to make the films more appealing to audiences in the United States, and in the case of *Hell Boats* this was James Franciscus who played the role of Lieutenant

Commander Jeffords, an American serving with the Royal Navy.

Jeffords is given the task of commanding a flotilla of MTBs for a secret mission and is allowed to take his friend, the Israeli/Palestinian Chief Petty Officer Yacov (Reuven Bar Yotam) with him. After obtaining spare parts from several scrapped vessels, Jeffords is able to put together a flotilla of three boats for a secret mission: an attack on a former Italian submarine base at Augusta, Sicily which is now being used to store deadly *Fritz-X* radio-controlled glide bombs, guided weapons which have proved effective against Allied shipping. The bombs are stored deep inside a mountain, making an air attack impossible.

Jeffords opts for an initial reconnaissance of the target, assisted by members of the Sicilian Resistance. The mission is successful, although it results in the deaths of the Resistance members.

The Lieutenant Commander then concocts a plan to steal a German E-Boat which can be used as a 'Trojan Horse' to infiltrate the enemy base. His plan involves sending a fake radio message which states that General Alexander's aircraft has crashed in the Mediterranean. When the Germans send a boat to investigate, Jeffords and his crew (who are floating in a rubber dinghy posing as German aircrew) seize the vessel and use it to infiltrate the enemy base. This part of the plot was based on Operation Ruthless, a scheme proposed by Ian Fleming when he was a wartime Intelligence Officer with the RNVR, in which a group of commandos posing as downed aircrew would seize a German ship in order to capture an Enigma machine and codebooks. The plan was never executed.

The lead, James Franciscus, was never a major Hollywood star, but had appeared in a large number of film and TV productions. He was the cowboy Tuck Kirby in *The Valley of Gwangi* (1969), the astronaut Clayton Stone in *Marooned* (1969), and Brent in *Beneath the Planet of the Apes* (1970). He also provided the voice of Jonathan Livingston Seagull in the 1973 film of the same name. That movie made such an impression on actress Barbara Hershey that she changed her name to Barbara Seagull, although she later changed it back to her original surname.

The cast also included Ronald Allen as Commander Ashurst. Allen was famous for appearing in two *Doctor Who* stories, *The Dominators* (1968) and *The Ambassadors of Death* (1970). He later had a long-running role in the ITV soap *Crossroads* (1964-88) and a year before his death in 1991 he married actress Sue Lloyd, who is best-known for playing Harry Palmer's girlfriend Jean Courtney in *The Ipcress File* (1966) and John Mannering's assistant Cordelia in the ITC series *The Baron* (1966), which was very similar to *The Saint* (1961-69) which starred Roger Moore.

Another notable cast member was the Welsh actor Philip Madoc (who played a German E-Boat captain), who holds the distinction of appearing in four different *Doctor Who* stories – *The Krotons* (1967-68), *The War Games* (1969), *The Brain of Morbius* (1975) and *The Power of Kroll* (1979), as well as the Peter Cushing feature film *Daleks: Invasion Earth 2150AD* (1966). Madoc spoke fluent German, and appeared as a German policeman in *Operation Crossbow* (1965) and as a U-Boat Captain in the *Dad's Army* episode *The Deadly Attachment* (1973).

John G. Heller, who had played German officers in a huge number of war movies including *Where Eagles Dare*

(1968) and *Kelly's Heroes* (1970), portrayed Rheinhardt, while David Savile – who played military roles in *Doctor Who* serial *The War Games* (1969), *The Man Who Hunted Himself* (1972), *Warship* (1973), and the *Doctor Who* twentieth anniversary special *The Five Doctors* (1983) – was Lieutenant Wallace R.N. Elizabeth Shepherd, who played Alison Ashurst, was the original contender for the role of Emma Peel in *The Avengers* (1968-69), and actually filmed some scenes before being replaced by Diana Rigg.

Many of the film crew had worked on previous Oakmont productions. Cinematographer Paul Beeson had been the Director of Photography on *Mosquito Squadron*, while composer Frank Cordell had done the music for that film. Producer Lewis J. Rachmil had worked on both *Mosquito Squadron* and the film which inspired it, *633 Squadron*.

The entire film was shot on the island of Malta. Many scenes were shot in the Grand Harbour at Valetta. Most of the training scenes were filmed at Manoel Island and Fort Manoel, while the interiors were lensed at Malta Film Facilities Limited facilities at Fort St Rocco in Kalkara. This location had also been used to shoot all of the miniature sequences for *Mosquito Squadron* (1968).

By the 1960s, motor torpedo boats were being phased out in favour of craft armed with anti-ship missiles. These have proved very popular with the navies of small nations, as they offer a good punch for their size. Armed patrol craft are also still in widespread use, and crop up in more modern films such as *Rambo: First Blood Part II* (1985), so this class of vessel may appear again in future Hollywood blockbusters.

2
RAIDS FROM THE SEA

DURING WW2, Britain launched a series of commando raids from the sea as a way of hitting back at the Germans. Not long after the evacuation of Dunkirk (Operation Dynamo), which concluded in early June 1940, Prime Minister Winston Churchill called for the creation of a suitable raiding force and proclaimed that 'they must be prepared with specially-trained troops of the hunter class who can develop a reign of terror down the enemy coast'.

The force – which became known as the Commandos – came under the operational control of the Combined Operations Headquarters. The man initially selected as the commander was Admiral Sir Roger Keyes, a veteran of the Gallipoli Campaign and the Zeebrugge Raid during the First World War. A call went out for recruits to join the new force and, by the autumn of 1940, 2,000 men had volunteered for active service with this unit.

The first mission carried out by this new force was Operation Collar, on 24-25 June 1940, against German installations in the Pas-De-Calais area. Having no suitable ships of their own, the fledgling commando force had to use four RAF Air Sea Rescue boats based at Dover, Ramsgate and Newhaven. However, these were not really suitable for the task as they were lightly armed and lacked suitable compasses and navigation equipment.

Operation Collar achieved little, other than killing two German sentries. But important lessons had been learned, particularly the need for proper training, weapons and equipment, and the next major commando raid – Operation Claymore, against German facilities in the Lofoten Islands, off Norway – took place on 4 March 1941. The Lofoten Islands were an important centre for the production of fish oil and glycerine, which were both used in the manufacture of explosives.

This time the British sent a large enough force to overwhelm the German garrison, consisting of men from No 3 and 4 Commando, a Royal Engineers Section, and 52 men from the Royal Norwegian Navy. Two new troop transports were used, HMS *Queen Emma* and HMS *Princess Beatrix*, while five destroyers – HMS *Somali*, HMS *Bedouin*, HMS *Tartar*, HMS *Eskimo* and HMS *Legion* – provided naval gunfire support.

The mission was a complete success. Ten merchant ships were sunk, and 228 of the enemy taken prisoner. 3,600 tons of fish oil were destroyed and 314 Norwegians taken back to Britain, where they joined the Free Norwegian Forces. The British suffered no casualties other than one officer who injured himself with his revolver.

Another successful raid during the early war years was Operation Biting (aka The Bruneval Raid) on the night of 27-28 February 1942, when a force of 120 paratroopers and commandos attacked a German radar station at Bruneval on the French coast north of Le Havre, and returned to Britain with many key components from a German *Wurzburg* radar station. At that point in the war, British night bombers were suffering severe losses as a result of new German radar systems. One of the Government's scientific advisors, Dr R.V. Jones, studied aerial reconnaissance photos and deduced that the Germans were using two very different types of radar. *Freya* was a long-range system which employed a large mattress-like antenna, while *Wurzburg* was a short-range, precise technology using a dish aerial.

Jones realised that effective countermeasures to the new *Wurzburg* radars could only be devised if a complete set (or at least its more important components) could be captured and brought back to the UK for study.

The installation at Bruneval, which was close to a cliff edge, seemed to offer the best target for such a raid, and a request for such a mission – eventually called Operation Biting – was passed on to Lord Louis Mountbatten, the new commander of Combined Operations. The original plan was for an assault from the sea, but Mountbatten ruled this out as the area was too heavily defended and the Germans could theoretically destroy the *Wurzburg* before it could be captured. An alternative plan was therefore devised in which a force of paratroopers would land at night near the objective, capture the equipment, and then be evacuated by Royal Navy landing craft. On 8 January 1942, Mountbatten contacted Major-General Frederick 'Boy' Browning to ask if the 1st Airborne Division could carry out the job. Browning was very enthusiastic about the operation, as it would raise morale and demonstrate the value of airborne troops. Browning later became well-known for his role in the planning of Operation Market Garden in September 1944, and was portrayed in the film *A Bridge Too Far* (1977) by Dirk Bogarde.

Several weeks of planning and rehearsals followed, including practice evacuations by landing craft on Loch Fyne, and a detailed model of the radar site at Bruneval was constructed. Eventually the decision was made to hold the operation on the night of 27-28 February 1942, when there would be a full moon and a rising tide, which would be needed to operate landing craft.

On the evening of 27 February 1942, a force of Armstrong Whitworth Whitley bombers of 51 Squadron, carrying paratroopers, set off from England led by Wing Commander Percy Charles 'Pick' Pickard. The Whitley was a twin-engine medium bomber used in the early stages of WW2 by the RAF. Although obsolete as a conventional bomber by 1942, it was still being used as a paratrooper-dropping aircraft and maritime patrol plane.

Pickard was one of the outstanding bomber pilots of WW2, and was already familiar to the British public as he had appeared as the pilot of a Wellington bomber in the propaganda film *Target for Tonight* (1941). He was later killed during Operation Jericho, a raid by RAF Mosquitos on Amiens jail on 18 February 1942 which involved bombing the prison walls to allow French Resistance members to escape. This raid was one of the inspirations for the plot of the film *Mosquito Squadron* (1968), which includes a scene in which a *Highball* bouncing bomb is used to breach the main wall of the fictional Chateau Du Charlon, to enable RAF POWs to flee.

After landing near the radar site at Bruneval, the force of British paratroopers led by Colonel John Frost (who was later to achieve fame for his actions at Arnhem in 1944 and was portrayed by Anthony Hopkins in the 1977 film *A Bridge Too Far*) assaulted both the radar station and the nearby chateau, where most of the garrison were accommodated. As Frost's men held off the Germans, an RAF technician dismantled much of the radar equipment which was then transported to the beach on a trolley. Several landing craft then arrived to take Frost's men out to waiting Motor Gun Boats (MGBs), which took the raiding force back to England.

The raid was an almost total success. Two of Frost's men were killed, six were wounded and another six were captured. German losses were five dead, two wounded, two captured and three missing. More importantly, the vital parts of the *Wurzburg* radar system were now in British hands, enabling effective countermeasures to be developed – particularly *Window*, strips of tinfoil cut to the same wavelength as the radar it was jamming. Further intelligence was also gleaned from interrogation of the two captured prisoners.

No feature film has ever been made of the Bruneval raid, but it is alluded to in the film *The Red Beret*, aka *Paratrooper* (1953). *The Red Beret* is of great interest to film historians as it was the first production by Warwick Films, which was established by Albert R. Broccoli and Irving Allen. Broccoli later created Eon Productions with a new business partner, Harry Saltzman, and the two were responsible for the James Bond series of films which are still being made to this day. Many of the production crew on *The Red Beret* went on to work on the early Bond films. Director Terence Young helmed the first Bond film *Dr No* (1962) plus *From Russia with Love* (1963) and *Thunderball* (1965), and had a great influence on the way Sean Connery played Bond – particularly his penchant for Savile Row suits.

The Red Beret was also the start of Bob Simmons' long career as a stunt arranger. Simmons arranged the action sequences in most of the Bond films made between 1962 and

1985. Other notable credits included *The Wild Geese* (1978) and *Who Dares Wins* (1982). Screenwriter Richard Maibaum also wrote or co-scripted many of the Bond films, with his last being *Licence to Kill* (1989).

The plot of *The Red Beret* concerned a Los Angeles-born Canadian national, Steven 'Canada' McKendrick (Alan Ladd), who joins the fledgling British 1st Airborne division in 1940. 'Canada' has a skeleton in his closet, as he is actually a former pilot who believes he was partly responsible for the death of a colleague in a parachute accident. The parachute training sequences were shot at RAF Abingdon (which was also used in a similar capacity for *Carve Her Name with Pride* in 1957 and *Operation Crossbow* in 1964). The film is of great interest to aviation historians as it contains unique colour footage of the RAF's last Vickers Wellington bombers, which play the part of paratrooper-dropping aircraft. Seven Wellington T.Xs were used in the filming, with one later being flown to Malta for use in *The Malta Story* (1953). All of these aircraft were scrapped in late 1953.

In reality, although the Wellington was indeed considered for the parachute-dropping role in WW2 it was found to be wholly unsuitable for this task. The main problem was that a large hole would have to be cut in the underside of the aircraft to allow the fitting of a hatch through which parachutists could exit. In the case of the Wellington, this would have fatally weakened the aircraft's unique geodetic structure (which consisted of a criss-cross aluminium framework covered with wooden formers and fabric). In addition, the Wellington had a very narrow, cramped fuselage unsuitable for the carriage of passengers, particularly parachutists who would be wearing bulky clothing and carrying heavy equipment. The Wellingtons in the film were thus used to represent Armstrong Whitworth Whitleys which were used to drop paratroopers in the early years of the war, but which had all been scrapped some time before.

Part of the film features a recreation of the Bruneval raid, which in this case is called 'Operation Pegasus'. The Commanding officer on this fictional mission is Colonel John Snow (Leo Genn), an obvious reference to the real-life Colonel John Frost.

A recreation of the Bruneval raid is also featured in the TV drama *Pathfinders* (1972-73), a 13-episode series made by Toledo Productions and filmed mainly at RAF West Malling in Kent and Pinewood Studios. Supposedly based on the exploits of the RAF's Pathfinder Force during WW2, the series was notable for its poor production values. Although some interior and exterior filming was carried out with the RAF's last airworthy Avro Lancaster PA474 (which at that time lacked a mid-upper turret and was based at RAF Waddington), the production relied heavily on stock footage, including clips from *The Dambusters* (1955) and the wartime colour documentary *Night Bombers* (1943). Some shots were achieved using large radio-controlled model Avro Lancasters, and several rather unconvincing full-sized wooden mock-ups of Lancaster bombers were created at Pinewood Studios for some scenes. Overall, though, this was a cheapskate production despite the involvement of a distinguished technical advisor, former bomber pilot Captain Hamish Mahaddie, who had previously been involved with *633 Squadron* (1964), *Battle of Britain* (1969), and other aviation films.

The second episode – *For Better, For Worse* – which was first broadcast on the ITV network on 4 October 1972 dealt with a commando raid on a German radar station on the French coast which has been carried out in order to bring key components of the system back to England for examination. Laurence Hardy played a character called Dr Goodliffe, who was clearly based on the real-life Dr R.V. Jones.

In 1954, Warwick Films made another colour war movie, *The Cockleshell Heroes*, about Operation Frankton – a commando raid on the occupied French port of Bordeaux in December 1942. The raid was carried out by ten men of the Royal Marines Boom Patrol Detachment who had been landed in the Gironde Estuary by the Royal Navy submarine HMS *Tuna* (N94) captained by Lieutenant Commander Dick Raikes. The attacking force travelled in six specially-designed canoes, each carrying several limpet mines. Six merchant ships were damaged in the attack, though five were subsequently refloated and repaired. This was a recurring problem in WW2, as ships sunk in the relatively shallow depth of a harbour can usually be raised and refitted unless they have exploded or turned turtle. All but three of the US Navy ships sunk at Pearl Harbour were repaired and put back into service by mid-1943.

Only two of the commandos, Major Herbert 'Blondie' Hasler and Bill Sparks, survived the raid. Two of the raiders died of hypothermia, while the remaining six were executed by the Germans – even though they were wearing uniforms. This unfortunate outcome happened as a result of Hitler's infamous 'Commando Order' issued on 18 October 1942, which stated that captured Allied Commandos were to be executed even if they were wearing uniforms and had surrendered. A flagrant breach of the Geneva Convention, this order even disturbed some German commanders.

Like *The Red Beret*, *The Cockleshell Heroes* was made in colour and had an impressive cast, although the names of individuals were changed. José Ferrer (who also directed the film) played a character called Major Stringer, representing Major Herbert G. Hasler who was the leader of the actual operation. Trevor Howard played Colonel Thomson, a World War 1 veteran who believes in the value of strict discipline in sharp contrast to the maverick Stringer. War movie stalwart Victor Maddern was Sergeant Craig, while the rest of the cast included several actors who appeared in a number of British war movies of the fifties including Percy Herbert, Anthony Newley and Peter Arne. Future *Dracula* actor Christopher Lee had a small part as the commander of the British submarine HMS *Tuna*, while Walter Fitzgerald was a Gestapo officer who interrogated the captured commandos.

The film was shot in Cinemascope on location in Eastney Barracks, Southsea, Hampshire (representing Portsmouth) and at Portsmouth itself, with the French estuary scenes being shot off the coast of Portugal. The two surviving 'Cockleshell Heroes', Major 'Blondie' Hasler and Bill Sparks, served as technical advisors on the film.

The greatest commando raid of the early war years though, was the attack on the docks at St Nazaire on 28 March 1942 (Operation Chariot), whose main aim was the destruction of the Normandie Dock, a large dry dock which had been originally built in 1932 to house the French liner S.S. *Normandie*, a huge vessel similar in size and appearance to the RMS *Queen Mary*. As such, this dock was the only one in this part of Europe which could house the larger German capital ships such as the *Tirpitz* and *Scharnhorst*. Its destruction would force these ships to return to Germany for any repairs that might be required.

One option might have been to bomb the dock (something that was indeed tried many times during the war), but at this stage in the conflict most bombing was highly inaccurate and RAF Bomber Command still used relatively small bombs which were too puny to do much damage to the dry dock or capital ships within it. Another tactic might have been to shell the dock from the sea, but this would have put the Royal Navy's capital ships at high risk of being sunk by shore batteries and air attack

The solution that the British planners came up with was to fill the front end of an expendable naval vessel with as much explosive as possible and then ram it through the gates of the dock and blow it up. In addition, an accompanying force of Commandos in small motor launches would attack and destroy all the surrounding installations before being evacuated and returned to the UK.

The main problem facing the Commandos was that St Nazaire was one of the most heavily-defended ports in Europe, garrisoned by a large number of German troops and equipped with a huge number of guns of every calibre (plus radar and searchlights) which could wreak havoc with the attacking force. The solution was to carry out the attack at night and use various means to disguise the raiders as German vessels.

The vessel chosen to lead the assault was HMS *Campbeltown*, an elderly four-funnelled destroyer which had been launched in 1919 and originally served in the US Navy as the USS *Buchanan*. In late 1940 the *Buchanan* was one of 50 old US destroyers given to Britain under the 'ships for bases' deal made between Churchill and Roosevelt in which the USA obtained naval facilities in British colonies (such as Bermuda) in exchange for these vessels.

The 50 vessels were in poor condition and required a lot of work to put them back into serviceable condition, but at this stage in the war Britain was desperately short of convoy escorts and put them to use as soon as possible. By the spring of 1942, though, the *Campbeltown* was well past its sell-by date and was ideal for conversion into a floating bomb.

The Royal Navy altered the *Campbeltown* to make it look like a German destroyer. Two of the four funnels were removed and the remaining pair were modified with angled tops to look like those found in German warships. The ship's three four-inch guns were removed and a single light 12-pounder QF gun and eight 20mm Oerlikon automatic cannon were fitted for self-defence. The vessel was lightened as much as possible so that she could clear the sandbanks in the Loire Estuary, and extra armour was fitted to key areas to protect her crew. The bow of the ship was filled with a huge explosive charge consisting of four-and-a-half tons of Amatol (a material made from a mixture of TNT and ammonium nitrate) sealed in behind concrete and detonated by a time pencil.

The force which set out from Falmouth, England on 27 March 1942 consisted of the *Campbeltown,* 17 motor launches and a single motor torpedo boat (MTB). Unfortunately, things didn't go exactly to plan. A small force of RAF bombers had been instructed to bomb targets in the St Nazaire area in the hope that the Germans would concentrate their attention on the skies rather than the sea, but these pinprick raids had the reverse effect and actually aroused the defenders who then became convinced that a seaborne raid was imminent.

To begin with, the attacking force was mistaken for a German flotilla – especially as messages flashed from ship to shore by Aldis lamp were replied to in German. Eventually, with the *Campbeltown* just one mile from the drydock, the Germans realised what was happening and opened fire. Ca*mpbeltown* pulled down her *Kriegsmarine* flag, hoisted the

White Ensign, and charged towards the dock at full speed. As she burst through the dry dock gates, commandos landed from the accompanying motor launches and attacked surrounding facilities, such as the pump house.

Initially the raid was considered a failure, as the huge bomb in *Campbeltown's* bow did not explode. But at 1.30 p.m. on 28 March it blew up, killing a large number of German personnel. The delay in the charge going off is thought to have been due to deterioration in the time pencil which detonated the explosive. In 1942 electronic timers didn't exist, and the usual method for creating a time bomb was to use a 'time pencil', a device which – once activated by crimping the end with pliers – used acid to dissolve an internal wire. Once this had burned away a spring would be released, setting off a small detonator.

The raid was a complete success, although casualties were heavy as only 228 out of the 811 men who took part returned to the UK. 169 servicemen were killed and 215 were taken prisoner, while five escaped to Spain. On the credit side, the Normandie Dock was severely damaged and was not put back into service until long after the end of the war. 360 German soldiers were killed and 89 decorations were awarded to members of the British force, including five Victoria Crosses.

No feature film has ever been made about the St Nazaire Raid, but it was the inspiration behind two movies: *Gift Horse* (1952) and *Attack on the Iron Coast* (1967). *Gift Horse* was an excellent movie, directed by Compton McKenzie, about the exploits of HMS *Ballantrae* – an ex-WW1 vintage four-stack US Navy destroyer which is given to the Royal Navy in 1940 (the title of the movie comes from the proverb 'Never look a gift horse in the mouth'). The cast includes Trevor Howard as the *Ballantrae's* Captain, Lieutenant

Commander Hugh Algernon Fraser, with war movie stalwarts Richard Attenborough, James Donald and Bernard Lee in supporting roles. Another notable cast member was William Russell (aka Russell Enoch), who appeared in several British war movies including *The Great Escape* (1963) before playing schoolteacher Ian Chesterton in the BBC TV series *Doctor Who* (1963-89 and 2005-present).

The first half of the film depicts the *Ballantrae* being used on convoy protection duties in the North Atlantic, but the latter section of the movie deals with its participation in an attack on an enemy drydock for which purpose it is converted into a floating bomb, with its bows filled with explosive – exactly as happened to the real *HMS Campbeltown*.

The actual ship used in the film was HMS *Leamington*, which had been built in the USA in 1919 as the USS *Twiggs*, a *Wickes*-class destroyer. One of the 50 obsolete US Navy ships given to Britain in 1940, she had an interesting history. In 1942 she was of the escorts to the ill-fated Arctic convoy PQ17. The following year she was transferred to the Royal Canadian Navy (where she became the HMCS *Leamington*). In 1944 she was given to the Russians, who renamed her the *Zguchik* ('Firebrand'). In 1950 she was returned to the Royal Navy and took part in the filming of *Gift Horse* before being scrapped.

Another film inspired by the St Nazaire raid was *Attack on the Iron Coast* (1967), the first film made by Oakmont Productions and which was directed by Paul Wendkos. Oakmont came about as a result of the success of *633 Squadron* (1964) which had been produced by the Mirisch Corporation, owned by Walter Mirisch and his brothers Marvin and Harold.

Mirisch set up Oakmont Productions as a low-cost subsidiary which would make 90-minute war films with a budget not exceeding $1 million, suitable for use as part of a 'double bill' (something that has now disappeared from British cinemas, but which was very popular in the sixties). Usually they had an American leading man, with the only exception being *Mosquito Squadron* (1968) which starred Glasgow-born David McCallum as Squadron Leader Quint Munroe (who was supposedly Canadian). However, McCallum had just spent four years playing Ilya Kuryakin in the TV series *The Man From UNCLE* (1964-68) and was very well-known in the USA. Most of the Oakmont Productions films were shot on location and at MGM's British studios in Borehamwood.

Attack on the Iron Coast was not a faithful retelling of the St Nazaire raid, but was clearly inspired by it. The film opens with Canadian commando officer Major Jaimie Wilson (Lloyd Bridges) looking at film footage of a recent disastrous commando raid he led on the French port of La Plage, an operation clearly based on the real-life attack (Operation Jubilee) on Dieppe on the French coast on 19 August 1942.

Wilson then proposes another suicidal mission ('Operation Mad Dog') which involves ramming an explosive-laden vessel into the drydock at Le Claire, which can be used to repair German capital ships such as the (fictional) *Ostwind*. As this was a low-budget Oakmont Films production, the destroyer used in the real St Nazaire raid was replaced with a rusty old minesweeper, and the supporting force travelled in just four motor launches.

The raid practice sequences were filmed at St Catharine's Docks in London, which was also used in *Battle of Britain* (1969) and *Who Dares Wins* (1982). The same location, suitably redressed and filmed at night, was also used for scenes of the actual attack. The exterior shots of the German HQ employed the mock French chateau which had been built on the backlot at MGM Studios in Borehamwood for *The Dirty Dozen* (1967), while the interiors of the HQ were filmed at the Royal Pinner School in Middlesex.

As was to be the norm in films made by Oakmont Productions, a considerable amount of stock footage was re-used from previous productions. The RAF night bombing sequence, for example, was lifted from *The Dambusters* (1955). Although an original score was composed by Gerard Schumann, some of Ron Goodwin's music from *633 Squadron* was re-used for a few scenes, including the end titles, although his very familiar main title theme was not used as it was too well known.

The cast included Andrew Keir as Captain Franklin, who has lost his son in the Le Plage operation and believes Wilson was to blame for this tragedy. Sue Lloyd also appears as Wilson's wife. Lloyd is best known for playing spy Harry Palmer's love interest, Jean Courtney, in *The Ipcress File* (1966) and John Mannering's assistant Cordelia in the popular ITC TV series *The Baron* (1966). Actors Walter Gotell and George Mikell, who had both played German soldiers in several British war movies including *The Guns of Navarone* (1961), appear as officers in charge of the defending garrison. Gotell later played the Chief Constable in the BBC TV series *Softly, Softly: Task Force* (1969-76), a spin-off from *Z-Cars* (1962-78), and also portrayed KGB Chief General Gogol in several James Bond films during the Roger Moore era.

The producer and writer of the film was John C. Champion who had previously been responsible for *Zero Hour* (1957), the very serious airliner drama which was the inspiration for the hit comedy *Airplane!* (1980), which also starred Lloyd Bridges. The director was Paul Wendkos, who had helmed three *Gidget* films (which starred *The Guns of Navarone* star, James Darren) plus two Westerns, *Guns of the Magnificent Seven* (1969) and *Cannon for Cordoba* (1970), which were both shot in Spain for Mirisch Films.

The worst feature of the film is the rather poor miniature effects which were the work of Les Bowie (who at that time was trading as 'The Bowie Organisation'). Bowie was renowned for producing convincing effects on a very small budget and had worked on a number of Hammer films. He also reportedly created the effects for the pre-title sequence of *One Million Years BC* (1966) for just £1,500, and later worked on *2001: A Space Odyssey* (1968) and *Superman* (1978). However, his work for *Attack on the Iron Coast* was not very convincing.

Attack on The Iron Coast was released in the UK in 1968 as part of a double bill with *Yellow Submarine* (1968), an animated film featuring The Beatles which has since become a cult classic. In the USA the film was released as a double feature with a long-forgotten Bond imitation, *Danger Route* (1968).

No further films were made about the St Nazaire raid, but there have been countless books, articles and TV documentaries on the subject. In 2007, the BBC screened a documentary about the mission – presented by Jeremy Clarkson – which was entitled *The Greatest Raid of All Time*. Rather oddly, in this production it was claimed that this was one of the lesser-known raids of WW2. In fact, it was one of the most famous commando missions of the conflict, and highly successful.

The largest commando raid carried out in WW2 was Operation Jubilee, the attack on the French port of Dieppe which took place on 19 August, 1942. A force of approximately 6,000 troops – consisting of 5,000 Canadians, 1,000 British troops and 50 US Rangers – landed at 5.00 a.m. The aim of the mission was to destroy port facilities and coastal defences, and learn lessons that could be applied in the subsequent invasion of Europe.

At that time, Winston Churchill was under great pressure from both Roosevelt and Stalin. The Americans were keen for an invasion of France to be carried out as early as the summer of 1942 (Operation Roundup), while the Russians felt that Britain was not doing enough to help them. An attack on the French coast might persuade Hitler to divert some of his divisions to coastal defence.

The plan was drawn up by Lord Louis Mountbatten of Combined Operations HQ, and was essentially a re-mount of a raid (Operation Rutter) that was originally to have taken place the previous month. That particular attack had been cancelled after four German Focke-Wulf Fw-190s bombed some of the landing ships as they lay at anchor. Unfortunately this delay in the operation meant that the Germans were expecting an attack, and were more than ready to repel the invaders.

The raid was an unmitigated disaster. Of 6,086 Allied troops who landed on the beaches, 3,623 were killed, wounded or captured. The Royal Navy lost 33 landing craft plus one destroyer, HMS *Berkeley*.

Operation Jubilee saw the combat debut of the new Churchill tank, manufactured by Vauxhall, which was deployed by the Calgary Regiment of the 1st Canadian Tank Brigade. Unfortunately most of the Churchills were abandoned by their crews as they were unable to get off the beach. The problem was that tracked vehicles couldn't operate on a shingle beach, as the small round stones jammed in the tracks and broke the pins securing the links. This became a slur on the reputation of the Churchill, as it then became known as 'the tank that got stuck on the beach at Dieppe' when in fact *any* tank would have the same problem with a shingle beach.

The RAF supplied 60 squadrons of fighters to cover the operation, and these included Spitfires and Hurricanes plus the relatively new Mustangs and Typhoons. At the time, the RAF thought that it had shot down 250 German aircraft, but post-war research has shown that true German losses were just 48 aircraft as against 106 RAF planes shot down. One Fw-190 was shot down by an RAF Allison-engined Mustang I (P-51A), the very first Mustang kill of WW2, while another Fw-190 was destroyed by a Hurricane II. This is thought to be the only occasion in WW2 when this obsolete fighter downed a Fw-190.

Although Dieppe was a military disaster, important lessons were learned. Churchill had proved his point that the Allies were not yet strong enough to invade France with any chance of success. Also, it would be suicide to attack a well-defended port.

In recent years some evidence has emerged which has suggested that the true purpose of Operation Jubilee was the capture of a German Enigma machine from a building in Dieppe. According to this theory, proposed by author David O'Keefe, the true architect of the mission was none other than future James Bond creator Ian Fleming, who at that time worked for the Naval Intelligence Division.

No film has ever been made of the Dieppe raid, but it is mentioned in the film *D-Day: Sixth of June* (1956) which starred Robert Taylor, Richard Todd and Dana Wynter.

Operation Jubilee was the largest commando raid carried out in WW2, and was regarded as a failure. But one of the smallest such raids during the war was the successful Operation Jaywick on 26 September 1943, which involved just 14 commandos in an attack on Japanese ships in Singapore Harbour. The mission was the brainchild of 28-year-old Captain Ivan Lyon (of the Allied Intelligence Bureau and Gordon Highlanders) and Bill Reynolds, a 61-year-old Australian citizen, and had some similarities with Operation Frankton – the attack on ships in Bordeaux harbour in December 1942 which formed the basis of the book and film *The Cockleshell Heroes* (q.v.).

The plan involved a force of Allied commandos travelling from Australia to Singapore in a fishing boat and carrying out an attack on shipping in the harbour using collapsible canoes (folboats) and limpet mines. Bill Reynolds possessed a 70-foot Japanese fishing boat, the *Kofuku Maru*, which he had used to evacuate refugees from Singapore and was now in India. Lyon ordered the boat to be shipped to Australia, where it was renamed the MV *Krait* after a small but deadly Asian snake.

In mid-1943 the *Krait* travelled from a training camp at Broken Bay, New South Island to Thursday Island. Aboard were thirteen men – two British and eleven Australian – from Z Special Unit (also known as Z Force), which included Major Lyon.

On 13 August 1943 the *Krait* left Thursday Island for Exmouth Gulf, Western Australia where it was refuelled and repaired. After acquiring all the necessary folboats required for the attack, the *Krait* sailed towards Singapore, with the crew disguised as Asian fishermen.

On 24 September the *Krait* arrived off Singapore, and six commandos left in three folboats. After paddling 31 miles, they established a forward operating base on a small island near Singapore harbour and lay up until 26 September, when they launched an attack on several Japanese ships lying in the harbour. Seven Japanese ships – comprising a total of 39,000 tons – were sunk in the attack, and the commandos returned to their hiding place on the island where they waited for a few days before returning to the *Krait* on 2 October.

The *Krait* subsequently sailed back to Australia. Apart from a brief encounter with a Japanese patrol boat in the Lombok Strait, the voyage passed without incident and the *Krait* arrived back in Exmouth Gulf on 19 October.

The reaction of the Japanese authorities in Singapore to the attack was sudden and vicious. Unable to believe it had been carried out by commandos, they assumed that pro-Communist Chinese guerrillas had been responsible and instigated a series of brutal reprisals against the civilian population. The Allies never admitted responsibility for the sinking of the ships, largely because they wanted to preserve the secret of the *Krait* so that it could be used for further missions.

The mission has therefore come in for some criticism, as the loss of seven ships must be balanced against the terrible suffering inflicted on the civilian population. This was a common problem in WW2, as many successful missions carried out by resistance groups and the Special Operations Executive (SOE) and its American equivalent, the Operation for Special Services (OSS) often resulted in terrible reprisals against the civilian population.

Nonetheless, Operation Jaywick is still regarded as one of the great Allied commando raids of WW2, and in 1989 it was the subject of an Australian TV mini-series – *The He-*

roes – which was directed by Donald Crombie, with Paul Rhys as Ivan Lyon. One notable cast member was actor/singer Jason Donovan, who played Australian commando 'Happy' Huston. At that time Donovan was extremely well-known for playing Scott Robinson in the TV series *Neighbours* (1985-present), and for being a successful pop star and former boyfriend of *Neighbours* co-star Kylie Minogue.

The Heroes was very well-received by critics and the general public, particularly as it eschewed Hollywood-style action in favour of gritty realism. In 1991 a sequel – *Heroes 2: The Return* – was made, which dealt with Ivan Lyon's second commando mission in 1944, Operation Rimau, which ended in tragedy and failure with all the commandos being killed.

Operation Rimau had a similar *modus operandi* to the earlier Jaywick, as it involved an attack by folboats (naval canoes) using limpet mines. Originally, Rimau was to be part of a much larger attack on Japanese shipping which was to be called Operation Hornball and would have involved semi-submersible canoes, known as 'Sleeping Beauties', which could function almost as mini-submarines with the operators wearing breathing apparatus.

The original plan was much more ambitious than Jaywick, and involved transporting 15 'Sleeping Beauties' and their crews by submarine to Merapas Island in Indonesia, where the commandos would lie up with enough supplies to last three months and capture a local fishing boat which could be used in the operation. 23 commandos were to be used in the operation, instead of the 14 employed in Jaywick.

On 11 September 1944, Lyon and his men left their base in Garden Island, Western Australia and headed towards Singapore in the submarine HMS *Porpoise*. The vessel reached the island of Merapas off the coast of Paula Bintan on 23 September 1944. Although the island was thought to be uninhabited, a periscope reconnaissance showed that there were three Malay natives with a canoe on the beach. Accordingly, one crew member – Lieutenant Walter Carey – had to be left on the island to guard the stores that had been left.

On 28 September the porpoise intercepted a junk, the *Murika* from Ketapang, off the west coast of Borneo. The Malay crew were taken on board the submarine, and seven commandos boarded the junk. A forward operation base was then established at Pedjantan Island. The *Mustika* subsequently transferred the raiding force to Merapas, from where an attack was launched on Singapore island.

Unfortunately things didn't go to plan, and on 10 October the *Murika* was discovered by a Malay Police patrol boat, the *Hei Ho*. Regrettably, one of the Australian commandos on board the *Murika* panicked and opened fire on the *Hei Ho*. Lyon realised that the mission had been compromised, as the patrol boat would report this incident to the occupying Japanese authorities, and he ordered the 'Sleeping Beauties' to be destroyed.

Lyon and some of his men then carried out a limited attack on some ships on Singapore harbour using the folboats and limpet mines, possibly sinking three of them, but from this point on the hunter had become the hunted as the Japanese gradually killed or captured all of the Allied soldiers, with all those taken prisoner being eventually executed. The mission was therefore a heroic failure rather than the clear-cut success that Jaywick had been.

Heroes 2: The Return, therefore had a more bleak tone than *The Heroes*, as the mission had ended in tragedy and failure. This time round, Ivan Lyon was played by Nathaniel

Parker – son of former British Rail chairman Sir Peter Parker – who had made a big impression as pilot 'Flash' Gordon in the LWT mini-series *A Piece of Cake* (1988) about an RAF Spitfire squadron in 1939 and 1940.

Another film about a naval commando mission in the Far East theatre was *The Great Raid* (2005), directed by John Dahl and which starred Benjamin Bratt, James Franco, Connie Nielsen, Marton Csokas and Joseph Fiennes. The movie dealt with the raid on Cabanatuan on the island of Luzon in the Philippines during WW2, when men of the 6th Ranger Battalion under Lt. Colonel Mucci were ordered to attempt the rescue of 500 US prisoners of war before they were executed by the Japanese. Unfortunately the film was a critical and commercial failure, making only $11m at the worldwide box office against a budget of $80m.

The last naval commando raid in recent history would be the attack on the airfield at Pebble Island which took place during the night of 14-15 May 1982 as part of the Falklands War. At that point in the conflict, the Argentine forces had deployed a number of FMA IA 58 Pucara and Beechcraft T-34 Mentor light attack aircraft on the island, which would have posed a considerable threat to any British invading force.

A reconnaissance of the area was initially carried out by men from the Boat Troop of D Squadron, 22 SAS using Klepper canoes, and on the night of 14 May 1982 two Westland Sea King HC4 helicopters of 846 Naval Air Squadron lifted off from HMS *Hermes* carrying 45 SAS Troopers plus a Naval Gunfire Support Forward Observer (NGSFO). Their target was a number of Pucara and T-34 Mentor light attack aircraft which were based on the airstrip. The SAS men attacked the planes using L16 81mm mortar bombs and 66mm LAW rockets. Explosive charges were placed on some aircraft, while others were sprayed with bullets from the troopers' M-16 rifles. The only casualties were one SAS trooper wounded and an Argentine officer killed by shrapnel. Argentine losses comprised six Pucaras, four T-34 Turbo-Mentors, and one Short SC.7 Skyvan light transport plane destroyed, plus the destruction of the ammunition and fuel dumps.

No cinema film or TV drama has ever been made about this raid, but an excellent reconstruction of the attack was staged for the BBC TV documentary series *Soldiers* (1985) which was presented by author Frederick Forsyth. This footage has since turned up in many documentaries about the Falklands War, and can be viewed on YouTube (search under 'Pebble Island Raid').

3
OPERATION DYNAMO

OPERATION Dynamo was the name given to one of the most important rescue missions of the Second World War, when the Royal Navy rescued 338,000 British and French troops from the beaches of Dunkirk between 26 May and 4 June 1940. Although it might be regarded as a defeat, it was a victory of sorts as it kept Britain in the war. Had the Germans prevented the evacuation, then Britain would have been forced to sue for peace, allowing the Nazis to become masters of Europe and turn on Russia. As things happened, these 338,000 troops became the core of the force which invaded France four years later, paving the way for the final Allied victory over Germany in May 1945.

Bearing in mind its historic importance, the Dunkirk evacuation has featured in several movies over the last eight decades. William Wyler's *Mrs Miniver* (1942) had some scenes of the civilian-manned 'Little Ships' leaving England for Dunkirk. Regarded as a propaganda film, this movie is credited with helping to change American public opinion in favour of the British cause. The Dunkirk evacuation is also briefly depicted in *In Which We Serve* (1942) – which was directed, produced and written by Noel Coward, who also starred as the lead, Captain Kinross – about the adventures of the crew of British destroyer HMS *Torrin*. Sailor Shorty Blake (John Mills) gives out cocoa and biscuits to evacuated soldiers of the British Expeditionary Force (BEF) while, on the bridge, Captain Kinross offers them his favourite naval tipple: Bovril laced with sherry.

Mills also starred in what was, until recently, the definitive film about the evacuation: *Dunkirk* (1958), directed by film critic Barry Norman's father, Leslie Norman. The screenplay was written by David Divine, based on the book *The Big Pick-Up* by Elleston Trevor and the play *Dunkirk*, co-authored by Lieutenant Colonel Ewan Hunter and Major J.S. Bradford. Elleston Trevor was one of ten pen-names used by prolific British author Trevor Dudley-Smith, who also wrote *Flight of the Phoenix* which was made into a film starring James Stewart in 1965 (and remade in 2004 with Dennis Quaid in the starring role). Additionally, he was the creator of the *Quiller* series of spy thrillers which inspired the film *The Quiller Memorandum* (1966) directed by Michael Anderson and scripted by Harold Pinter and which starred George Segal, and the short lived BBC TV series *Quiller* (1975) starring Michael Jayston.

The film describes Operation Dynamo from the viewpoint of two people, Corporal 'Tubby' Binns (John Mills) who is trapped in France, and a newspaper reporter back in England, Charles Foreman (Bernard Lee). Another key character in the film is Foreman's friend, the cowardly John Holden (Richard Attenborough), who owns a garage and light engineering firm which makes belt buckles for the Army and is unwilling to take a boat over to France because his wife has just had a baby. Feeling he is not doing enough to help the war effort, the guilt-stricken Holden eventually makes it to

France where he rescues some soldiers and ends up being treated as a hero.

The beach sequences were filmed at Camber Sands in south-east England, with thousands of British Army troops playing extras, while a scene early in the film – in which Binns' men blow up a bridge – was shot at Teston Bridge on the River Medway in Kent. Dunkirk town centre was recreated using part of Rye Harbour in Sussex, England. Scenes of boats leaving England were shot on the Thames at Teddington Lock, and near Tower Bridge in Central London.

As was the norm in films of this era, considerable archive footage was employed throughout the production, although this was not always correct for the period. Some of the Stuka footage shows the later Ju-87D version (which didn't enter service until 1942), and shots showing the German army advancing through France depict a German Tiger I tank (which didn't see combat until late 1942).

A considerable amount of miniature and studio water tank work was used for the scenes showing Royal Navy destroyers being attacked at the East Mole in Dunkirk. The musical score was by Malcolm Arnold, and the main title theme was reused for *The Heroes of Telemark* (1965). Interestingly, this same piece had also appeared a few years before as incidental music in the BBC TV documentary series *The War in the Air* (1954).

The film was premiered at the Empire, Leicester Square, London on 20 March 1958 and was the second most popular film in the UK that year, making over $2m at the worldwide box office, set against a budget of just £400,000. It did not do well at the US box office though, making a total of only $310,000 in the US and Canada. The film was restored in 2017 in association with the Luna Cinema and Vintage by

Hemingway to coincide with the release of the new Christopher Nolan film about the evacuation (q.v.), and was then released on DVD and Blu-Ray. Screenings of the restored film were held at a temporary outdoor cinema on the beach at Camber Sands on 20 and 21 September 2017. Before the first screening, actress Hayley Mills introduced a compilation of colour home movie footage which her late father, John Mills, had taken during the filming on the beach.

Weekend at Dunkirk (1964) was a French film, directed by Henri Verneuil, which focused on Operation Dynamo from the French viewpoint. It was similar to the earlier John Mills picture, but was made in France and was the first colour depiction of the Dunkirk evacuation. The picture starred popular French actor Jean-Paul Belmondo, and the score was by Maurice Jarre. The late French composer Jarre, who was the father of pop musician Jean Michel Jarre, wrote the scores for numerous French, British and American films between 1962 and 2001. He died in 2009. His most famous scores were for *Lawrence of Arabia* (1962) and *Doctor Zhivago* (1965).

As was the norm in sixties war films, the Messerschmitt fighters which appear on screen were played by French-made Nord 1002s (licence-built versions of the Messerschmitt Bf108), which were available in large numbers at that time as they were being retired by the French Navy and were being sold to civilian operators.

The Dunkirk evacuation also features in the pre-credits sequences of *Battle of Britain* (1969). First of all, we see a shot of German vehicles entering the town of Dunkirk comprising an American M37 105mm self-propelled gun, two modified White M3 half-tracks and two M35 Reo trucks. All the vehicles were supplied by the Spanish Army and painted grey with German markings applied.

An impressive tracking shot (filmed at Huelva Beach in Spain) then follows, showing a landscape littered with all the vehicles and guns left behind by the British Army at Dunkirk. Many of these were old lorries and cars found in Spain, while those in the background were two-dimensional flats. Old 75mm field guns (also seen in the 1965 film *Battle of the Bulge*) were fitted with barrel extensions made of lead, which were cut and 'flared out' with tinsnips to resemble spiked guns.

Further shots of the Dunkirk evacuation, particularly those showing British soldiers wading out to sea, were filmed for the production but ended up on the cutting room floor. Some of these scenes have survived, owned by a company called World Backgrounds, and have turned up in a number of documentaries.

The Dunkirk operation also featured in an Italian war movie, *Eagles Over London* (1969), which was directed by Enzo G. Castellari. The film forms part of a little-known genre known affectionately as 'Macaroni Combats' (similar to 'Spaghetti Westerns'), movies presenting an alternative view of WW2 in which the Italians are heroes, the British are buffoons, and the Nazis are villains. Often these films also involved the French and Spanish movie industries, and had scant regard for historical accuracy.

The film opens with Captain Paul Stevens (Frederick Stafford) of the British Expeditionary Force leading a desperate rear guard action against German Panzers (played by postwar vintage American M47 and M48 tanks). Stevens's troops destroy a bridge (as in the 1958 John Mills' movie *Dunkirk*), and then proceed to the beachhead to await evacuation. The strafing Luftwaffe fighters are played by North American T-6 trainers.

Stevens eventually makes it back to London while, in an interesting plot twist, German SS Commandos led by Major Krueger (Luigi Pistilli) murder some British soldiers, steal their uniforms and go back to England where they attempt to attack British radar stations. The radar stations in the film have large rotating bedstead antennae, something that is wrong for the period as the 1940 Chain Home installations had huge fixed aerials made of wood and metal looking a bit like the Eiffel Tower (as correctly depicted in *Battle of Britain*).

The movie would give almost anyone who cares about historical and technical accuracy a heart attack. Some of the film was shot at Tablada airfield in Spain, using some of the same Hispano HA-1112 M-1 Buchons and CASA 2-111s which had been used in *Battle of Britain* a few months before. But the Buchons were painted to represent RAF fighters, while the sole German 'Messerschmitt' seen in the film is a Spitfire with German crosses applied! The RAF fighters seen starting up and taxying in the film were the 'taxying Buchons' used in *Battle of Britain* for ground scenes set on a Luftwaffe airfield. All were painted in British camouflage and had RAF markings applied. None of the airworthy Buchons used in *Battle of Britain* would have been available, because they were all flown to Britain in the spring of 1968 for use in that far superior film.

Most of the aerial sequences in *Eagles Over London* were created in the studio using some rather dubious miniatures and mock-ups which don't look like any recognisable aircraft type. One particularly laughable scene shows Air Marshal George Taylor (Van Johnson), making no attempt to disguise his American accent, sitting in a very cardboard-looking aircraft mock-up, asking the authorities to send up more reinforcements in dialogue laced with Americanese!

One fan of the film though, was Quentin Tarantino, who thought the film was wonderful and considered *Battle of Britain* to be 'boring' because it contained elements of soap opera (presumably he was referring to the plot thread involving Christopher Plummer's Squadron Leader Harvey and his wife Maggie, played by Susannah York).

One person who objected to the Italian film (according to the author of *Flying Film Stars*, Mark Ashley) was the director of *Battle of Britain*, Guy Hamilton, who allegedly threatened the filmmakers with legal action if they released the film in the UK as he feared it would affect the success of his own meticulously-made epic. As a result, *Eagles Over London* was never released in the UK, and was only shown to American cinema audiences in 1973 with a new title – *Battle Squadron*. Director Enzo G. Castellari got into similar legal problems with his *Jaws* rip-off, *The Last Shark* (1981) (aka *Great White*), which was the subject of a legal case brought by Universal Studios. As a result, the film was withdrawn in the US.

The next recreation of Operation Dynamo appeared in the film *Atonement* (2007), directed by Joe Wright, with miles of beach at Redcar – near Middlesbrough in north east England – being littered with period vehicles and abandoned guns. The event is presented in the form of a five-minute tracking shot without any cuts, which perfectly conveys the horror and chaos of Dunkirk.

In July 2017, a new film about Operation Dynamo premiered in cinemas across the world. Filmed mainly in the large-format IMAX process, *Dunkirk* (2017) was directed by the highly-acclaimed and talented British director Christopher Nolan. For Nolan this was a very personal project, the roots of which started about 20 years earlier when he made a hair-raising trip across the English Channel with his then-girlfriend (and now wife and producer) Emma Thomas, and friend Ivan Cornell, in a small boat.

Some critics have described Christopher Nolan's film as 'a remake of the 1958 John Mills film', but nothing could be further from the truth as the two movies are completely different in mood and style. Leslie Norman's film was a patriotic flag-waver, rather like *The Dambusters* (1955) and *Reach for the Sky* (1956), while the Nolan film has a very 'modern' feel.

As this author has related in his previous books, there are a number of stylistic trends in modern cinema which have often ruined movies – the use of 'washed-out' colour, jerky camera work (especially during action sequences), dim lighting, excessive political correctness, the 'F' word in just about every line of dialogue, and a lot of very unconvincing CGI.

To his credit, Nolan eschewed all these current clichés in film-making and determined that the film would be made 'in camera' as much as possible with a minimal amount of CGI. In this respect, Dunkirk resembles the highly-praised WW1 air movie *The Blue Max* (1966), which did not use a single matte or miniature shot in the entire film. *Dunkirk* also features a minimal amount of dialogue and only a few characters, and is very short at only 1 hour 47 minutes. This works in the film's favour, as there is an underlying theme of time running out – a factor which is enhanced by Hans Zimmer's stunning score.

The structure of the Nolan film is quite brilliant, as it features three distinct timelines: 'The Mole', lasting one week; 'The Sea', lasting one day; and 'The Air', lasting an hour.

Each timeline features different characters, and they all merge by the end of the film. At the start of the movie we are introduced to a number of young British soldiers including Tommy (Fionn Whitehead), Alex (Harry Styles), and Gibson (Aneurin Barnard). Best known as the lead singer of boy band One Direction, Harry Styles gives a very credible performance. There is nothing new about the concept of pop stars appearing in war movies to make them appeal to youngsters. Johnny Leyton appeared in both *The Great Escape* (1963) and *Von Ryan's Express* (1965), and a number of 60s singers including Paul Anka and Fabian featured in *The Longest Day* (1962). Incidentally, Johnny Leyton even released a single of *The Great Escape*, with strange lyrics added to Elmer Bernstein's main theme. Other characters featured in 'The Mole' segment include Naval Commander Bolton (Kenneth Branagh) and Army officer Colonel Winnant (James D'Arcy).

The second timeline, 'The Sea', largely centres around one of the small boats heading for *Dunkirk* – the *Moonstone* – and its crew, owner Mr Dawson (Mark Rylance), son Peter (Tom Glynn-Carney), and his friend George (Barry Keeghan). On their way to the French coast, the *Moonstone's* crew rescue a British soldier who is clinging to the upturned hull of a sunken ship. Played by Cillian Murphy, he is never named in the film and is referred to in the script as the 'shivering soldier'.

The third timeline, 'The Air', focuses on two Spitfire pilots – Farrier (Tom Hardy) and Collins (Jack Lowden) – part of a 'Vic' of three British fighters which have been sent to battle the Luftwaffe.

Nolan's film was the very first feature about Operation Dynamo to be made in Dunkirk itself, and this posed a number of practical problems. Dunkirk is a large industrial town with a beach ten miles long, which goes right up to the Belgian border. This meant that a large number of modern structures in the background had to be disguised.

Almost 1,400 extras were used in the film, and their apparent numbers were increased by using two-dimensional painted cut-outs in the background. This is an old technique, but a very effective one which has been used in a number of classic war movies including *Operation Crossbow* (1965), *Where Eagles Dare* (1968), *Battle of Britain* (1969), *A Bridge Too Far* (1977) and *Memphis Belle* (1990).

Despite this, one fault of the finished film is that there don't seem to be enough troops or vehicles on the beach. If you look at photos and paintings of the actual evacuation, the beach was teeming with hundreds of thousands of soldiers and cluttered with thousands of vehicles (the British Expeditionary Force left behind 75,000 trucks, plus guns and motorcycles). Though the British attempted to wreck all these guns and vehicles before abandoning them, many were salvaged by the *Wehrmacht* who put them back into service as the German Army was short of vehicles. So many British 2-pounder anti-tank guns were captured in France that the Germans started manufacturing their own ammunition for it. In subsequent German service, the gun was known as the 4.0cm PAK 192e or 4.0 cm PAK 154e.

Yet in the film, the beach looks almost deserted in some scenes, as 1,400 extras plus some cut-outs can never convincingly represent a third of a million men. In this respect, the beach sequences in the 1958 *Dunkirk* film and *Atonement* are more accurate. Another notable omission in the film was the lack of smoke, as Dunkirk was blanketed in emissions from burning oil tanks for the period of the evacuation.

Another problem facing the film-makers was a shortage of ships. Hundreds of Royal Navy and civilian vessels were involved in the original evacuation. In May/June 1940 the Royal Navy had 202 destroyers, and 41 of them took part in Operation Dynamo along with many civilian vessels and ships from other Allied navies.

In 2016, only one WW2 Royal Navy destroyer – HMS *Cavalier* (launched in 1944) – still existed as a museum ship at Chatham docks. She could not move under her own power, but in theory could have been towed to the filming location. Unfortunately permission to do this could not be obtained, and the producers had to look elsewhere for ships.

Although no suitable vessels existed in the UK, the producers located a former French destroyer, the *Maille-Breze*, a 3,900 ton T-47 class destroyer which entered service in 1957. The *Maille-Breze* lacked working engines and was currently a museum ship based in the Loire Estuary near Nantes, but could be towed to Dunkirk where she was anchored and used for some shots.

To make her resemble a WW2 Royal Navy destroyer, her radar towers were removed and a modern missile launcher was concealed behind a dummy gun turret. Fake Royal Navy pennant numbers were applied to her forward hull, and she subsequently portrayed two different vessels in the film – HMS *Vivacious* (D36) and HMS *Vanquisher* (D54) – although, to be pedantic, she really looked too modern to be a 1940 Royal Navy warship as she resembled an American *Fletcher*-class destroyer.

Three other vessels portrayed Royal Navy warships in the film. The Dutch minesweepers HNLMS *Naaldwijk* (M/PW809) became the British minesweeper HMS *Britomart* (J22), while HNLMS *Sittard* (M380) played two different destroyers – HMS *Havant* (H32) and HMS *Jaguar* (F34). The Dutch multi-purpose ship MLV *Castor* (A810) became HMS *Basilisk* (H11).

Two other real naval vessels used in the film were the British Harbour Defence Motor Launch HMS *Medusa* (ML1387) and the British Torpedo Boat MTB *102*, which took part in the real-life evacuation in 1940. It also participated in the D-Day landings, and portrayed a captured MTB being used by the German Navy in *The Eagle Has Landed* (1976). A Norwegian steamer, the *Rogaland*, also appears in the movie as a British hospital ship, painted white and marked with red crosses.

Hundreds of 'little ships' were used in the evacuation, and 150 of them are still extant thanks to the efforts of the Association of Little Ships. 20 of these were used in the film, although the main 'hero' boat, the *Moonstone*, was actually a 100-year-old cabin cruiser – the *Revlis* – which was found in Inverness and shipped to Dunkirk by flat-bed truck. It was refitted with period accessories for the film.

The air component of Operation Dynamo was also well-represented in the film, with three genuine Spitfires being used in the filming. Two of these were correct 1940 Mark I Spitfires, AR213 and X4650, with the third being a cosmetically-modified Mark LFVb Spitfire EP122 which was altered to resemble a Mark I by having 1940-pattern exhausts stubs fitted and its two 20mm Hispano cannon removed. All the aircraft were supplied by Comanche Fighters, based at Duxford near Cambridge, with the pilots being Dan Friedkin, Steve Hinton and Ed Shipley.

Director Christopher Nolan wanted to film the aerial scenes using huge IMAX cameras. As it was not practical to fit these huge cameras onto a real Spitfire (as this would involve drilling holes in what was essentially a priceless artefact), a modified Yakolev Yak-52TW trainer N699DP was employed in the filming. Called the 'Yakfire', the two-seat aircraft was fitted with a fake Spitfire canopy over its front cockpit, in addition to Spitfire-type exhausts, fibreglass elliptical wingtips, and a 1940 'spinach and sand' camouflage colour scheme. IMAX cameras were fitted above both wings. The one on the port wing was mounted high on lightweight scaffolding and could film the front cockpit, while that on the starboard wing was set low and could shoot forward with the canopy and exhausts in shot to the left of the frame. Another camera filmed to the rear, along the starboard side of the fuselage.

The Yak was normally flown by a stunt pilot from the rear cockpit, with the port wing camera filming an actor in the front cockpit. Thus the actor really did appear to be flying the plane; a degree of realism which had never been achieved before in the history of the movies. In the 'Making of' documentary which features in the 2018 Blu-Ray release, producer Emma Thomas revealed that both herself and Christopher Nolan had looked at earlier aviation pictures and decided that they were often let down by very phoney-looking cockpit shots. A good example would be *633 Squadron* (1964), in which cockpit interiors filmed at MGM Studios, Borehamwood using a blue screen technique looked very unconvincing, even though they were shot using a real Mosquito nose section and what were then regarded as state-of-the-art techniques.

As has always been the case with WW2 aviation movies, shortage of German aircraft was a problem. Early in the production it had been hoped to use a genuine Messerschmitt Bf109E (the type which was used in 1940) in the flying scenes, but none was available. Microsoft founder Paul Allen owned an airworthy 109E which was part of his Flying Heritage Collection in the USA, but was not willing to allow his rare and precious aircraft to be used in the filming. Another 109E was owned by the Biggin Hill Heritage Hangar in the UK, but it was not airworthy at the time of shooting. The Airbus company owned a flyable late-war 109 G-4 but this had a completely different nose from the E-model (the 'Emil'), so in the end the producers chose to use a Spanish-built Hispano HA-1112 MıL Buchon, G-AWHK, which was owned by the Aircraft Restoration Company at Duxford near Cambridge, and had been used in the filming of *Battle of Britain* in 1968. The Buchon was essentially a Spanish version of the Messerschmitt Me109G fitted with a Rolls-Royce Merlin 500 in place of the original Daimler-Benz DB605 engine. As such, it had a completely different nose from an E-model ('Emil') as the Merlin was fitted right way up with the exhaust stack at the top whereas the 'Emil' had an inverted engine with the exhausts at the bottom. In addition, the Buchon's radiator was fitted directly under the engine inside a large air scoop, giving it a very different look from the 'Emil' which had an underwing radiator like the Spitfire.

As well as the three Spitfires and the Buchon, a fourth genuine WW2 warbird makes a brief appearance in the film in the shape of Bristol Blenheim IF L6739, G-BPIV. This is currently the only airworthy Blenheim in the world and – like most of the surviving Blenheim airframes – is actually a Canadian Fairchild Bolingbroke. Originally rebuilt to represent a Blenheim IV (hence the UK civil registration G-BPIV), the aircraft crashed at Duxford in 2003 and was rebuilt as a Mark I using an original nose section which had been used for some years as the body-shell of an electric car.

A number of airfields were used during the filming of *Dunkirk*. Merville was the base for filming aircraft over the beach, while the flying unit moved to Lelystad in the Netherlands later in the shoot. For the dogfight scenes set over the English Channel, the former Royal Naval Air Station (RNAS) at Lee-on-Solent was employed.

A well as the aforementioned Yak 52, three other aircraft were employed as camera ships in the production including two helicopters, an Ecureuil and a Twin Squirrel supplied by Will Banks of GB Helicopters, while a Piper Aerostar 601P flown by Craig Hosking was used for some scenes as it had a similar performance to a Spitfire.

Two other aircraft types appear in the movie, namely the Junkers Ju-87B Stuka dive-bomber and the Heinkel He-III medium bomber. There are now only two complete Stukas left in the world – one in the RAF Museum, Hendon and another in the Museum of Science and Industry in Chicago – and neither is airworthy, so large radio-controlled models had to be employed in filming (as had been used in *Battle of Britain* in 1968 for the Ventnor Radar Station attack sequences, although the real raid had been executed by Junkers Ju-88 twin-engined bombers).

The Heinkel He-III also had to be represented with radio-controlled models as there are currently no airworthy examples anywhere in the world. In 1968, the producers of *Battle of Britain* employed 31 airworthy CASA 2-111s (Spanish-built versions of the He-111 with British Rolls-Royce Merlin 500 engines) which were loaned by the Spanish Air Force. Some of these aircraft subsequently appeared in *Eagles Over London* (1969) and *Patton* (1970). In the mid-seventies, the Spanish Air Force attempted to sell off their remaining CASA 2-111s but only a few were purchased by collectors and museums and the majority were scrapped. The world's last airworthy CASA 2-111 was the example owned by the Commemorative Air Force, N72615, which crashed on 10 July 2003 near Cheyenne Municipal Airport in the USA. At the time of writing there are plans for two CASA 2-111s to be restored to airworthy condition with one, owned by the Flying Heritage Collection in the USA, to be refitted with original German engines.

The radio-controlled Heinkels used in *Dunkirk* looked very authentic, particularly in the scenes in which they are hit and trail smoke. The model Stukas are similarly effective, especially in a scene near the end of the movie where one is hit by a Spitfire and plummets into the sea next to a Royal Navy destroyer.

Shooting of the movie began at Dunkirk beach on 23 May 2016 using 1,400 extras. The East Mole – which plays a very important part in the plot – had to be rebuilt at great expense using vast quantities of wood, and required extensive repairs after it was damaged in storms. Despite being filmed in the summer months, the production was dogged by bad weather. As had been the case with *Saving Private Ryan* (1998), new uniforms had to be manufactured for the production, in this case by a clothing factory in Pakistan. Thousands of them were made up and then artificially aged by the costume department. 1940-pattern boots were also made in Mexico and 'distressed' after production to look old and used.

Nolan's intention had been to film as much as possible of the movie using IMAX cameras. In the end 75% of the film was shot in IMAX, with the remaining 25% being filmed with regular 65mm cameras. The main problems with IMAX cameras were that they were very bulky, incredibly expensive, and also noisy which meant they weren't really suitable for dialogue scenes.

After filming as much as they could in the Dunkirk area, the production team moved to the Netherlands on 25 June to continue shooting on the Ijsselmeer Lake. This is a large inland sea which was created in 1932 by the building of a 32km dam across the Zuiderzee. This resulted in a huge freshwater lake just 14 feet deep, which offered a much safer environment in which to film the English Channel scenes. Four weeks of filming were carried out at this location, and also at Weymouth Harbour and Swanage Station in England, before the remainder of the shooting was carried out in Warner Brothers' studio facilities in Los Angeles.

Some scenes where shot on the Warner Brothers backlot, while the shots of destroyers sinking were filmed at Falls Lake at Universal Studios. These employed a half-scale mockup of a destroyer made of steel and plywood which was 100 feet long and weighed 50 tons. It was mounted on a gimbal so that it could be rolled over in an entirely controllable way. Some scenes of Collins' Spitfire sinking in the English Channel were also shot in Falls Lake, and were matched to earlier footage lensed in Ijsselmeer Lake in the Netherlands.

Some remaining cockpit scenes were shot on a clifftop at Palos Verdes, California using a replica Spitfire. This allowed a very realistic sea background and horizon to be incorporated in the shots without having to resort to green screen or front or back projection methods.

One thing that makes *Dunkirk* so effective is its very powerful use of sound. War and aviation movies have traditionally used stock sound effects. For example, almost any shot of an aircraft diving out of control is usually accompanied by the sound of a WW2 Stuka, since this makes it more exciting.

Another common error is the sound of a bomb dropping, which is usually depicted by a whistling sound which decreases in pitch. In fact, if you are on the ground and a bomb or artillery shell is heading towards you then you will hear a sound which gradually *increases* in pitch, due to the Doppler effect. This is the same reason that a police or ambulance siren increases in pitch as it heads towards you and then decreases as it moves away from you. This common error in films was corrected in *Dunkirk*, in which many sounds were created from scratch.

An airworthy Spitfire at Duxford had its engine run up as different parts of the noise it made – exhaust, supercharger, propeller, etc. – were recorded by sound engineer Richard King for use in the film. Some recording was also carried out on board two preserved WW2 ships: HMS *Belfast* on the Thames in London, and SS *Lane Victory* at San Pedro, California. (The *Lane Victory* had appeared as a troop transport in *The Thin Red Line* in 1998, and in *Flags of Our Fathers* in 2007.)

Another thing that helped the mood of the film – that of rising tension and of time running out – was the brilliant musical score by Hans Zimmer which employed the concept of Shepard Tones. Shepard Tones are a series of multiple overlaid musical sounds which give the impression that they are continually rising in pitch but are actually going nowhere. They can be thought of as the musical equivalent of the famous 'impossible staircase' drawn by artist M.C. Escher, which appears to be going uphill but is never actually rising.

Shepard Tones have actually featured in the popular BBC TV series *Doctor Who* on a few occasions. The track *White Void* by Brian Hodgson was used in *The Mind Robber* (1968), and different versions of it have also appeared in the serials *The Wheel in Space* (1968) and *Inferno* (1970), in which it was used for all the scenes in which the Primord creatures appeared. It was also employed in the ITV series *The Tomorrow People* (1973), and the track is also sometimes known by the alternative title of *Souls in Space*.

Dunkirk premiered on 13 July 2017 in the UK and has since done extremely well at cinemas in the UK and US, making $525.6 million at the box-office against a budget of $100 million.

One critic of the film though, is respected author and historian James Holland. In his blog *Griffon Merlin*, the writer has highlighted a number of historical and technical inaccuracies in the film. As well as the fact that Dunkirk beach appears almost empty in some scenes and there is a lack of smoke in the film, Holland has pointed out that Nolan's film has implied that most of the evacuated troops were rescued by the armada of little ships when in fact it was the Royal Navy that did most of the work. Holland has also questioned the depiction of the RAF in the film. Though accurate Spitfires were used, only one 'Vic' of three aircraft was shown, flying at low altitude. In reality, anything between one and three squadrons – each with 18 aircraft – would be sent over at a time, flying at high altitude so they could dive on any German bombers they saw. Holland has also doubted whether a Spitfire could land on the beach with its wheels down. In fact, during the war several Spitfires (and other aircraft) landed on beaches with wheels down, and the Spitfire beach landing seen in the film was real, although of course it required careful planning.

My main personal criticism of the film would be the lack of numbers of soldiers and vehicles seen on the beach. Also the four destroyers look wrong. As described earlier, one looks too 'modern', and the other three look like current-day minesweepers with fake gun turrets added (which is exactly what they were). In addition, in the real Dunkirk evacuation there would be dozens of vessels lying offshore. This could have been achieved using CGI, but it was Christopher Nolan's intention to use as little CGI as possible with its main use being to depict the Spitfires' tracer fire.

However, these are all niggling criticisms, and I think Christopher Nolan deserves great credit for making a WW2 movie which doesn't have any Americans in it and goes against all the current trends in filmmaking, eschewing action movie clichés. I would the hope that the success of this film leads to other productions – such as Ridley Scott's Battle of Britain movie, Peter Jackson's *Dambusters*, and *Destroyer* (about HMS *Coventry* during the Falklands War) – being greenlighted.

4
BENEATH THE WAVES

ONE of the decisive weapons in WW2 was the submarine, and at times Germany came very close to achieving its goal of sinking enough merchant shipping to knock Britain out of the war. It failed for a number of reasons. One was that Hitler did not give enough priority to the building of a sufficiently large fleet of U-Boats to starve Britain into submission. In addition, most of the German craft were Mark VII and Mark IX boats, vessels which soon became obsolete as the war progressed. During WW2, submarines were really just torpedo boats which could submerge for a short period. On the surface a U-Boat could make 17 knots, but while underwater its electric motors gave it a speed of just six knots, making it vulnerable to attack. Towards the end of the war the Germans developed a much more advanced U-Boat, the Type XXI, which could do 17 knots underwater and would have been difficult to hunt down. Fortunately this class of vessel arrived far too late to influence the course of the war.

At the same time the Allies won the technological war, developing new tactics, weapons, sensors, aircraft, ships and equipment which would enable them to hunt down U-Boats with increasing efficiency. For example, HF/DF ('Huff Duff') radio direction-finding technology in Allied vessels enabled them to pinpoint surfaced U-Boats with great precision, and the invention of the cavity magnetron allowed the development of airborne microwave radar (ASV Mk III) which could pick up even the periscope of a submarine.

Better anti-submarine weapons were also developed. At the start of the war, the RAF used rather ineffective anti-submarine bombs – munitions which were more likely to damage or destroy the attacking aircraft than sink a sub. Later, the RAF replaced these with far more effective depth charges, and from mid-1943 onwards these were supplemented by the Mark 24 mine – an air-dropped acoustic homing torpedo invented in the USA, which accounted for 37 submarines destroyed and 18 damaged during the war.

In addition, the British broke the naval codes used by the *Kriegsmarine*, enabling them to re-route convoys away from U-Boat wolf-packs and send hunter-killer groups of anti-submarine vessels to locations where they could be most effective.

While this was happening, after early problems caused by torpedo failures, the US Navy gradually destroyed much of Japan's merchant fleet with a force of just 140 submarines, and achieved an effective blockade of the Japanese home islands. Along with increasingly effective air raids by Boeing B-29 Superfortresses, this brought Japan to her knees.

This battle beneath the waves in the Atlantic, Mediterranean and Pacific theatres has been the subject of a large number of feature films, many made during the war itself, with the most recent big-budget submarine film being *U-571* (2000).

One of the earliest films to depict submarine warfare in WW2 was the 1941 Powell and Pressburger epic *49th Parallel* which – rather unusually for its time – depicted events from the German point of view. A German submarine, *U-37*, attacks shipping in the Gulf of St Lawrence in Canada and then enters Hudson Bay where it puts a six-man landing party ashore to scavenge supplies. While the men are looking for food, the *U-37* is bombed and sunk by several twin-engined Lockheed Hudson maritime patrol bombers of the Royal Canadian Air Force. The Hudson was derived from a pre-war airliner, the Lockheed Model 14 Super Electra – the same type which took British Prime Minister Neville Chamberlain to Munich in September 1938 – and 2,941 were built between 1938 and 1943.

The six surviving German submariners encounter a number of characters at the Hudson Bay Company Depot at Wolstenholme Post, including Nick the Eskimo (Ley On) and hunter Johnnie (Laurence Olivier), complete with checked shirt, moustache and an incredible French accent which wouldn't have seemed out of place in an episode of *'Allo! 'Allo!* The Germans steal a seaplane, but it runs out of petrol and crashes. Eventually the remaining German, Leutnant Ernst Hirth (Eric Portman), tries to cross the border using a train heading for the neutral US but is thwarted by a Canadian deserter (Raymond Massey) who makes sure he is returned to Canada. Rather like the later *Mrs Miniver* (1942), the film was a propaganda piece designed to convince ordinary Americans that they should enter the war on the British side.

We Dive at Dawn (1943), directed by Anthony Asquith, was one of several naval war movies to feature John Mills. The previous year he had appeared in *In Which We Serve* (q.v.). However, this film is set in April 1942 and concerns the fictional submarine P61 *Sea Tiger*. After a humdrum patrol, the *Sea Tiger* is sent on a mission to destroy the new

German battleship *Brandenburg* which is heading for the Baltic via the Kiel Canal.

On their way, they pick up three downed Luftwaffe airman from a 'rescue buoy', one of whom is portrayed by Walter Gotell, who played German servicemen in a large number of British war movies made between the forties and sixties. The captured Germans reveal that the *Brandenburg* has already entered the Baltic, and Captain Taylor (John Mills) decides to go after her, even though the area is heavily defended. Taylor fires all six of the *Sea Tiger's* forward torpedo tubes at the battleship before crash-diving and enduring a lengthy depth-charging session from German destroyers.

Eventually Taylor fools the Germans by expelling oil, a dead German, and other debris from the torpedo tubes, which makes its way to the surface. (This was indeed a common ploy used by both sides in WW2, and has since become a cliché in submarine films.) The *Sea Tiger* escapes because of this ruse, but now lacks enough diesel oil to return home.

Taylor is preparing to abandon his vessel near a Danish island when Hobson (Eric Portman) comes up with an alternative plan – he can sail into a port on the island and refuel using captured fuel supplies. The plan is risky but Taylor agrees to give it a try and, as Hobson and other crew members hold off the German garrison with rifles and machine guns, the submarine takes on enough oil to get home. Unfortunately the cook, Pincher (Robb Wilton), is killed and Oxford (David Peel) and Lieutenant Johnson (Ronald Millar) are wounded, but the rest of the crew are unharmed and – when the *Sea Tiger* gets home – they learn that they had succeeded in sinking the *Brandenburg*.

Crash Dive (1943) was an impressive submarine movie which was made in Technicolor (something that was very unusual and expensive at the time). Directed by Archie Mayo and written by Jo Swerling and W.R. Burnett, it starred Tyrone Power, Dana Andrews and Anne Baxter. At the time the film was made, Tyrone Power had already enlisted in the United States Marine Corps and had to be given four months special leave to complete the production. The title is rather odd, as 'Crash Dive' was a term used in the Royal Navy and the US Navy instead tended to talk of a 'Quick Dive'.

The plot concerns a US Navy submarine (the USS *Corsair*) which is operating in the North Atlantic, hunting down German merchant raiders that have been preying on Allied shipping. A new Executive Officer, Lieutenant Ward Stewart (Tyrone Power) – who had previously commanded a PT (Patrol Torpedo) Boat – is assigned to the vessel. During a weekend leave, he meets a New London school teacher, Jean Hewlett (Anne Baxter), on a train bound for Washington D.C. and the two start dating. There is a complication, though, as – unbeknown to Stewart – Jean is already romantically involved with Lt. Cdr. Dewey Connors (Dana Andrews). The plot therefore includes a 'love triangle' which has featured in many war movies including *D-Day: Sixth of June* (1956), *Mosquito Squadron* (1968), *Pearl Harbor* (2001) and *Dark Blue World* (2001).

Although much of the film is concerned with this romantic sub-plot, there is considerable action. While out on patrol, the *Corsair* encounters what appears to be a Swedish merchant vessel, but it is actually a German Q-ship with concealed weaponry hidden behind fake deckhouses. In the battle which follows, Stewart sinks the Q-ship while Connors is injured.

The final part of the film features a raid by the *Corsair* on a harbour being used as a U-Boat base. Some of the crew of the submarine paddle ashore and sabotage vital installations, while the *Corsair* torpedoes ships in the harbour. The two principal characters make peace and the film ends with Stewart and Jean getting married, after which there is a brief patriotic advert for War Bonds.

Destination Tokyo (1943) was another top-notch submarine picture which starred Bristol-born Cary Grant as Captain Cassidy, commander of the USS *Copperfin*. The film was made by Warner Brothers and involved an interesting 'star swap' in which Cary Grant was loaned by Columbia Pictures who, in return, received the services of Humphrey Bogart for the lead role in the desert action picture *Sahara* (1943), which is discussed in detail in another of my books, *Battles on Screen: World War II Action Movies* (Extremis Publishing, 2017).

The film begins just 17 days after the Pearl Harbour attack, on 24 December 1941, when Cassidy receives orders to sail from San Francisco to the Aleutian Islands where he is to pick up a meteorologist – Lieutenant Raymond (John Ridgely) – whose job is to obtain important weather data to help the forthcoming air attack on Tokyo by General Doolittle's force of B-25 bombers (as depicted in the 1944 film *Thirty Seconds Over Tokyo*).

While en-route to the Aleutian Islands, two Japanese aircraft attack the *Copperfin*. Both planes are shot down, but one of the pilots survives and subsequently stabs one of the submarine's crew when they attempt a rescue. (Although this may seem like Allied propaganda, this was entirely accurate as the Japanese obeyed the ancient warrior code of *Bushido* in which surrender to an enemy was forbidden. This code was later used as an excuse for their barbaric treatment of Allied POWs.) The aggressive pilot is then shot dead by Tommy

Adams (Robert Hutton), who blames himself for not reacting sooner and tries to atone for his guilt by volunteering to defuse a live bomb which is trapped beneath the deck. Mike is later buried at sea and, when Greek-American 'Tin Can' refuses to attend the ceremony, he has to explain that it is because he feels so upset.

Eventually the *Copperfin* reaches Tokyo Bay and has to wind its way through minefields and past an enemy submarine screen. Cassidy eventually spots a Japanese ship and follows it into the bay. That night, the submarine lands a small party by rubber dinghy and they set up equipment to make weather observations while, back at the submarine, Tommy has developed appendicitis and has to be operated on by the pharmacist's mate (William Prince) using a surgery book, ether, and primitive instruments.

In due course, the shore party returns safely to the *Copperfin* and Raymond broadcasts the important weather information back to the US Navy High Command. The Japanese realise there is a US submarine in the bay and make a search, but the *Copperfin* remains undetected and Cassidy's crew watch the Doolittle Raid through the periscope before departing.

On the way home, the *Copperfin* sinks a Japanese aircraft carrier but is then depth charged for hours by a destroyer. Eventually the US vessel manages to turn the tables on its opponent and sinks it with a torpedo, allowing the submarine to return safely to San Francisco.

Further submarine pictures were made in the decades following the war. *Operation Pacific* (1951) was set on the USS *Thunderfish*, and starred Ward Bond as Commander John 'Pop' Perry and John Wayne as Lieutenant Commander 'Duke' Gifford. Part of the plot dealt with the problem of unreliable torpedoes in the US Navy, an issue that was not solved until late 1943. At the time, the standard US torpedo was the Mark 14 which had a number of faults. It had an unreliable magnetic detonator, was slow running, and had a relatively small warhead (643lb) compared with its Japanese counterpart – the Type 91 torpedo – which carried 893lbs of explosive. There were many occasions in the first two years of the Pacific War when US Mark 14 torpedoes hit their targets but failed to explode. The later part of the film deals with Operation Victory, the Japanese fleet's attempts to repel the US invasion of the Philippines in October 1944.

One oddity of this period was *Submarine Attack* (1954), an Italian war movie directed by Duilio Coletti which had an underlying message of peace and reconciliation. Germany, Italy and Japan have always had some difficulty in coming to terms with their involvement in WW2, and – even today – it is a source of great embarrassment to these nations. It is probably true to say that the majority of the Italian people never wanted to join the war on Hitler's side, and this was reflected in the readiness with which Italian forces surrendered during the conflict.

Submarine Attack has an inappropriate title, because it is really concerned with the actions of a humane Italian submarine commander who goes out of his way to rescue survivors from Allied merchant ships he has sunk, providing them with food and shelter and – on one occasion – even permitting them to celebrate Christmas aboard his vessel. It must be one of the first pacifist war movies, and the cast includes a young Lois Maxwell as a captured Royal Navy officer, several years before she found fame for playing Miss Moneypenny in the James Bond films.

Run Silent, Run Deep (1958) starred the electrifying combination of Burt Lancaster and Clark Gable, and was directed by Robert Wise who later helmed some of the most highly acclaimed movies in motion picture history including *The Day the Earth Stood Still* (1951), *West Side Story* (1961), *The Sound of Music* (1965) and *The Sand Pebbles* (1966). He also directed *Star Trek: The Motion Picture* (1979) which, although vilified by critics and being considered overlong and lacking a coherent plot, proved extremely popular with fans and effectively re-launched the franchise which has now embraced countless films and spin-off TV series.

The film was based on a novel of the same name by Commander Edward L. Beach Jr., and covered a number of themes including vengeance, endurance, loyalty, and honour during combat. Commander Beach later complained that the finished film lacked the subtleties of his original book.

The plot concerned a US Navy submarine officer, Commander P.J. Richardson (Clark Gable), who is determined to get even with a Japanese destroyer captain who he has dubbed 'Bungo Pete' and who has been responsible for sinking three US submarines in the Bungo Straits, including his previous command. In this respect he resembles Captain Ahab in *Moby Dick*, who is obsessed with killing a huge whale. Eventually, Richardson persuades the Navy Board to give him a new vessel – the USS *Nerka* – with an experienced executive officer, Lieutenant Commander Jim Bledsoe (Burt Lancaster). Richardson sets off towards the Bungo Straits with the intention of vanquishing his opponent.

However, Bledsoe feels that the mission is too risky and also resents the fact that he has not been given command of the vessel – something which he feels is his right. Despite the tension between him and his executive officer, Richardson continues with his mission to find and destroy 'Bungo Pete'. He trains his crew in the highly risky practice of engaging enemy destroyers with a 'bow shot': a technique that often fails, as the oncoming torpedo can be easily 'combed'.

After entering the Bungo Straits, the *Nerka* comes across a large Japanese convoy. They succeed in sinking a large cargo ship and attack 'Bungo Pete', but are then engaged by enemy aircraft and forced to dive. For the next few hours they endure a lengthy depth charge attack. Three of the crew are killed, and Richardson is knocked out. The *Nerka* also narrowly avoids what its crew believes to be one of its own torpedoes coming back at them.

Eventually Bledsoe fools the Japanese by expelling dead bodies and other debris from the torpedo tubes, which then float to the surface. He assumes command of the vessel and heads back to Pearl Harbour. During the journey the crew listen to 'Tokyo Rose', who announces that the *Nerka* has been sunk. Bledsoe realises that – as the Japanese think their submarine has been destroyed – there is an opportunity for them to return to the Bungo Straits and complete the mission.

The *Nerka* makes its way back to the Bungo Straits, where it sinks the Japanese destroyer, the *Akikaze*. It is also nearly hit by a torpedo fired by a mystery submarine. Bledsoe realises that the *Akikaze* was working with a Japanese submarine all along. The *Nerka* tracks it down, forces it to the surface, and sinks it with a torpedo. His goal achieved, Richardson collapses and dies.

The *Nerka* was played by the USS *Redfish*, and the film received much praise for its accurate depiction of torpedo attacks – particularly the use of a Torpedo Data Computer (a purely mechanical analogue device which was often called the 'fruit machine') to achieve a shooting solution. The film also correctly depicts the common tactic of attacking at night on the surface, resulting in greater accuracy. This method was also used by the Germans and, although highly effective, it put the submarine at greater risk of counter-attack from enemy vessels equipped with radar.

The Enemy Below (1957), directed by Dick Powell, dealt with the duel of wits between Lieutenant Commander Murrell (Robert Mitchum) and his German counterpart, German U-Boat Commander Kapitan-Leutnant von Stolberg (Curt Jurgens), a man who is not enamoured with the Nazi regime.

The film was based on the 1956 book of the same name by British author Denys Rayner, who had served in the North Atlantic. Rayner's original novel was set on the Royal Navy destroyer HMS *Hecate*, but for the film version the action shifted to the South Atlantic and the warship became the USS *Haynes*, a *Buckley*-class destroyer. This vessel was portrayed by the USS *Whitehurst*, and filming was carried out off Hawaii.

The film deals with the cat-and-mouse game of wits between the American captain and his German opponent. Some of the destroyer crew initially doubt Murrell's tactics and ability – as he is a former merchant skipper – but they soon develop respect for his skill, as does the Captain of the U-Boat who realises he is dealing with a wily opponent. The two commanders are in fact evenly matched, and a stalemate develops with Murrell repeatedly depth charging his opponent to keep him down until reinforcements arrive.

Unfortunately the German commander seizes an opportunity to torpedo the *Haynes*, and it looks as though it is game over for the Americans. But Murrell has another trick up his sleeve – he tells the crew to build a few fires on the deck to make the destroyer appear more badly damaged than it actually is, and abandon ship. The U-Boat falls for the ruse and surfaces with the intention of finishing off the destroyer with its 88mm deck gun, allowing Murrell to ram the submarine and sink it after damaging it with gunfire.

Murrell and von Stolberg salute each other as the U-Boat sinks. Murrell then has a change of heart and throws von Stolberg a rope, which enables him to save both himself and his injured executive officer Heini Schwaffer (Theodore Bikel). Schwaffer subsequently dies, and the film ends with the surviving German and American crew being rescued by a US Navy ship. Schwaffer is buried at sea as the American crew watch respectfully. In the original novel, the ending is very different as the (British) destroyer captain tries to take a swing at the U-Boat Commander while they are in a lifeboat and there is none of the mutual respect and admiration depicted in the film version. In fact, two different endings of the film were made – one in which the U-Boat Captain dies, and another in which he is rescued.

The Enemy Below provided the blueprint for many submarine movies which followed, and was a clear influence on the highly successful *U-571* (2000). It also provided the plot outline for a 1966 episode of *Star Trek*, *Balance of Terror*, which was obviously based on the film. *Star Trek* creator and writer Gene Roddenberry later made a payment to the estate of Gary Cooper, who owned the rights to the film.

Killers from the Deep, an episode of the Irwin Allen TV series *Voyage to the Bottom of the Sea* (1965-68), was also based on *The Enemy Below* and used substantial amounts of footage from it. Actor David Hedison – who (as Al Hedison) had appeared in *The Enemy Below* as Lieutenant Ware – had a long-running role in *Voyage to the Bottom of the Sea* as Commander Lee Crane, captain of the SSRN *Seaview*. Hedison was a close friend of Roger Moore, and played the character of CIA operative Felix Leiter in two Bond movies, *Live and Let Die* (1973) and *Licence to Kill* (1989).

Torpedo Run (1958) was a highly-acclaimed war film directed by Joseph Pevney, which was made in Metrocolor and Cinemascope. It starred Glenn Ford as Lieutenant Commander Barney Doyle, a WW2 submarine commander who becomes obsessed with sinking the Japanese aircraft carrier IJN *Shinaru*. The film opens with the USS *Grayfish* looking for the *Shinaru*, but then Doyle learns that the Japanese carrier is accompanied by a number of vessels including the transport ship *Yoshida Maru*, which has a number of civilian passengers on board including his wife and child, who were captured in the Philippines.

Grayfish eventually finds the ships, and Doyle attempts to torpedo the *Shinaru* against the advice of his second-in-command, Lieutenant Archer (Ernest Borgnine). Archer's misgivings are proved correct, as the torpedoes miss the *Shinaru* and hit the *Yoshida Maru*, much to Doyle's horror. The Japanese make no attempt to rescue the survivors, and they are left to drown.

Doyle then follows the *Shinaru* into Tokyo Bay and tries once more to sink it, but he again fails and is forced to return to Pearl Harbour. Though Vice Admiral Setton (Philip Owen) wants to give Doyle a desk job in view of what happened, Sloan persuades him to allow Doyle one last crack at the Japanese carrier.

Later, on patrol off the Alaskan coast, the *Grayfish* finds the *Shinaru* once more. She fires off some torpedoes and immediately has to dive to avoid a depth charge attack by the carrier's escort. The *Grayfish* is damaged and sinks to the bottom of the ocean, forcing the crew to abandon the vessel using escape apparatus. They are picked up by another US submarine, which sinks the Japanese destroyer. Doyle and his men then learn that their earlier torpedo attack had sunk the *Shinaru*.

Up Periscope (1959) was a vehicle for rising star James Garner, who at that time was well-known for appearing in the TV series *Maverick* (1957-62), and was based on the 1956 novel by Robb White. A few years later Garner achieved great fame for appearances in *The Great Escape* (1963) and *Grand Prix* (1966), for which he had to learn how to drive a racing car.

Garner plays Lieutenant Kenneth Braden, a recently-trained US Navy frogman who is told to report for duty before he can inform his new girlfriend Sally Johnson (Andrea Martin). He subsequently discovers that she is a Naval Intelligence Officer who had been given the job of assessing his suitability for a forthcoming secret mission.

A US submarine captained by Commander Stevenson (Edmond O'Brien) takes Braden to the island of Kosrae to photograph a Japanese military code book at a radio station. Stevenson makes Braden's mission easier by taking his submarine into Lelu Harbour (against orders) so that Braden has a shorter and easier swim. After Braden has completed his mission, Stevenson dictates a letter in which he admits that he risked the submarine and his crew by going into the harbour. When the submarine returns to Pearl Harbour, Braden announces that his crew had accidentally mislaid the letter. Braden is overjoyed to discover that Sally Johnson is waiting for him on the dockside.

The Cruel Sea (1952), directed by Charles Frend and produced by Leslie Norman, dealt with Allied anti-submarine operations during the Battle of the Atlantic, with a screenplay by Eric Ambler based on the best-selling book by Nicholas Monsarrat. The film begins in the autumn of 1939 in Glasgow, when Captain Ericson (Jack Hawkins) takes command of a brand-new *Flower*-class corvette, HMS *Compass Rose*, which has been built on the Clyde. Ericson had previously commanded a merchant vessel, but had been conscripted into the Royal Navy when war began. His two sub-lieutenants – Lockhart (Donald Sinden) and Ferraby (John Stratton) – are both newly-commissioned officers with no prior naval experience. Their new first lieutenant, James Bennett (Stanley Baker), is a bad-tempered bully, but he soon has to go on long-term sick leave as he suffers from a duodenal ulcer.

Over the next three years, the crew of the *Compass Rose* become an effective fighting team and even destroy a U-Boat. In one disturbing scene (which is probably the best-remembered one from the whole film), Ericson is forced to ignore survivors of a U-Boat attack floating in the water in order to depth charge a submarine which his ASDIC (sonar) operator assures him is directly below the men. The resulting explosions kill all the floating seamen, but no submarine is found and Ericson is consumed with guilt. Did he make the right decision?

As I have observed, this scene is one of the most famous in film history, but when it came to be edited it was found that a point-of-view shot of the *Compass Rose* moving away from the survivors in the water had not been filmed. As it would be too expensive to re-mount the shot, the film editor Peter Tanner simply reversed a section of film which means that the seagulls appear to be flying backwards in the shot, although most people who have seen the picture have never noticed this trick being used.

The ASDIC mentioned in the film was the original name for sonar, and is an acronym for the Anti-Submarine Detection Investigation Committee which was set up in WWI to investigate new ways of locating submarines. The Germans never had sonar technology to match the Allies, and relied solely on hydrophones (underwater microphones) to detect vessels.

One weakness of wartime ASDIC was that it could only detect submarines which were ahead of the vessel. Any submarine directly below the ship could not be detected, which meant that depth charge attacks had to be made 'blind'. The problem was solved later in the war by the use of new weapons (namely the 'Hedgehog' and 'Squid' anti-submarine mortars), which fired forward. 'Hedgehog' – which used the same spigot mortar principle as the hand-held PIAT anti-tank weapon – was particularly effective, as it fired a volley of 12 contact-fused bombs ahead of the ship in an oval pattern. It was bought by the US Navy and one of its vessels, USS *England*, a *Buckley*-class destroyer, sunk six Japanese submarines using this weapon.

After three years of active service, the *Compass Rose* is herself torpedoed, and the crew is forced to take to life-rafts. There aren't enough to go round, and some of the crew die of hypothermia. The next morning, a British destroyer picks up the survivors.

Captain Ericson survives this ordeal and eventually takes command of HMS *Saltash Castle*, a *Castle*-class frigate which is far larger than the *Compass Rose*, with much better armament and equipment. Over the next three years the *Saltash Castle* takes part in numerous naval actions including the harrowing Arctic convoys, and sinks a U-Boat after a long action in which Ericson only manages to stay awake by using

Benzedrine tablets. Incidentally, the ship's doctor in these scenes is played by Andrew Cruickshank, who later played Dr Cameron in the long-running BBC TV series *Dr Finlay's Casebook* (1962-71).

The German submarine is forced to surface, and the frigate's crew spends a couple of minutes jumping for joy until Ericson orders them to open fire on the enemy vessel as it is still a threat. The crew then riddle the U-Boat with rounds from a 40mm Bofors anti-aircraft gun and a Lewis 0.303 inch machine gun until it is obvious that the enemy sailors want to surrender. They promptly swim across to the British frigate and are rescued. For the first time, Ericson sees the enemy at close hand and realise they are ordinary human beings and not Nazi supermen. The film ends with the German submarine fleet surrendering en-masse in May 1945, and Ericson reflects that in almost six years of combat his crew only sunk two U-Boats.

The real star of the film is the ship HMS *Compass Rose*. 267 *Flower*-class Corvettes were built during WW2, but by 1951 not a single one remained in service with the Royal Navy and the producers were forced to use the Greek ship RHN *Kriezis* (formerly HMS *Coreopsis*), which was itself awaiting scrapping. At the start of the film the *Kriezis* is supposedly playing a brand-new ship, but it is obvious it has seen better days as the paintwork is covered with chips and stains and streaked with rust. This would have been even more noticeable if the film had been made in colour.

Based on a pre-war whaler design and with a displacement of about 1,000 tons, the *Flower*-class corvette had a lot of deficiencies and would probably not have been accepted by the Royal Navy in peacetime. Its triple expansion reciprocating steam engine was 19th century technology and gave it a top speed of only 16 knots – one knot less than a surfaced U-Boat. It also had a very weak defensive armament which could be as little as a single 4-inch QF gun, one two-pounder pom-pom AA gun and two Lewis 0.303 inch machine guns, making it very vulnerable to air attack. It also rolled very readily – it was said that a *Flower*-class corvette could roll in wet grass – and had a tendency to flood in bad weather, making it a very 'wet' ship. In addition, it had limited refrigeration capacity which meant that the crew had to eat mainly canned and dehydrated foods on long missions. Despite these defects, the *Flower* class destroyed 47 German and four Italian submarines during the war, while 36 of the 267 built were lost due to accidents and enemy action.

The Cruel Sea premiered in the UK on 24 March 1953 and was a critical and commercial success, even doing well in the USA against expectations. It is now regarded as the best film ever made about the Battle of the Atlantic.

Another film which dealt with the subject of German U-Boat crews was *The McKenzie Break* (1970), which was filmed in Ireland and Turkey. The screenplay was by William V. Norton, based on the 1958 novel *The Bowmanville Break* by Sydney Shelley, which chronicled a real-life incident in Bowmanville POW Camp in Ontario, Canada in October 1942 when German prisoners staged a riot.

Later, four German submarine commanders attempted an escape which involved a pick-up by a U-Boat. The plan was thwarted by the Royal Canadian Navy. Another influence on the screenplay was the series of events at Grizedale Hall, Cumbria (including the construction of an illicit radio transmitter), where a number of *Kriegsmarine* officers were imprisoned during WW2. The film was directed by Lamont Johnson, who later helmed the very controversial rape drama

Lipstick (1976), and was produced by Arthur Gardner and Jules V. Levy.

The plot involved Captain Jack Connor (Brian Keith), an Irishman serving in the British Army, who is sent to a POW camp in the north-west of Scotland which has been experiencing serious breaches of discipline instigated by fanatical Nazi U-Boat Commander Kapitan zur see Willi Schluter (Helmut Griem). The situation is being aggravated by the camp's Commanding Officer, Major Perry (Ian Hendry), a weak individual who has difficulty establishing his authority.

The wily Captain Connor soon deduces that the various riots and breaches of discipline are being orchestrated by the prisoners to provide cover for a mass escape attempt. They are digging a tunnel and hiding much of the excavated earth in the attic space of their huts. A former crime reporter, Connor works out that the prisoners are sending and receiving messages via coded letters and, after having the letters decoded by an expert, he finds out that a mass escape is planned with the submariners being rescued by a U-Boat which will surface offshore. Connor then proposes that the escape should be allowed to go ahead but with careful monitoring by spotter plane, the Police and the Army, with the ultimate goal of capturing the submarine involved in the mission.

The best scenes in the film are those in which the prisoners break out and make their way across the damp Scottish countryside in a battered red lorry which has been disguised as a civilian truck carrying explosives, complete with police motorcycle escort. The sky is leaden and the ground is sodden for the full duration of the picture, and rural Ireland in 1970 does look very much like 1940s Scotland, complete with red telephone boxes, flocks of sheep and heavily potholed roads.

The POW's red lorry is initially spotted by an Auster AOP.6 observation plane, but the prisoners manage to give it the slip and Connor persuades another pilot to take him aloft in a Royal Navy Percival Proctor III liaison aircraft. Both these aeroplanes were accurate for the period, and cockpit scenes were done 'for real' with a camera inside the aircraft. The Percival Proctor used in the movie had the civil registration G-AIWA, and had the false serial R7524 and Royal Navy markings applied for filming. This aircraft was later written off in a crash at La Ferte Alais in France on 9 June 1984. The identity of the Auster used in the film remains unknown to this day.

The final scenes of the movie are especially thrilling. The German submariners abseil down a cliff and, using rubber dinghies, start to paddle out to a waiting U-Boat which has just surfaced off the coast. Unfortunately for them, Connor has spotted the U-Boat from his aircraft and gives its position to a nearby Royal Navy patrol vessel.

As the patrol boat speeds to the scene, Connor instructs his pilot to buzz the POWs in the dinghies in an attempt to put them off. Kapitan Schluter fires at the aircraft using a sub-machine gun, and the crew of the U-Boat also open fire with twin MG 42 machine guns. Connor's plane is hit and has to make an emergency landing on the clifftop, just as a Royal Navy patrol boat arrives on the scene.

The German U-Boat is forced to dive to escape attack, and Schluter is left stranded. The patrol boat immediately detects the submarine on ASDIC and launches an attack using sideward-firing depth charge throwers, while Captain Connor observes the scene from the clifftop. The whole operation has ended in a fiasco as the submarine has apparently got away unscathed and most of the prisoners have escaped, though Schluter and two colleagues have been recaptured.

The last ten minutes of the film are a tribute to the film editor's art, as all the scenes involving the submarine and the patrol boat were filmed in Turkey with the help of the Turkish Navy and were seamlessly edited into the footage shot in Ireland. The submarine in these shots was a former US Navy *Balao*-class, Guppy Type IIa, while the patrol boat was an ex-Royal Navy Fairmile Class B Motor Launch.

One of the last scenes in the film, which shows Connor (from behind) standing at the cliff edge beside the wingtip of the Proctor as he gazes down at the patrol boat, was filmed in Turkey using a double for Connor and a dummy Proctor wing section. The shots of the patrol boat's sonar set, and depth charge firings and explosions, were stock footage.

The film premiered on 28 October 1970 and was well-received, though there was some controversy at the time over the fact that it was set in Scotland but filmed in Ireland, with some Scottish politicians wondering why it was not made in their native land. Incidentally, the same questions were asked 25 years later when *Braveheart* (1995) – a film about the life of William Wallace – was made in Ireland.

A U-Boat plays a prominent part in the plot of *Murphy's War* (1971), an action-adventure which was directed by Peter Yates. Yates had served as an assistant director on *The Guns of Navarone* (1961), and was a former racing driver. With his interest in automobiles, he was keen that any films he directed should have realistic car chases. One thing that had always annoyed Yates was that up until the late sixties, car chases in films were always speeded up by under-cranking the camera. This can be seen in the early Bond films, such as *Goldfinger* (1964).

This, he felt, was not authentic, as the interesting thing about a car cornering at speed is the way it rolls and bounces up and down on its suspension. Yates first put his ideas into practice in the film *Robbery* (1967), which was loosely based on the real Great Train Robbery and featured what is now regarded as the first truly realistic car chase in the history of the movies.

The following year Yates directed *Bullitt* (1968), which included an exciting car chase between the bad guys' Dodge Charger and a Ford Mustang driven by Steve McQueen's title character, Police Lieutenant Frank Bullitt. McQueen did his own driving for the movie, and all car interior scenes were done for real without any studio work involving back projection or blue screen. The resulting few minutes of action is still regarded as the 'gold standard' for movie car chases.

Yates' flair for action and realism is evident in *Murphy's War*, which was scripted by Stirling Silliphant and based on a 1969 novel of the same name by Max Catto.

The film opens with the armed merchant cruiser RN/MS *Mount Kyle* sinking near the mouth of the Orinoco River in Venezuela after being torpedoed by a German U-Boat in April 1945. The German submarine has surfaced and its Commander, Lauchs (Horst Janson), has ordered his crew to machine gun the survivors in the water in order to preserve the secret of his vessel's location. Unfortunately for Lauchs, all this has been witnessed by the merchant's ship's floatplane, an American-built Grumman J2F Duck, which was airborne at the time of the attack. The Duck is slightly damaged by gunfire from the U-Boat, and subsequently beaches.

Apart from the Duck pilot, the only other survivor of the massacre is the *Mount Kyle's* aircraft mechanic Murphy (Peter O'Toole). As he struggles ashore, he sees the U-Boat making its way up the Orinoco River to a hiding place. Murphy later travels to a missionary settlement on the Orinoco where he is nursed back to health by a pacifist Quaker doctor, Dr Hayden, who is played by O'Toole's then-wife Sian Phillips.

Some of the U-Boat crew subsequently carry out a raid on the settlement, and their Commander shoots Lieutenant Ellis (John Hallam), the Grumman Duck pilot. But they don't know about Murphy, who vows to restore the Duck to flying condition and bomb the sub.

Helped by Frenchman Louis Brezon (Phillipe Noiret), Murphy repairs the Duck and takes it on a test flight, which is no mean feat as he isn't a trained pilot. Two real Grumman Ducks were used in the production, and were flown by top stunt pilot Frank Tallman. For one scene, Tallman piloted the aircraft from the rear cockpit while O'Toole sat in the front cockpit and apparently controlled the plane. O'Toole also learned to taxi the aircraft on the water, and – for the most dangerous flying stunts – Tallman was made up to look like O'Toole. Thus the film features a degree of realism in its flying scenes which had never been seen before in the movies, as very few of the cockpit scenes were shot in the studio.

The only inaccuracy in the film is that the Grumman Duck seaplane was never used by British Forces during the war. In Max Catto's book, the aircraft was a Fairey Swordfish floatplane, but no seaplane variant was available for filming as only one Swordfish – LF 326, which was a wheeled version and had taken part in the filming of *Sink the Bismarck!* in 1960 – was in flying condition in 1970. At that time, it was owned by the Royal Naval Air Station at Yeovilton.

Two Grumman J2F-6 Duck floatplanes, US civil registration N67790 and N1196N, were used in the making of the film, both supplied by Tallmantz Aviation and flown by Frank Tallman. Tallmantz Aviation was a company set up by fellow stunt pilots Paul Mantz and Frank Tallman. Mantz was killed while flying the Tallmantz Phoenix P-1 for the film *Flight of the Phoenix* (1965). Tallman had been due to carry out the flight, but had badly injured his leg in a go-kart accident. Eventually part of it had to be amputated, but he continued as a stunt pilot with a prosthetic leg.

After restoring the Duck to flying condition, Murphy manufactures two huge home-made petrol bombs and fits them under the Duck's wings. He then attacks the U-Boat, which is lying further up river. He releases the aircraft's ordnance and is rewarded by two huge fireballs. Murphy returns to the settlement triumphant, but unfortunately his air raid has been a failure as the bombs had actually missed. Soon afterwards, the U-Boat returns to the settlement and riddles the Duck with gunfire before destroying the buildings with explosives. The floatplane in this sequence was an expendable replica created mainly from spare parts.

But Murphy isn't finished yet and – with the help of Louis – he concocts a plan to ram the U-Boat with the Frenchman's boat, which is a flat-bottomed barge with a mounted crane, converted from a wartime tank landing craft. As the Irishman puts the plan into effect, news comes through on the radio that the European war is over, but Murphy is unrepentant. 'Their war 〚may be over〛... not mine.' Commander Lauchs pleads with him to stop, as hostilities have ceased, but Murphy is determined to execute his plan. The U-Boat riddles the barge with machine gun fire and cannon rounds, and then fires a torpedo which misses and gets stuck in a mud-bank. Murphy retrieves the torpedo using the barge's crane and then drops it on the sub, resulting in a massive explosion which destroys the U-Boat, killing himself in the process.

Murphy's War was filmed on location in the Orinoco River in Venezuela between February and July 1970. The scenes of the *Mount Kyle* sinking were shot in the large outdoor water tank at Malta Film Facilities, and some interiors were filmed at Pinewood and Twickenham Studios in England. The Type IX U-Boat was played by the Venezuelan Navy submarine ARV *Carite*, which was originally the USS *Tilefish*. The main title theme was by John Barry, though the incidental music was by Ken Thorne (as had been the case with the ITC TV series *The Persuaders* in 1970). The film was not a great success despite its realism and high production values, probably because of ongoing public disquiet about the Vietnam War.

An unusual film about submarine warfare was the little-known British picture *Mystery Submarine* (1963), which was directed by C.M. Pennington Richards and starred Edward Judd, James Robertson Justice and Laurence Payne. The plot concerns the German vessel *U-153*, which is damaged by an Allied air attack while on patrol in the Atlantic. Seawater gets into the battery compartment, causing the release of poisonous chlorine gas, and a British prize crew takes over the vessel and capture its secret papers. This part of the plot is similar to the later big-budget movie *U-571* (2000), and was based on a real-life incident in 1941 when the Royal Navy captured *U-570* and put her in into service as HMS *Graph* (pennant number P715).

Later, British Intelligence suggest that the vessel can be used as a Trojan Horse to infiltrate German wolf-packs, and a picked crew of volunteers led by Commander Tarlton (Edward Judd) is given the task. The mission is successful, and the captured sub even destroys the wolf-pack leader before being sunk by a British frigate. Fortunately all the crew escape before she goes down.

The greatest film ever made about submarine warfare, though, must be the West German production *Das Boot* (*The Boat*), which was filmed in 1980 and released in 1981. Directed by Wolfgang Petersen, it exists in four different versions: the original TV series of six 50-minute episodes, a 150-minute theatrical version (with English subtitles), a 200-minute 'Director's Cut' with optional dubbed English soundtrack and new digital sound effects, and finally a 123-minute English language version which was re-titled *The Boat*.

The film begins in the autumn of 1941, as the *U-96* is setting out on a long patrol from its base at La Rochelle on the Atlantic coast of France. The submarine pens shown in the film were the real thing, built in the early years of WW2 to protect German U-Boats from air attack.

One thing that comes over in the movie is just how cramped and uncomfortable WW2 submarines were. There was only one toilet for about 50 crew, no baths or showers, poor ventilation, and no air-conditioning or dehumidifiers. Every cubic inch of the submarine was packed with food supplies, with sausages, bread, hams and bananas hanging everywhere, and – as the sub had limited refrigeration capacity – everything went off quite rapidly. WW2 submarines dripped with condensation inside, and foods like bread soon rotted. Later in the war, the British and Americans introduced air conditioning, dehumidification and showers in their submarines, but U-Boats never had such comforts.

In the film, the crew start off clean-shaven and well-dressed and eat fairly decent meals, but as time progresses they become dirty, unshaven and unkempt, and have to exist on canned foods as all their fresh produce had rotted. WW2 submariners of all nations have spoken about the stench inside their vessels – a mixture of stale sweat, faeces, urine, diesel oil and vomit – so it is probably just as well that *Das Boot* was never made in *Smell-O-Vision*!

A highly accurate mock-up of a U-Boat interior was created at Bavaria Studios in Hamburg, using a real submarine as a reference, and much of the interior filming was carried out using a hand-held camera with inbuilt gyroscopes to steady the image. Thus when the crew race from one end of the boat to the other, swinging their way through multiple hatches, the camera follows them in a *tour-de-force* of subjective camerawork.

Several models of the *U-96* in different scales were built for various sequences, including a full-size towable replica. The latter was used for some sequences in *Raiders of the Last Ark* (1981), as were the submarine pens at La Rochelle.

The film cost $15m and was written for the screen by Dean Reisner, based on a 1973 novel by Lothar-Gunther Buchheim. It follows the crew of the *U-96* as they leave La Rochelle to hunt down Allied shipping in the Atlantic and the Bay of Biscay.

Early on in their patrol, they are attacked by a destroyer but manage to evade its depth charges by diving deep. Later, they receive reports of a convoy and launch an attack. Once again they are attacked by a destroyer escort, and dive even deeper than before to avoid damage. Pipes burst and bolts crack as the *U-96* heads for the bottom, far deeper than its intended operating depth. The submarine has to play dead for a while until it is safe to resurface (a familiar trope in submarine movies).

When the *U-96* resurfaces, they discover a severely damaged and sinking tanker ablaze from stem to stern. The Captain gives the order to finish it off with a torpedo and, after it has hit, the crew of the U-Boat watch in horror as the tanker crew jump into the sea which is covered with patches of blazing oil.

The *U-96*'s crew expect to be sent back to La Rochelle for repairs and replenishment of stores, but they are instead ordered to head for the Italian naval base at La Spezia. Unfortunately this means they will have to pass through the Straits of Gibraltar, one of the most heavily-defended stretches of water on the planet.

Rather gingerly, the *U-96* makes is way through the Straits of Gibraltar on the surface but is then attacked by an Allied patrol plane, which is represented by a solitary North American T-6 Harvard, a type which was never used for this purpose. The *U-96* is severely damaged and sinks to the bottom of the sea, with water pouring in. After spending some time on the seabed with the air slowly running out, the crew manage to repair the vessel. They reach the surface and then return to La Rochelle but, as their submarine is about to dock at the quayside with crowds cheering and a band playing, an Allied air raid begins.

The attacking aircraft are played by two T-6 Harvard trainers which apparently bomb the submarine and surrounding facilities (though no actual bombs are seen). A clip from *Battle of Britain* (1969), showing several CASA 2-111s (Spanish-built Heinkel He-111s) breaking formation, can also be seen at this point. Many of the crew are killed or injured in the attack, and the wounded Captain watches as the *U-96* sinks (though, as it was sunk in shallow water, it would a relatively simple matter to refloat and repair it!).

The most recent big-budget submarine picture to date, though, is *U-571* (2000) which was produced by Dino and Martha De Laurentiis and directed by Jonathan Mostow. Even before production had begun, the film attracted controversy as it became known that the screenplay would suggest that it was the Americans – and not the British – who had made the most crucial capture of an Enigma code machine during the war. As most historians know, the most significant retrieval of an Enigma machine occurred on 9 May 1941, when *U-110* was forced to the surface by HMS *Bulldog* and HMS *Aubretia*. Although the submarine was in danger of sinking, a boarding party led by Lieutenant David Balme got inside the U-Boat and retrieved an intact Enigma machine and current code books. All this was achieved without the German crew realising what had happened, and was one of the greatest intelligence breakthroughs of the war.

The film *U-571* suggested that this crucial Enigma capture occurred in April 1942 by members of the US Navy. One person who found about this was none other than David Balme, who was still alive in 1999 when the film was being planned and made his feelings known to director Jonathan Mostow. Mostow, to his credit, listened to Balme's point of view and gave him a job on the film as a technical advisor, although the basic plot was unchanged. Balme has since praised the film for its excitement and level of technical accuracy, although the aforementioned historical inaccuracy about Enigma captures during the war remains.

The film was made in Italy and Malta in 1999. As no working U-Boats were available, two full-sized towable submarine replicas were constructed, one of which was an American S-Class vessel which had been converted to look like a U-Boat.

The film begins with the *U-571* attacking an Allied merchant ship. A Royal Navy destroyer retaliates by depth charging the submarine, causing severe damage. Kapitan-Leutnant Gunther Wassner makes a distress call, but it is intercepted by the US Navy who realise that they have a golden opportunity to capture a vital Enigma machine. Their plan is to steal the Enigma machine and then sink the *U-571* before the Germans realise what has happened. An old S-Class vessel, the *S-33*, is modified to look like a resupply U-Boat (a 'Milk Cow'), and a crew is hastily put together which includes an Executive Officer, Lieutenant Tyler (Matthew McConaughey), who is unhappy that his request for promotion to Captain has been blocked by his current Commanding Officer, Lieutenant Commander Mike Dahlgren (Bill Paxton).

The *S-33* sails to its rendezvous with the crippled German submarine and meets up with the *U-571* on a stormy night. A large boarding party paddles from the *S-33* across to the German submarine but, with just yards to go, an alert German sailor sees that one of their 'rescuers' is carrying a sub machine gun and raises the alarm. A brief firefight breaks out, and several Germans and Americans are killed. But enough US sailors get on board to carry out their mission, and the Enigma machine is captured.

Just as the American sailors are congratulating themselves on their success, disaster strikes as the *S-33* is hit by a torpedo from the genuine 'Milk Cow' supply U-Boat which has arrived on the scene and observed what has happened. (This is a technical error, as 'Milk Cow' submarines did not carry torpedoes.) The *S-33* is hit and sinks, and Commander Dahlgren is blown into the water. A scene in which he is shown to have been decapitated was deleted, as it was considered too gruesome.

Tyler quickly takes command of the *U-571*, orders all hatches closed, and crash dives the vessel which is already damaged, with only one of two diesel engines working. He now only has a small crew and is not sure how to operate the craft. The 'Milk Cow' tries to sink the *U-571*, but its torpedoes all miss. The *U-571* fires back, and one torpedo scores a lucky hit.

Relieved that they have survived, Tyler orders his crew to patch up the U-Boat and head for the nearest friendly territory, which happens to be Land's End. They travel on the surface – which is entirely accurate, as WW2 submarines could only remain submerged for short periods, unlike modern underwater vessels which can stay beneath the surface for up to three months.

On their way they are spotted by a single-engined 'German reconnaissance fighter', which buzzes the submarine. One of the submarine crew wants to shoot it down using the U-Boat's 20mm anti-aircraft gun, but Tyler restrains him because – if he misses – the Germans will realise the *U-571* has been captured by the Allies.

In reality, the German aircraft should have been a four-engined Focke-Wulf Fw-200 Condor or a Junkers Ju-88 long-range fighter, but neither of these types exist in airworthy condition so an Italian Fiat G.59B two-seat trainer, I-MRSV, fitted with fake drop tanks and painted in German markings was used instead. Incidentally, the world's other airworthy Fiat G.59B, based in Australia, was also used to portray a German fighter in the 1995 version of *Sahara* which starred James Belushi.

Eventually the German fighter disappears, but soon afterwards a German destroyer appears on the horizon. It has obviously been summoned by the aircraft. This vessel was actually an Italian ocean-going tug which was fitted with fake gun turrets and had its apparent proportions altered in post-production using computer technology. The destroyer heaves to, and a boarding party is sent over to the submarine in two boats. Tyler realises the game will be up if the Germans get on board, so he orders his crew to destroy the enemy vessel's radio room with their deck gun before a message can be sent. The US sailors do as instructed and the Germans react violently, sounding klaxons and going to battle stations.

As the Germans man their guns and swing the destroyer's three gun turrets towards the submarine, the *U-571* closes all hatches and gets under way. Tyler orders the submarine to sail directly towards the enemy vessel so that it cannot depress its guns enough to fire. Then, as it dives, it passes beneath the hull of the warship.

The *U-571* dives deep, but the destroyer starts a depth charge attack. Meanwhile, the *U-571*'s original commander, Kapitan-Leutnant Wassner, escapes from captivity and kills one of Tyler's crew before he is restrained. Tyler tries to trick the destroyer's crew into believing that the *U-571* has been destroyed by ejecting debris and the body of the dead crew member out of a torpedo tube, but the attack continues because Wassner is tapping messages in Morse Code on the submarine's hull which are being picked up by the destroyer's hydrophones. The crew put an end to this by knocking Wassner unconscious, but their only hope for survival now is to sink the enemy vessel as the *U-571* is dropping uncontrollably to a depth of 600 feet.

Tyler comes up with a risky plan to save the situation. He will ascend rapidly and then torpedo the destroyer with their sole remaining functional torpedo tube. In order to do this, crewman Trigger (Tom Guiry) will have to submerge himself in the bilge water and repressurize the remaining torpedo tube. Trigger uses an air hose to breathe inside the flooded compartment. He closes the air valve to the stern tube, but finds a second leak which he cannot reach. *U-571* surfaces, heavily damaged and unable to fire its last torpedo. The destroyer opens fire and Trigger manages to close the crucial valve just before he drowns. Tyler orders Tank to fire the torpedo, which scores a direct hit, and the destroyer explodes and sinks. But the *U-571* is severely damaged and soon afterwards the surviving crew take to a rubber dinghy, with the precious Enigma machine on board. Soon afterwards they are picked up by a US Navy Consolidated PB-Y Catalina and taken back to England.

U-571 was released on 21 April 2000 and was a great success, making $127 million at the box office against a production cost of $62 million. It was praised by the critics for its excitement and high production values. Nonetheless, there were some concerns about the way it had distorted history and even Prime Minister Tony Blair spoke out on the matter, telling the House of Commons that it was 'an affront to British sailors'. It remains, though, the last major WW2 submarine movie made to date.

One way the Allies attempted to lessen the impact of U-Boats was to introduce convoys which became better defended as the war progressed, and these have been the subject of a few films. One of the earliest films about this topic was the Ealing Films production *Convoy* (1941), which was directed by Pen Tennyson and starred Clive Brooks, John

Clements and Edward Chapman. The plot centred around Lieutenant Cranford (John Clements), who is living the life of a playboy until WW2 breaks out. He then joins the Royal Navy and is assigned to convoy protection duties. The rest of the film deals with the cat and mouse game that ensues between a German warship and the convoy protection vessels.

Western Approaches (1944) was a Technicolor docufiction film directed by Pat Jackson, who later helmed several episodes of *Danger Man* (1962-68) and four episodes of *The Prisoner* (1967) including what is arguably the very best episode of the series, *The Schizoid Man* (1967).

The film is the fictional account of 22 sailors adrift in a lifeboat, and attempts by the British to rescue them. A ship arrives but is hit by a torpedo fired by a U-Boat. When it surfaces it is severely damaged by 20mm Oerlikon cannon fire from the Allied vessel and has to be scuttled.

San Demetrio London (1943), directed by Charles Frend (who later helmed *The Cruel Sea*), tells the true story of the tanker MV *San Demetrio* which was abandoned by her crew after being attacked by the German heavy cruiser *Admiral Schneer* and abandoned, during the Battle of the Atlantic. The crew departed the vessel in three lifeboats, with two of them being found by rescue vessels. The third boat was adrift for three days, at which point the crew re-boarded the *San Demetrio*, extinguished her fires, got her engines working again and sailed to the Clyde, making landfall at Rothesay on the Isle of Bute after ten days.

The cast included future *Doctor Who* producer and director Barry Letts as Apprentice John Jones, and one of the earliest screen appearances of Gordon Jackson as Messboy John Jamieson.

Two Humphrey Bogart films have dealt with the war at sea from the perspective of armed merchant vessels. *Action in the North Atlantic* (1943) was directed by Lloyd Bacon, Byron Haskin and Raoul Walsh. The film starred Bogart as Joe Rossi, First Officer of the American oil tanker, SS *Northern Star*, while Raymond Massey played Captain Steve Jarvis.

The *Northern Star* is sunk by a U-Boat and the crew is re-assigned to a new vessel, the Liberty Ship SS *Seawitch* which is well-armed with a 5-inch gun and 20mm and 40mm anti-aircraft guns. The vessel becomes part of convoy 211 which is sailing to Murmansk with vital war supplies. The convoy is stalked by a wolf-pack of U-Boats, but the German submarines cannot attack by day because of the *Seawitch's* formidable defensive armament and at night the cargo ship eludes detection by hydrophones by shutting down its main engine.

As the convoy near land, the submarine calls in two Luftwaffe Heinkel He-59 twin-engine floatplane torpedo bombers, depicted entirely by miniatures flown on wires. But these elderly biplanes prove vulnerable to anti-aircraft fire and are both shot down. The *Seawitch* is then torpedoed by a U-Boat, but the Captain makes the vessel seem more damaged than it is by setting fires on deck. He then rams the U-Boat and sinks it. (You will notice this plot point is identical to the end of *The Enemy Below*, made 14 years later.) Russian fighters then arrive to cover the convoy.

Passage to Marseilles (also known as *Message to Marseilles*) was a 1944 war film directed by Michael Curtiz, which was designed to cash in on the success of *Casablanca* (1942) as it had many of the same cast and crew, including stars Humphrey Bogart, Sydney Greenstreet and Claude Rains, Curtiz as director, and composer Max Steiner.

The story centres around Jean Matrac, a French patriot and former newspaper publisher who is framed and wrongly imprisoned on the French penal colony of Cayenne in French Guiana. Along with four other convicts, he makes an escape attempt in a canoe and is eventually rescued by a French freighter, the *Ville De Nancy*.

As the vessel nears Marseille the ship's master, Captain Malo (Victor Francen), learns that France has surrendered to Nazi Germany and elects to head for an Allied port. Pro-Vichy passenger Major Duval (Sydney Greenstreet) attempts to take control of the ship, but is thwarted by the patriotic convicts. The vessel comes under attack by a German Focke-Wulf Fw-200 Condor long-range reconnaissance bomber, but Matrac – who is an ace marksman – does some highly accurate shooting with a Lewis 0.303 in machine gun and brings the enemy aircraft down.

The four-engine Focke-Wulf Fw-200 Condor was converted from a pre-war airliner, and was known as the 'Scourge of the Atlantic'. Although it usually operated only in a reconnaissance role, it could carry a small bombload under its wings, and occasionally made attacks on merchant ships which were sailing alone. It had one major weakness though – because it was a conversion from an airliner, it was lightly constructed and could not take much battle damage. Rather like the Japanese Zero fighter, it did not take a lot of rounds to bring it down, and even rifle-calibre machine gun bullets proved effective against the aircraft. It was thus appallingly vulnerable to fighter attack, and once the Allies deployed fighters at sea in small escort carriers the day of the Condor was over.

The Condor sequences in *Passage to Marseilles* were created entirely with miniatures and mock-ups, but look very convincing. They are the only cinematic depictions of this aircraft attacking a merchant vessel in any feature film to date.

Matrac and his comrades make it to Allied territory, and he eventually joins a Free French bomber squadron in England, flying as a waist gunner in a Boeing B-17 Flying Fortress. Real B-17s were used in these scenes, although Free French bomber squadrons never used the type. Matrac eventually dies during a mission when his aircraft comes under attack by multiple fighters.

Convoy was a 13-episode NBC TV series which was screened in the USA between 17 September and 10 December 1965. The series featured John Gavin as Commander Dan Talbot of the US Navy destroyer escort DD-181, and John Larch as the civilian merchant Captain Ben Foster of the cargo vessel *Flagship*. The cast also included James Doohan before he became famous for playing chief engineer Lieutenant Commander Montgomery 'Scotty' Scott in *Star Trek*. The series was made in black and white to allow the use of much wartime footage, and is believed to be the last major American TV production to be produced in monochrome. It was cancelled after just one season due to poor ratings.

The series is of interest to film historians as it starred John Gavin, who very nearly became the third actor to play James Bond. Gavin was an established film and TV actor who had appeared in a number of films including *Psycho* and *Spartacus* (both 1960). He also appeared in a Bond-like role in *OSS 117: Double Agent* (1968). In 1971 he was earmarked to play James Bond in *Diamonds Are Forever*, but was side-lined when Sean Connery returned to the role. He was then considered for the part of Bond in *Live and Let Die* (1973), but lost out to Roger Moore when the producers insisted that a British actor be cast instead.

5
UNDERWATER SABOTAGE

ALTHOUGH full-sized submarines carrying torpedoes didn't appear until the late 19th century, small submersible vessels armed with explosive mines were proposed about a hundred years earlier. During the American War of Independence in 1776, inventor David Bushell created the world's first submersible, the *Turtle*, which was entirely man-powered and was designed to affix simple explosive mines to the hulls of Royal Navy warships. Between 1793 and 1797, the American inventor Robert Fulton (1765-1815) built what would now be regarded as the world's first submarine, the *Nautilus*. (This was also the name of the submarine in Jules Verne's 1870 novel *20,000 Leagues Under the Sea*, and the name of the world's first nuclear-powered submarine which was commissioned in 1954.)

Constructed using copper sheets over iron ribs at a shipyard in Rouen, France, the vessel was powered by a small collapsible sail while on the surface. Once submerged, it was propelled by a small, hand-cranked propeller and was capable of a speed of two knots. With a length of 25 feet, it could stay underwater for up to four-and-a-half hours, and was fitted with devices which would be found on any modern submarine, namely a breathing tube (now known as a 'schnorkel') and adjustable horizontal fins ('hydroplanes' in a modern sub) to assist diving. The armament consisted of a number of mines which Fulton called 'carcasses'. These contained explosive charges of between ten and 200lbs, and were attached to enemy vessels using a spike which could be driven into the wooden hull of contemporary warships. As ships' hulls were then made of wood (which was often clad in copper sheeting), there was no point in using magnets to attach the bombs.

The *Nautilus* was apparently demonstrated to French Emperor Napoleon Bonaparte who was not impressed, particularly as it leaked water. In 1804, Fulton switched sides and worked for the British Admiralty. Unfortunately the Royal Navy did not see a future for these early, man-powered submarines, and Fulton eventually returned to the USA where he designed and built one of the earliest steamboats, the *North River Steamboat of Clermonts*, in 1807.

No feature film has ever been made about Fulton's inventions, but they were the inspiration for a four-part serial *Triton* which was broadcast on BBC Television, from 30 June 1961. Written, produced and directed by Rex Tucker, it starred future *Doctor Who* companion William Russell as Captain Belwether and Francis Matthews as Lieutenant Lamb. Matthews is well-known for providing the voice of Captain Scarlet in the Gerry Anderson puppet TV series *Captain Scarlet and the Mysterons* (1967), and also for playing the titular character in the BBC detective series *Paul Temple* (1969-71). Other notable cast members were Reed De Rouen as Fulton, Robert James as Admiral Nelson, and also Roger Delgado as 'The Man with a Patch'. A decade later, Delgado was to find fame as the very first (and best) Master in the 1971 season of *Doctor Who*, which starred Jon Pertwee.

The plot of *Triton* involved Belwether and Lamb travelling to France as undercover agents to thwart Napoleon and Fulton's plans. The serial proved very popular, attracting favourable reviews, and just seven years later the BBC remade the production using the same script but with a completely new cast. It must be almost unique for a TV series to be remade so soon after the original transmission, particularly as the only technical advantage the remake offered over its predecessor was that it was made in 625-line black-and-white UHF rather than the earlier 405-line VHF system. Had the BBC waited another 17 months, the second version of *Triton* could have been made in colour as BBC 1 started broadcasting in colour on 16 November 1969. (BBC 2 had originally started with 625-line black-and-white transmissions on 21 April 1964, and had moved to colour on 1 July 1967.)

This new version – which again consisted of four 30-minute episodes, screened from 30 June 1968 onwards – featured Jonathan Adams as Captain Julius Belwether and Paul Grist as Lieutenant Simon Lamb. Grist was a popular TV actor in the sixties and seventies. Although he was born in Glamorgan in Wales, he often played American or Canadian characters, such as CIA agent Bill Filer in the classic *Doctor Who* story *The Claws of Axos* (1971).

This time round Nelson was played by Terry Scully, Robert Cawdron was Fulton, and Hamilton Dyce portrayed Earl St Vincent. The following year, Hamilton Dyce played General Scobie in Jon Pertwee's first *Doctor Who* story, *Spearhead From Space*. The producer of this updated version was John McRae, with Michael Ferguson directing. Ferguson had a long career in television, directing four Doctor Who serials *The War Machines* (1966), *The Seeds of Death* (1969), *The Ambassadors of Death* (1970), and *The Claws of*

Axos (1971). He also helmed episodes of *Z-Cars* (1962), and several Yorkshire TV productions including *The Sandbaggers* (1978-80), *Airline* (1981) and *The Glory Boys* (1984). The incidental music for this version of *Triton* was by Dudley Simpson, who composed most of the incidental music for *Doctor Who* between 1967 and 1979. The highlight of *Triton* was a scene in which Belwether and Lamb escape from captivity by climbing down an open sewer directly below their prison cell's latrine, lit candles clutched tightly between their teeth (a period variation on the 'escaping via the man-sized air conditioning duct' cliché which features in many 60s and 70s action TV series and films). The following year, the BBC made a sequel to *Triton* called *Pegasus*. This time Fulton had switched sides and was working with Belwether and Lamb to thwart a French invasion plan which involved balloons.

Mini-submarines (and other forms of underwater sabotage) didn't really become practical until the Second World War because of all the technical challenges that had to be overcome. One of the problems with Fulton's submarine design was that it lacked a suitable engine, as the electric motor had not yet been invented. Eventually ship designers came up with the idea of a petrol or diesel engine as a submarine's main power-plant, which would give it a speed on the surface of up to 17 knots. This main engine would charge a bank of lead/acid batteries (similar to car batteries) which would power electric motors when the craft was fully underwater. The only snag was that submarines (including mini-submarines) could only travel slowly when using electric power – a speed of just six knots was typical – and could only stay underwater for a short time because of limited battery life and air supply.

In the early years of WW2, the Italian Navy proved highly proficient in the use of frogmen and mini-submarines to place explosives under the hulls of British warships. Probably their greatest success came on 19 December 1941 in Alexandria harbour in Egypt, when members of the Decima Flottiglia MAS of the Italian Navy sunk two WW1-vintage Royal Navy battleships, HMS *Valiant* and HMS *Queen Elizabeth* (plus the 8,000 ton tanker *Sagona*), as they lay at anchor. At a stroke the balance of naval power in the Mediterranean changed, particularly as the aircraft carrier HMS *Ark Royal* and the battleship HMS *Barham* had both been sunk in the western Mediterranean by German U-Boats only a few weeks before.

As both the *Valiant* and the *Queen Elizabeth* had been sunk in the relatively shallow waters of a harbour they were eventually refloated, and put back into service by mid-1943. In the meantime, the Royal Navy fooled the Italians by putting a full complement of men aboard the partially-sunken *Valiant*, as they knew that aerial reconnaissance photos would then appear to show a fully-manned (and presumably undamaged) battleship. The attack on the *Valiant* (and this successful ruse by the British) formed the subject of the film *The Valiant* (1962), which starred John Mills.

The attacks on HMS *Valiant* and HMS *Queen Elizabeth* also feature in the immediate post-credits sequences of *The Silent Enemy* (1957), about the wartime career of Royal Navy frogman Lionel 'Buster' Crabb. The attack is shown in some detail thanks to some excellent miniature and matte work by effects maestro Wally Veevers, and correctly shows Italian divers using manned *Maiale* torpedoes (which the British later copied and called '*Chariots*') which could each carry two men plus a large, detachable mine. The timeline of the film is wrong, though, as the Italians actually attacked shipping in Gibraltar harbour in September 1941, three months *before* the Alexandria raid and not after it, as implied in the movie.

The rest of the film is set in and around Gibraltar, and recounts how Crabb set up a small team of Royal Navy divers to counter the efforts of the Italian forces of the Decima Flottiglia MAS (Tenth Light Flotilla of assault vehicles) who attempted to blow up Royal Navy ships as they lay at anchor. The film depicts an early attack on British ships being repelled by Crabb and his men, who drop small depth charges over the side of a motor launch, resulting in one Italian frogman being captured and another killed. The single *Chariot* manned torpedo used in the mission is later salvaged by the British, repaired and put back into service.

In reality, Crabb and his men also made use of the advanced scuba (self-contained underwater breathing apparatus) gear (with large oxygen cylinders), rubber diving suits, masks and flippers, which they captured from the Italians and which were all far superior to the equipment the British had been using up to that point. Throughout the film all the British divers use the Davis Submerged Escape Apparatus (DSEA) consisting of goggles, nose-clip, oxygen mask and a bag worn on the chest which contained a small oxygen cylinder and a barium hydroxide rebreather device to absorb ('scrub') exhaled carbon dioxide. This equipment was originally designed by Sir Robert Davis in 1910 to enable the crew of a sunken submarine to reach the surface using a special chamber fitted to a submarine, and was not originally intended for use as scuba diving gear since the oxygen cylinder only had enough gas to last 30 minutes. In addition, the DSEA gear lacked weights to help divers submerge easily, and also did not provide insulation against the cold.

The film is of great interest to aviation enthusiasts, as it contains unique footage of a detachment of Avro Shackleton MR.2 four-engine maritime patrol aircraft of 224 Squadron which were based in Gibraltar in 1957 when the film was made. The Shackleton was designed by Sir Roy Chadwick and was based on the Avro Lincoln bomber, which itself was an improved and more powerful version of the famous Lancaster. Powered by four 2,500 h.p. Rolls-Royce Griffon engines, the Shackleton was replaced by the jet-powered British Aerospace Nimrod in the late sixties, although six converted aircraft were used in the Airborne Early Warning (AEW) role until 1991.

One of 224 Squadron's aircraft, WL792, crashed at Gibraltar on 14 September 1957 when it suffered a catastrophic engine failure during a Battle of Britain Air Display. None of the crew were injured, but the aircraft was written off. As space was very limited at Gibraltar, the wreck was simply dumped offshore in the ocean, enabling it to be used in a key scene halfway through the movie when Crabb's men battle with Italian frogmen who are trying to take possession of a vital briefcase belonging to Polish General Sikorski.

This incident – which is one of the highlights of the movie – is based on a real historical event on 4 July 1943, when an RAF Consolidated Liberator II bomber AL253 crashed in the sea immediately after take-off, resulting in the death of one of its passengers, General Wladyslaw Sikorski of the Polish Free Army. It has always been believed that the aircraft had been sabotaged by the Russians, as Stalin had a great hatred for the Poles and feared the Free Polish forces. The perpetrator of the sabotage is thought to have been the

MI6 double agent Kim Philby, who was in Gibraltar at the time of the accident and supposedly jammed the aircraft's control rods in the rear fuselage with a mailbag, preventing it from gaining height after take-off.

In the film recreation of these events, Sikorski's Liberator (represented by a Shackleton) crashes in the sea off the coast of Gibraltar (courtesy of some excellent miniature work from Wally Veevers). Sikorski's body is washed ashore, but Crabb's men are ordered to dive on the aircraft and retrieve the General's briefcase which is full of secret documents.

Crabb has almost freed the trapped briefcase when one of his men spots several Italian frogmen, clad in black rubber diving suits, heading towards them. A knife fight then ensues between the Royal Navy and Italian divers, which ends in a British victory.

Soon after this, the Italian underwater commandos return to Gibraltar harbour and blow up several merchant vessels which are assembling for the forthcoming invasion of North Africa. This is where the film's timeline again departs from reality. The crash involving General Sikorski happened in July 1943, while Operation Torch (the Anglo American invasion of French North Africa) took place in November 1942, seven months earlier.

Crabb already knows that the Italians are using the nearby Spanish town of Algeciras (which looks onto Gibraltar) as a base, and carries out an unauthorised reconnaissance mission to find out what is going on. He discovers that an impounded Italian cargo vessel, the *Olterra*, has been adapted to launch *Chariots* using an internal water-filled dock and an exit port under the waterline.

Crabb subsequently carries out a dangerous mission in the captured *Chariot* to place mines under the Italian vessel, just as she is about to launch her own divers sitting on manned torpedoes. The vessel explodes and sinks, and Operation Torch is saved. This episode is a great piece of cinema, but is a largely a work of fiction as neither the underwater knife fight or the mining of *Olterra* ever happened. The film ends with Crabb being awarded the George Medal – but that was far from the end of his career.

In 1947, Crabb left the Royal Navy but returned in 1950, carrying out a number of diving missions. In 1956 Crabb was recruited by MI6 to investigate the Russian cruiser *Ordzhonikidze* which was lying in Portsmouth harbour, having brought Soviet leader Nikita Kruschev and Premier Nikolai Bulganin to Britain for talks. British Naval Intelligence asked Crabb to take a look at the cruiser's propellers, which were supposedly of a new design. On 19 April 1956 Crabb dived into Portsmouth harbour and was never seen again.

Eventually the story of Crabb's mission and his disappearance broke in the British newspapers, and the Admiralty was forced to release a cover story which claimed that Crabb had vanished when he had taken part in trials of a secret underwater apparatus in Stokes Bay on the Solent.

14 months after Crabb's disappearance, on 9 June 1957, a headless body in a diving suit was brought to the surface in a net by two fishermen off Pilsey Island in Chichester harbour, and the body was brought to the shore in a landing craft operated by members of RAF Marine Craft Unit No 1107.

The body was missing both head and hands, and was clad in a Pirelli two-piece rubber diving suit. Crabb's ex-wife was unable to positively identify the body and neither was his girlfriend, Pat Rose. A post-mortem examination (in the days before DNA testing) was also inconclusive, as two very distinctive scars on Crabb's body could not be found.

The strange circumstances surrounding Crabb's death have led to various conspiracy theories which continue to this day. Some sources have suggested that Crabb was apprehended by underwater sentries and then died during interrogation, with his body being dumped. Another version of events suggested he was shot by a Russian sniper, while the most fanciful theories proposed that he had been captured and brainwashed or possibly even defected, ending his days working for the Soviet Navy.

Thunderball and *The Silent Enemy*

There will always be differences of opinion about what happened to 'Buster' Crabb. What is undisputable, though, are the similarities between some scenes in the James Bond film (and book) *Thunderball* and *The Silent Enemy*.

As described in my earlier book *Dying Harder: Action Movies of the 1980s* (Extremis Publishing, 2017*)*, *Thunderball* started life as a 1959 screenplay by Ian Fleming, Kevin McClory, Jack Whittingham and Ivor Bryce, entitled *Longitude 78 West*. Originally this was to be made into a film in 1960 as the very first Bond movie, but Elstree Studios turned it down, considering the nuclear blackmail plot to be preposterous and being of the opinion that no-one would go and see it! In 1961, Ian Fleming turned the rejected screenplay into a novel, *Thunderball*. Rather unwisely, he did not obtain permission from his co-authors, resulting in a lawsuit from McClory and Whittingham which ended with a court case in 1963. The judge ruled in favour of McClory and Whittingham, and this had implications for the James Bond films which have continued until fairly recently.

As a result, McClory was made one of the producers of the 1965 film *Thunderball* (along with Albert R. Broccoli and Harry Saltzman), and was allowed to make a new version of the film after ten years had elapsed. (It was this provision that allowed *Never Say Never Again* to be made in 1983.) Interestingly, anything that was in the 1959 draft screenplay and 1961 book, but was not in the 1965 film, could be included in the new film without any legal problems.

The Silent Enemy contains a scene in which Crabb defeats an Italian frogman attack by throwing explosive charges into the sea. There is also a section of the film in which Crabb carries out an underwater reconnaissance of the Italian merchant ship *Olterra* in Algeciras harbour and discovers an underwater port, leading to an internal dock inside the ship which is used to launch and recover *Chariots*. In the film *Thunderball*, Bond inspects the underside of Largo's yacht, the *Disco Volante*, in Nassau harbour and is then attacked with explosive charges. Bond subsequently discovers that the *Disco Volante* has an underwater hatch and internal dock to allow the operation of underwater craft similar to wartime *Chariots*.

There is also the fact that both films feature underwater action around a sunken aircraft – a Shackleton in the case of *The Silent Enemy*, and a *Vulcan* in Thunderball. Both aircraft were built by Avro and designed by Roy Chadwick.

Thunderball features a final battle in which US Navy SEALs parachute into the sea and fight SPECTRE frogmen using spear guns. In Fleming's original novel, the American servicemen were the crew of a US Navy submarine who are all armed with knives, as are the two lots of divers in *The Silent Enemy*.

As a wartime Naval Intelligence Officer in the Royal Navy Volunteer Reserve (RNVR) who was sometimes based at Gibraltar, Fleming would have been aware of Crabb's underwater feats, and *The Silent Enemy* premiered in 1958 – the year before he started work on *Longitude 78 West* – so it is very likely that the film influenced the content of what eventually became *Thunderball*.

Other films featuring underwater sabotage

Above Us the Waves (1955) was a British war film directed by Ralph Thomas and starring John Mills which dealt with attacks on the German battleship *Tirpitz*, using *Chariot* manned torpedoes and later midget submarines, known as X-Craft.

The first operation was known as Operation Title and involved four *Chariots* which – as recounted earlier – were British copies of a successful Italian design which was basically a manned torpedo in which the two operators wearing diving gear sat on the craft as though they were on horseback. The plan was to transport the craft from the UK to Norway concealed beneath the hull of a converted fishing vessel, the *Arthur*. Unfortunately the *Chariots* became dislodged in heavy weather, and the mission had to be abandoned with the crew landing in Norway and escaping via Sweden.

The rest of the film describes the preparation for – and execution of – Operation Source, an attack on the German battleship *Tirpitz* as it lay at anchor in Kafjord, which in reality took place on 22 September 1943. The mission involved the use of six X-Craft, midget submarines weighing about 30 tons. Twenty of these craft were built during WW2 and were powered by a single-shaft Gardener diesel engine (the same type used in contemporary London buses) generating 42hp, plus a 30hp Keith Blackman electric motor which provided propulsion while the vessel was submerged. The X-Craft were not armed with torpedoes like a conventional submarine. Instead, they were fitted with two 4,400lb detachable Amatol charges, which were dropped beneath the hull of the vessel they intended to sink and detonated via time fuses.

The screenplay was based on a best-selling book, *Above Us the Waves* by C.E.T. Warren and James Benson, which was published in 1953 and sold 350,000 copies. Shooting started on 20 September 1954 at Guernsey, with the British Admiralty providing complete cooperation. Surviving *Chariots* and X-Craft left over from the war were used in filming. The technical advisor on the film was Commander David Cameron, who commanded X-6 as a Lieutenant and won a Victoria Cross during Operation Source. The mission was only partially successful, as the *Tirpitz* was not sunk as planned and all six X-Craft were lost. However, severe damage was inflicted on the battleship and it was out of action for several months.

The events of Operation Source were recreated again in *Submarine X-1* (1968), one of six war movies made by Oakmont Productions, which specialised in fictional stories very loosely based on real events. For example, *Attack on The Iron Coast* (1968) was a low-budget re-telling of the raid on St Nazaire, while the plot of *Mosquito Squadron* (1968) incorporated elements of Operation Jericho, the bombing raid on Amiens prison in February 1944.

Submarine X-1 was directed by Walter Graham, who had previously worked mainly in television, and produced by John C. Champion who also co-wrote the story with Edmund

H. North, who had scripted *Sink the Bismarck!* (1960). Their story was turned into a screenplay by Donald Sanford (who co-wrote *Mosquito Squadron* with Joyce Perry) and Guy Elmes.

Submarine X-1 opens with Canadian Royal Navy officer Commander Bolton (James Caan) wading ashore on a deserted beach with a few of his crew after his submarine, HMS *Gauntlet*, has been sunk by the German battleship *Lindendorf*. (Curiously, Kenneth Branagh's fictional character in the recent *Dunkirk* movie is also called 'Commander Bolton'.)

Bolton is soon given a chance to exact revenge on the Germans and the *Lindendorf*, as he is given the opportunity to train in the new X-Craft midget submarines which are due to attack the German battleship as it lies at anchor in a Norwegian fjord. James Caan later became a major Hollywood star, but the rest of the cast were better known for their appearances in various British TV productions.

Rupert Davies, who played British Admiral Redmayne, was at that time very well known for playing *Maigret* in the long-running BBC series. Norman Bowler had a long career in television, with his most famous role being Detective Harry Hawkins in the BBC's *Z-Cars* spin-off series *Softly, Softly* (1966-76). Scottish actor William Dysart (who played villain Regan in the 1970 *Doctor Who* story *The Ambassadors of Death* in 1970) was cast as Lieutenant Gogan.

Filming was carried out in 1967 at MGM British Studios at Borehamwood and on location at Loch Ness, near Inverness. Aldourie Castle was used as the submariners' headquarters at their training base at the fictional 'Inverwell' in Scotland. The film featured some black-and-white archive footage of a Messerschmitt Bf110 twin-engined fighter and a

Junkers 52/3m, the latter appearing in a scene in which German parachutists conduct a raid on the training base.

The film features some impressive diving scenes, with James Caan apparently doing his own stunts as he did on *A Bridge Too Far* (1977). Less impressive is the miniature work by Les Bowie, particularly in the final scenes of the *Lindendorf* being attacked in a Norwegian fjord. The musical score by Ron Goodwin is first class though, probably some of his finest work. Rather like John Barry, Goodwin never produced a mediocre score, even when the film was a 'B'-movie.

Submarine X-1 was rated 'U' in January 1968 in the UK, and was 'G'-rated in the USA for distribution by United Artists. Though the film has never been released on any home entertainment format in the UK, it does turn up on terrestrial and satellite television occasionally.

6
CARRIER WARFARE

AIRCRAFT carriers played a decisive role in the Second World War, and have been involved in every major conflict ever since. Development of this class of vessel started in 1914, at the start of the First World War, when the Royal Navy converted several ships into seaplane carriers. Three of these – the *Engadine*, the *Riviera* and the *Express* – launched aircraft which took part in a raid on German airship hangars at Nordholz on Christmas Day, 1914. Three years later, the battlecruiser *Furious* had its forward 16-inch gun turret removed to provide space for a flight deck. In 1918, the aft turret was removed to provide space for a landing on deck, and further reconstructions took place in 1925, 1932, and 1939 to turn her into a modern carrier.

On 19 July 1918, *Furious* launched what is now considered to be the first successful attack by an aircraft carrier, when seven Sopwith Camels took off to attack the airship sheds at Tondern in northern Germany, resulting in the destruction of airships L.54 and L.60. Pleased with the success of *Furious*, the Admiralty commissioned a second carrier – the *Argus* – which was built using a partly-completed Italian liner.

A third carrier – the *Eagle* – followed, based on the hull of the incomplete Chilean battleship the *Almirante Cochrane*. The resulting vessel was the first carrier to have the familiar 'island' – incorporating the bridge, funnel and flying control – on the starboard side of the ship. The rationale behind the positioning of the island on the starboard side is the well-known fact that aircraft in trouble tend to veer to port. All carriers built since then have adhered to this convention, with the only exception being the Japanese carriers *Akagi* and *Hiryu*, which had islands on the port side. The fourth vessel of the Royal Navy's initial quarter of flat-tops was the *Hermes*, which was laid down in January 1918. This was the first ship to be designed from the outset as an aircraft carrier. Carrier development was also proceeding in other nations. The first US Navy carrier was the *Langley*, based on a collier – the *Jupiter* – while the Japanese built a small carrier, the *Hosho*.

The next stage in the evolution of aircraft carriers came with the Washington Naval Treaty of 1922, which limited the number and size of naval vessels. In the case of aircraft carriers, maximum tonnage was limited to 27,000 tons. Under the terms of this treaty (which was later grossly violated by Germany and Japan), the USA and the UK were limited to a maximum aircraft carrier tonnage of 135,000 tons each, while Japan was limited to 81,000 tons. Italy and France were restricted to just 60,000 tons of aircraft carrier tonnage each.

At the start of the Second World War, therefore, only Britain, the USA and Japan had large aircraft carrier fleets. Nazi Germany built just one aircraft carrier, the *Graf Zeppelin*, which was never completed. Intended to carry navalized versions of the Messerschmitt Bf109 fighter and the Junkers

87R dive-bomber, this vessel could have given the Allies serious problems if it had ever entered service.

The first film to depict Royal Navy carrier operations in WW2 was *Ships with Wings* (1941), a Michael Balcon production made at Ealing Studios, directed by Sergei Nolbandov, who was also one of four scriptwriters involved in this production. Much of the carrier footage was lifted from *Find, Fix and Strike*, a documentary about HMS *Ark Royal*. In the film, the *Ark Royal* depicts the fictitious HMS *Invincible* (which, by a coincidence, was also the name of the modern aircraft carrier which led the Falklands Task Force in 1982).

The plot of the film is ludicrous. A Fleet Air Arm test pilot, Lieutenant Dick Stacey (John Clements), falls in love with a Vice Admiral's daughter, Celia Weatherby (Jane Baxter). In order to impress her, he puts on a daring display in a new fighter (in reality a Fairey Fulmar) while she is visiting HMS *Invincible*. Things go wrong, though, as the wings of the aircraft fail and he is forced to bail out. Unbeknown to him, his girlfriend's brother – who had accompanied him on the flight – stays with the aircraft and crashes on the deck of the *Invincible*, resulting in his death. Stacey is court-martialled and thrown out of the Royal Navy, and subsequently ekes out a living flying for a small airline in the Greek islands. While there, Stacey learns of an Axis plot to invade the fictional Greek island of Panteira. His aircraft is shot down by Italian fighters, but he is picked up by *Invincible* and allowed to join his old air group which is carrying out operations to defeat the invasion, during which the carrier receives two bomb hits on the flight deck.

Eventually Stacey atones for his previous errors by lowering his Fulmar fighter's undercarriage and crashing it onto the back of a German bomber, piggy-back style. With the two aircraft locked together, Stacey steers them towards a dam, destroying it and causing a flood which thwarts the invasion.

The film is notable for its poor miniature work and preposterous plot. British Prime Minister Winston Churchill wanted it to be withdrawn from circulation as it suggested that the outcome of a military campaign could hinge on the actions of a single man, though it should be noted that this was the theme of most of John Wayne's war pictures – plus many 1980s action movies, particularly those featuring Arnold Schwarzenegger or Sylvester Stallone! It was undoubtedly a jingoistic propaganda film, but it proved very popular with the British public who needed a morale boost at a time when the war was going very badly for the British.

The film also offers fascinating glimpses of the inferior aircraft with which the Fleet Air Arm was equipped in the early years of WW2. Although Britain effectively pioneered the use of carrier-based air power (and later invented three important innovations in this field; namely the angled flight deck, the mirror landing system and the steam catapult), it lagged behind in the development of naval aircraft. At the start of the war, the Fleet Air Arm's standard fighter was the Gloster Sea Gladiator, a navalised version of the Gloster Gladiator which was the RAF's last biplane fighter. Though highly manoeuvrable and a delight to fly, it had a puny armament of just four 0.303in machine guns and only had a top speed of 260 mph; less than some of the bomber aircraft it was likely to face, such as the Junkers Ju-88. After the Norwegian campaign in 1940, it was withdrawn from service and replaced by the Fairey Fulmar Mark I, which was the Fleet Air Arm's first eight-gun fighter. Although it was powered by a Rolls-Royce Merlin engine, like the RAF's Spitfire and Hurricane fighters, the Fulmar carried a second crew member (who carried out the roles of navigator, observer and wireless operator) in addition to the pilot, resulting in a much larger and heavier airframe. Consequently the Fulmar only had a top speed of 265mph – almost 100mph slower than a Spitfire Mk I – and was not very manoeuvrable. Despite these handicaps, Fulmars shot down 122 enemy aircraft during WW2, more than any other Fleet Air Arm (FAA) fighter. 600 Fulmars were built during WW2, and the one surviving example – N1854 – can be seen in the Fleet Air Arm Museum, Yeovilton.

Another FAA aircraft that can be seen in the film is the infamous Blackburn Skua dive-bomber-cum-fighter. This odd-looking aircraft was powered by a Bristol Perseus engine of just 890hp and consequently had a limited performance, with a top speed of just 225 mph. For the dive-bombing role, the Skua could carry a single 500lb bomb in a trapeze under the fuselage, and its greatest achievement came on 10 April 1940 when 16 Skuas – flying from their base at RNAS Hatston in the Orkneys – sunk the German cruiser *Konigsberg* while it was at anchor in Bergen. This was the first occasion in WW2 when dive-bombers sunk a warship. The Skua could also be used as a makeshift fighter, as it carried four 0.303in Browning machine guns in its wings and one accounted for a Heinkel He-111 during the Norwegian campaign. A development of the Skua (which can also be seen during the film) was the Blackburn Roc naval fighter, which mounted four 0.303in Browning machine guns in a turret behind the pilot, rather like the RAF's Boulton-Paul Defiant. Though handicapped by poor performance, a Roc shot down a single Junkers Ju-88 on 28 May 1940. This was the sole kill attributed to the type.

The final aircraft type which makes an appearance in *Ships with Wings* is the famous Fairey Swordfish biplane. Although obsolete at the start of WW2, the Swordfish took part in a number of important carrier actions, such as the attack on the Italian fleet at Taranto in November 1940 and the hunt for the German battleship *Bismarck* in May 1941.

The British air raid (Operation Judgement) on the Italian naval base at Taranto on 11-12 November 1940 was one of the Royal Navy's greatest successes in WW2. Just 21 obsolete Fairey Swordfish biplanes from the carrier HMS *Illustrious* carried out a night attack on the Italian fleet, with torpedoes and bombs, as it lay at anchor in Taranto. For the loss of just two aircraft, the Royal Navy sunk one Italian battleship, the *Conte di Cavour*, and severely damaged two others, the *Caio Dullo* and the *Littorio*. One heavy cruiser, the *Trento,* and two destroyers, the *Libeccio* and the *Pessagno*, were also damaged. At a stroke, the balance of naval power in the Mediterranean swung in favour of the British.

The Italians had believed that their battleships would be immune from torpedo attack at Taranto because the harbour was only 45 feet deep and air-dropped torpedoes usually required a minimum depth of 75 feet to work correctly. But the British solved the problem by fitting wooden fins to their torpedoes, enabling them to run in shallow waters. This lesson was noted by the Japanese, who modified their own aircraft-launched torpedoes in a similar fashion for the devastating attack on the US Navy's base at Pearl Harbour in Hawaii 13 months later.

The Pearl Harbour raid on 7 December 1941 was a tactical victory for the Japanese, but a strategic disaster as it brought American into a war it could not lose due to its massive industrial capacity. 351 naval aircraft from six carriers, led by Commander Mitsuo Fuchida, attacked warships lying at anchor, in two waves. 21 naval vessels were hit, although 18 of those were subsequently salvaged and repaired and only three – the battleships *Oklahoma*, *Arizona* and *Utah* – were damaged beyond repair. Furthermore, the most important Japanese target – the American Pacific Fleet aircraft carriers – were all at sea at the time of the raid.

The Pearl Harbour attack had been briefly depicted in a number of films and TV series in the fifties and sixties, such as *From Here to Eternity* (1953), but the most accurate and spectacular recreation of the raid was the movie *Tora, Tora, Tora* (1970) which was directed by Richard Fleischer, Toshio Masuda and Kinji Fukasaku, and filmed in Washington, Hawaii and Japan.

Tora, Tora, Tora was effectively two movies; one made in Japan and the other in Hawaii and the mainland USA. After completion, the two films were expertly cut together. The biggest problem facing the film-makers was a lack of airworthy Japanese aircraft. A survey showed that only a few Zeroes were left, and none were airworthy. A single Aichi D3A Val dive-bomber also existed, but there was not a single Nakajima B5N 'Kate' torpedo bomber left anywhere in the world. Eventually the producers solved the problem by creating a fleet of replica Japanese aircraft using converted North American T-6 Texan/Harvard and Vultee BT-13 and BT-15 Valiant trainers. 12 Zeroes, nine Kates and 10 Vals were built in California for filming in Hawaii, while three Zeroes and five Kates were constructed in Japan using conversion kits supplied from the USA. In addition, a few unmodified T-6 aircraft were used in Japanese carrier scenes. The Japanese film unit also built a plywood replica of the aircraft carrier *Akagi*, plus another of the battleship *Nagato*, which appears in the opening title scene.

The highlight of the film is a stunning sequence in which the Japanese air group takes off to attack Pearl Harbour against a backdrop of the rising sun. This was filmed on the US Navy carrier *Yorktown* off San Diego on 3 and 4 December 1968 using 31 replica aircraft. This striking footage has since been used in several other productions, including *Midway* (1976) and *Pearl* (1980). A highly detailed account of the making of *Tora, Tora, Tora* can be found in one of my other books, *Planes on Film: Ten Favourite Aviation Films* (Extremis Publishing, 2016).

The attack on the US Pacific Fleet's main base was also recreated for the film *Pearl Harbor* (2001), directed by Michael Bay and produced by Bay and Jerry Bruckheimer, which had a budget of $140 million. When the film was first announced, it was revealed that it would feature scenes set during the 'Battle of Britain, the Pearl Harbour attack, and the Doolittle Raid'. The storyline centred around the friendship between two young Americans, Rafe McCawley (Ben Affleck) and Danny Walker (Josh Hartnett), and a 'love triangle' involving the two young men and US Navy nurse Evelyn Johnson (Kate Beckinsale). After a brief prologue, the film proper begins in January 1941 when McCawley and Hartnett, having joined the US Army Air Corps, are assigned to a squadron flying Curtiss P-40 fighters. McCawley begins a romance with Evelyn Johnson, but craves action and decides to join one of the RAF's 'Eagle Squadrons' which are crewed by American volunteers. In the summer of 1941 he is involved in defending England from air attack (though in reality, by this point in the war the Luftwaffe had largely abandoned daylight raids on Britain and had moved most of its bombers to the Russian front; the RAF was largely engaged in fighter sweeps over France). In combat with German Messerschmitt Bf109s, Rafe crashes in the English Channel and is listed as missing, presumed dead.

Back in Hawaii, Evelyn hears the news and, thinking Rafe has passed away, begins a romance with Danny. But Rafe has actually survived the crash and turns up at Pearl Harbour on the eve of the Japanese attack. The following day, Sunday 7 December 1941 – after a hard night's partying – Rafe and Danny are woken by the noise of the surprise Japanese air attack on their base. Still wearing civilian clothes, the pair take to the air in two P-40s and shoot down several Japanese aircraft. (This segment of the film is based on the real-life exploits of two USAAF pilots Lieutenants Taylor and Welch, who shot down six Japanese planes during the attack. This action was recreated in the film *Tora, Tora, Tora*).

28 aircraft were used in the production, including four Spitfires, a Hurricane, a Sea Hurricane, two Hispano Buchons, four P-40s, three Kate replicas, three Val reproductions, three Zeroes, and also four B-25s which were used in the Doolittle Raid scenes (q.v.). The Vals and Kates were replicas which had been built in 1968 for *Tora, Tora, Tora*, but the Zeroes were the genuine article. One of them was owned by the Planes of Fame museum at Chino, California, and the other two were 'Flight Magic' Zeroes built using recovered derelict airframes, a lot of new parts, and American Pratt & Whitney R-1830 engines. The 'Planes of Fame' Zero is the only one in the world still flying with its original Sakae engine.

Filming of 'Pearl Harbor' took place in England, California and Hawaii in the summer of 2000. Many of the special effects sequences were achieved using CGI rather than miniatures and matte paintings (as had been the case with *Tora,*

Tora, Tora) and this meant that some scenes have a 'cartoony' look to them. A prime example would be the shot where a Val dive-bomber drops a large bomb on the *Arizona*. The camera then follows the bomb down until it pierces the deck of the ship, causing it to explode. Neither shot looks real.

Some sequences using full-size mock-ups of sections of ships were lensed in a large water tank at Baja Film Studios in Mexico, which had been created for *Titanic* (1997) and also used for the naval scenes in *Tomorrow Never Dies* (1997). But overall, the film was slammed by critics for its trite plot, unrealistic special effects, laughable dialogue, and multiple historical and technical inaccuracies.

It is often said that *Pearl Harbor* contains elements of previous Hollywood blockbusters, particularly James Cameron's *Titanic* (1997) and Tony Scott's *Top Gun* (1986). Thus, lifted from *Titanic* we have a love triangle (a plot point in many war movies) plus scenes of ships sinking and people struggling in the water. Also, the famous shot where Rose stands at the prow of the *Titanic* – helped by Jack – and imagines she is flying has its equivalent in *Pearl Harbor* in the sequence where Evelyn is taken aloft in the cockpit of a P-40 to see Pearl Harbour from the air at night. *Titanic* ends with Jack dying, while Danny is killed towards the close of *Pearl Harbor*, and both films have an end title song sung by a popular female artiste; namely *My Heart Will Go On* by Celine Dion (*Titanic*) and *There You'll Be* by Faith Hill (*Pearl Harbor*).

Pearl Harbor also borrows a few ideas from *Top Gun*, including the maverick pilot who is really a genius at air combat but has a problem obeying orders, and of course the famous scene from the Tony Scott film – in which Maverick (Tom Cruise) flies past a control tower at high speed and causes an officer to spill his coffee – which is duplicated in its entirety in *Pearl Harbor*.

Despite being panned by the critics, *Pearl Harbor* was nominated for four Academy Awards and won one (for Best Sound Editing). It was, though, also nominated for six Golden Raspberry Awards, including Worst Picture. This was the first time a Worst Picture-nominated film actually won an Academy Award. It was also moderately successful, making almost $450 million at the box office set against a budget of $132.2 million.

Pearl Harbour was a devastating psychological blow to the Americans, and they did not take long to strike back. On 21 December 1941, President Franklin D. Roosevelt asked his Chiefs of Staff if it would be possible to carry out a bombing raid on Japan. The problem was the vast distance involved in flying aircraft from the mainland USA or any Pacific island that America held, which was well outside the range of any bomber that the USA possessed.

One option was to use US Navy carrier aircraft, but they could only carry a small bombload and had a limited range, which meant the carriers from which they launched would be at high risk of being sunk by land-based aircraft. However, Captain Francis Low, Assistant Chief of Staff for anti-submarine warfare, suggested that it might be possible to launch US Army medium bombers from the deck of an aircraft carrier, and he sent a memorandum along these lines to Admiral Ernest J. King who was the Chief of Naval Operations. The idea was then passed on to Captain Donald D. Duncan, King's Naval Operations Officer, who concluded that the idea was technically feasible. General Henry H. 'Hap' Arnold then ordered Lieutenant Colonel James 'Jimmy' Doolittle, a former test pilot, to look into the matter further. Doolittle was a famous pre-war aviator who had worked for the Shell Oil Company, and was one of the first people to advocate the use of 100-octane petrol to improve the performance of aero engines.

Doolittle studied all the light and medium bomber aircraft that were in the US Army Air Force (USAAF) inventory, including the Lockheed Hudson, the Douglas A-20, the Douglas A-18 Bolo, the Douglas B-23 Dragon and the Martin B-26 Marauder, and concluded that the only plane that could carry out the mission was the new North American B-25B Mitchell – primarily due to its weight and wingspan, which would allow it to operate from the deck of a *Yorktown*-class carrier. On 3 February 1942, Captain Donald Duncan and Doolittle successfully flew two B-25Bs from the deck of the USS *Hornet* (CV-8). Although the bombers could take off, they could not land back on the carrier, so it was hoped that they could land on airfields in China or the USSR. Unfortunately Stalin had signed a neutrality pact with Japan in April 1941 and thus could not help the Allies in the Pacific theatre, so the B-25s would have to be flown to Chinese airfields and thereafter be incorporated into the Chinese Air Force.

The 17th Medium Bomb Group of the USAAF had been operating B-25s since September 1941, and was chosen to carry out the mission. Training was carried out at Eglin Field, Florida, where the crews received instruction from US Navy aviator Lt. Henry L. Miller. Eventually the B-25 crews learned how to get a fully-loaded Mitchell airborne in just 450 feet, just above stalling speed.

To save weight, the B-25s were modified for the mission. As all flying was to be carried out at low-level, the unmanned, periscope-aimed ventral gun turret was removed, saving 600lbs in weight, and the top-secret Norden bombsight

– which employed an analogue computer linked to the aircraft's autopilot – was taken out and replaced with a simple instrument (the 'Mark Twain' sight) suitable for low-altitude work. Additional fuel was also carried in extra tanks inside the fuselage and bomb bay, increasing fuel capacity from 646 to 1,141 gallons. Some petrol was carried inside the fuselage in small cans, which could be used during the flight to top up the tanks.

Ordnance was restricted to just four 500lb bombs per aircraft, with one bomb in four being specially designed incendiaries. To deter attacking fighters, two broomsticks painted black were fitted in the Plexiglas tail cones of each aircraft, and total defensive armament consisted of two fifty-calibre Browning M2 machine guns in the dorsal turret plus a single thirty-calibre Browning in a flexible nose mount.

On 25 March 1942, 22 B-25s flew from Eglin to McLellan Field in Sacramento, California at just 500 feet altitude to give the crews practice in low-level flying. From there, the B-25s flew to Alameda Naval Base in San Francisco, where 16 of the bombers were loaded onto the USS *Hornet*. The extra crew members then went on board as back-up personnel for the mission.

On 2 April 1942 the *Hornet* left San Francisco, and eleven days later she linked up with Task Force 16 – including the carrier USS *Enterprise* (CV-6) – which had been assigned to provide close protection. The voyage towards Japan was uneventful until 7.38 a.m. on 18 April, when a Japanese picket boat Number 23 – the 70-ton *Nitto Maru* – spotted the US force at a distance of 650 nautical miles from the home islands. The vessel was quickly sunk by 6-inch and 5-inch gunfire from the US cruiser USS *Nashville*, but not before it had sent out a radio message warning of an imminent attack.

Although the original intention had been to launch the B-25s just 380 nautical miles from Japan, the captain of the *Hornet*, Mark Mitscher, ordered the Army pilots to man their planes and take off immediately. By 09.19 a.m. all sixteen aircraft were airborne and on their way to Japan. The aircraft arrived over Japan around noon and attacked targets in Yokohama, Yokosuka, Kobe, Nagoya and Tokyo.

Complete surprise was achieved by the American force. Although the Japanese picket boat had sent out a warning that a US Task Force was heading for the Home Islands, the Japanese Air Force was expecting an attack by carrier aircraft the following day and was unable to intercept the low-flying bombers. Three Japanese fighters were shot down by the B-25s – one by *Whirling Dervish*, piloted by First Lieutenant Harold Watson, and two more by *Hari Karier*, commanded by First Lieutenant Ross Greening.

None of the B-25s were shot down, and 15 of them made it to China. Unfortunately due to communication problems and bad weather, none of the B-25s landed at Chinese airfields. 11 crews bailed out, four had to crash-land, and one touched down at Vladivostok in the Soviet Union, resulting in the crew being interned until 1943 when they made their way back to the USA via Iran.

Eight of the Doolittle Raiders were captured by the Japanese and tortured, and only four of these survived the war. The Japanese responded to the raid by massacring 250,000 Chinese civilians in one of the worst atrocities of the war.

Doolittle initially believed that the raid was a failure as all the aircraft had been lost, and he thought that he would be court-martialled. In reality, he was promoted to Brigadier

General when he returned to the USA and was awarded the Medal of Honor by President Roosevelt.

The raid did little material damage to Japan, but the psychological and strategic consequences were enormous. From that point on, the Japanese High Command was forced to retain four fighter groups in Japan for defence of the Home Islands; aircraft that were badly needed elsewhere. In addition, Admiral Yamamoto had to postpone his plan to invade Australia and attacked Midway Island instead. The resulting Battle of Midway (q.v.) was Japan's first great defeat of the war, and the beginning of the end for the Nipponese Empire. The bombing mission also gave a great boost to Allied morale.

In 1943, one of the pilots on the Doolittle raid, Captain Ted Lawson, wrote a book about the mission: *Thirty Seconds Over Tokyo*. This was a smash hit, and the following year it was made into a film by MGM with Van Johnson playing Lawson and Spencer Tracy as Doolittle.

The USAAF cooperated fully in the production, and supplied 20 B-25D Mitchells from the 952nd B-25 Transition Group at Mather Field, California. The aircraft were repainted in 1942 markings and camouflaged by the North American plant at Mines Field. Lawson's aircraft, *Ruptured Duck*, was played by B-25D – NC No 41-29754 – which performed most of the short take-offs in the film.

Ted Lawson and fellow Doolittle Raider Dean Davenport were technical advisors on the film, and Davenport carried out all short take-offs and low-flying sequences, including a hair-raising shot in which a B-25 flies under the Golden Gate Bridge in San Francisco.

As no US Navy aircraft carriers could be spared from war work and the real USS *Hornet* had been sunk off Guadalcanal in late 1942, extensive use was made of miniatures, studio mock-ups and matte shots. Indeed, the film is notable for its very realistic model shots involving large miniature B-25s flown on wires. The carrier take-offs are particularly impressive, as is a sequence in which an industrial complex is bombed. This was achieved using a huge outdoor miniature, and it is no surprise that the film won an Oscar for Special Effects in 1944. In fact, the model shots are noticeably better than those which appear in *633 Squadron* (1964), made twenty years later.

For the carrier deck scenes, a huge mock-up of the island and flight deck of the USS *Hornet* was created indoors at MGM's Stage 15 at Culver City, California. The studio doors were opened at each end, while four real B-25s did engine runs on the set. Some archive combat footage of the actual take-offs on 18 April 1942 was also edited into the film.

Most of the film was shot at Eglin Main Field, Florida, with the take-off practices being shot at Eglin Auxiliary Field Number 9 (aka Hulbert Field) which was used by the real Doolittle Raiders in 1942. Some shooting was also carried out at Mines Field, Los Angeles, and Alameda Naval Air Station near San Francisco. The low-level flying scenes were lensed in the Gulf of Mexico off the Florida coast, and the ports of Oakland and Los Angeles were used for Tokyo. The large column of black smoke which appears in one shot was a real fuel-oil fire in Oakland which was captured on film.

As mentioned earlier, a reconstruction of the Doolittle Raid forms part of the plot of *Pearl Harbor* (2001), but this time with little attention to period detail. Pilots Rafe McCawley and Danny Walker are assigned to Doolittle's B-25 Squadron because of their 'combat experience' (even though it was in fighters, not bombers). During WW2, pilots would sometimes be transferred from fighters to bombers and vice-versa, but this would require a lengthy period of re-training. For the 2001 film, just four late-war B-25J Mitchells (which bristled with defensive guns, unlike the B-25Bs used in the raid) were employed in filming on the carrier USS *Lexington*, which was now a museum ship at Corpus Christi in Texas, although the launch sequences themselves were filmed on another aircraft carrier, the USS *Constellation*.

Like the rest of the film, the Doolittle Raid sequences were shot like a pop video, with lots of slow-motion action. One of the most annoying inaccuracies was the scene in which Doolittle orders mock broomstick guns to be fitted in the B-25s, and armour plating to be removed, just minutes before take-off, when in fact these decisions were made weeks before. Some surviving Doolittle Raiders who were present on set pointed out these errors, but were persuaded that it was more dramatically effective to portray what happened in that way. Another major error was that the B-25s are seen to fly in formation towards the target when in reality they took off one at a time and made their own way towards Japan. Another mistake occurs almost at the end of the film, when a voiceover by Kate Beckinsale's character informs the viewer that Japan 'backed off' after the Doolittle Raid – when in actual fact they did nothing of the sort!

As mentioned earlier, one of the consequences of the Doolittle Raid was the Battle of Midway, which took place between 4-7 June 1942 and ended with a decisive victory for the Americans. The Japanese lost four aircraft carriers – the *Kaga*, *Akagi*, *Soryu* and *Hiryu* – plus the cruiser *Mikumu*. The US Navy lost the carrier USS *Yorktown*, plus the destroyer USS *Hammann*.

The Battle of Midway had been the subject of a number of documentaries, including an 18-minute colour feature made at the time of the battle by John Ford, who is best-known for directing Westerns. It was also depicted in *Wing and a Prayer* (1944), which featured the newly-commissioned USS *Yorktown* (CV-10) and its air group complement of F6F Hellcats (a type which did not enter service until 1943). In this film, Zeroes were portrayed by Grumman F-4F Wildcats in Japanese markings. The Midway battle was also mentioned in *Task Force* (1949), which used just two aircraft – a single SDB-5 Dauntless and an FM-2 Wildcat – which were both painted in an inaccurate gloss midnight blue and grey colour scheme. Filming was carried out on the carrier USS *Antietam* (CV-36), and much archive footage was also used.

In 1976 Hollywood producer Walter Mirisch made the definitive feature film about the battle, *Midway*, which was directed by Jack Smight (and known as *Battle of Midway* outwith the USA). Mirisch's company, the Mirisch Corporation, had been responsible for a number of earlier war pictures, including *The Great Escape* (1963) and *633 Squadron* (1964) which were both highly successful. Mirisch also had a low-budget subsidiary, Oakmont Productions, which made six war films in the 1960s – namely *Attack on the Iron Coast* (1967), *Submarine X-1* (1969), *The Thousand Plane Raid* (1969), *Mosquito Squadron* (1968), *Hell Boats* (1970), and *The Last Escape* (1970).

With an eye on cost, Mirisch had all the action sequences storyboarded and used colour stock footage wherever possible to depict these scenes, and he reportedly spent $60,000 on acquiring the rights to various pieces of archive film. The scenes which play behind the main titles are lifted from *Thirty Seconds Over Tokyo* (1944), with the addition of some sepia tinting and new sound effects. A lot of shots were from the little-known Japanese colour movie *I Bombed Pearl*

Harbour (1961), which featured excellent miniature work. The scene where a Japanese carrier deck is hit by bombs resulting in the destruction of a number of Kates, Vals and Zeroes was lifted from this movie, and was created by converting a seaside dock to resemble an aircraft carrier, complete with working deck elevator and authentic Japanese Type 96 triple-barrelled 25mm anti-aircraft guns.

Midway also includes some clips from *Battle of Britain* (1969), *The Flying Leathernecks* (1951), *Dive Bomber* (1941), and some action scenes also came from John Ford's 1942 documentary about the Battle of Midway and a later documentary *The Fighting Lady* (1944), which dealt with carrier operations in the Pacific. In fact, footage from 12 different films appears in *Midway*. This meant that a number of out-of-period aircraft appear in the film, including Grumman F-6F Hellcats and Curtiss SB2 Helldivers; planes which were not used until later in the war. A Grumman TBM Avenger is also seen taking off from a carrier deck. This aircraft did make its combat debut at Midway, as six examples flew from the airfield on Midway Island, but it was never launched from the deck of a carrier during the Midway battle. A lot of footage was also re-used from *Tora, Tora, Tora* (1970), including the carrier launch sequences, the P40 takeoffs, the airfield strafings, and the B-17 crash scene.

Two versions of the film were made – a theatrical release which was 120 minutes long, and a TV version with an extra 40 minutes of footage, including a depiction of the Battle of the Coral Sea which took place in May 1942. This extra footage includes an odd scene in which a Japanese Kawanishi H8K2 Emily flying boat is portrayed by a modern Lockheed C-130 Hercules, with cockpit close-ups achieved using a PB-Y Catalina painted in Japanese markings!

Little new aerial footage was shot for the production, though some period aircraft were obtained. Scenes set on Japanese carriers used several North American T-6 'Zero' and Vultee BT-13 'Val' replicas, which had been originally created for *Tora, Tora, Tora*. Two Grumman FM-2 Wildcat fighters, N6290C and N90541, were employed in the filming – though they retained their incorrect three-tone 1943 colour schemes for the movie – as was a single Consolidated PBY-6A Catalina N16KL which was hired from the American Air Museum Society of San Francisco. This aircraft was originally operated by the Danish Navy, and was written off in 1984. Permission was not granted for the two Wildcats to fly off the *Lexington*, so stock footage had to be used to depict carrier take-offs.

A Grumman Duck seaplane N1214N appears as background set dressing in one scene, while a single Douglas SB-D Dauntless Bu Bo 28536 was used for studio cockpit filming. Although only used as a static aircraft in this production, it was subsequently restored to airworthy condition and featured in the TV series *War and Remembrance* (1988). Aerial footage of an airworthy Douglas Dauntless (actually an A-24A model), N15749, which was originally shot for *Tora, Tora, Tora* but not included in the final cut of the film, appears in the production.

Studio close-ups of actors in aircraft also employed a Vultee BT-13 Valiant fuselage which doubled for the Douglas TBD Devastators of the ill-fated Torpedo Squadron 8. Some background footage of Vought SB2U Vindicator bombers, lifted from the Errol Flynn movie *Dive Bomber* (1941), was used in some back projection scenes.

The film had an all-star cast, comprising both real and fictional characters. Henry Fonda played Admiral Chester W. Nimitz, while Glenn Ford was Admiral Spruance and Robert

Mitchum had a brief cameo as Admiral 'Bull' Halsey, who was confined to bed with a skin condition during the battle. Other characters were fictional, such as Captain Matt Garth (Charlton Heston), a US Navy officer who is posted to the *Yorktown*.

The screenplay was by Donald Sanford, who had previously co-scripted *Mosquito Squadron*, a low-budget Oakmont production which relied heavily on footage from *633 Squadron* and employed many of the same locations and aircraft to save money. *Mosquito Squadron* featured a love triangle – presumably to give the film an element of human interest – and *Midway* also had a 'soap opera'-plot thread involving Garth's son Tom (Edward Albert), a US Navy fighter pilot in love with a Japanese-American girl, Haruko Sakua (Christina Kokubo), who is facing internment.

Midway was filmed in 1975 at the Terminal Island Naval Air Base, Los Angeles, California; at the US Naval Air Station at Long Beach, California; and at the Naval Air Station at Pensacola, Florida. The *Lexington* sequences were filmed in the Gulf of Mexico.

One problem with *Midway* is that with footage originating from so many sources, the film has a 'patchwork quilt' feel to it, with some scenes being very grainy and others pin sharp. There are also gross continuity errors, as shown by the scene near the end of the film where Charlton Heston's character climbs into a Douglas Dauntless, takes off in a Grumman Avenger, fights in a Douglas Dauntless, approaches the carrier in a Curtiss Helldiver, and then crashes in a Grumman Panther (which was a Korean War-era jet!). Despite these issues, the film is still an enjoyable and exciting account of the Midway battle. One thing that holds the film together is the magnificent score by John Williams, who is best-known for his long-term collaboration with Steven Spielberg and his themes for the *Superman, Indiana Jones* and *Star Wars* films. The theatrical version of the film also benefitted from the use of 'Sensurround', a highly innovative sound system employing ultra-low frequency speakers which greatly enhanced the effect of on-screen crashes and explosions. It was originally developed by Cerwin-Vega and Universal Studios for the Charlton Heston picture *Earthquake* (1974), and was subsequently used in four other films.

A more authentic depiction of the Battle of Midway can be found in the TV mini-series *War and Remembrance* (1988). Based on the book by Herman Wouk, it was a sequel to the highly acclaimed ABC production *The Winds of War* (1983), which was 18 hours long, and both series chronicled the exploits of various members of the Henry family as they became involved in both the European and Pacific conflicts. Overall, the 30-hour series was short on action and long on dialogue – it was a bit like *Dynasty* set during WW2 – but one episode featured a spectacular recreation of the Battle of Midway. This used more original aerial footage than the earlier Mirisch production, though it did use a lot of stock film – including some of the same shots that were used in *Midway*, plus some of the new footage lensed for the 1976 film.

Filming for this Midway segment took place on the US Navy training aircraft carrier USS *Lexington* (AVT-16) in the autumn of 1987. The *Lexington* has been used to depict both American and Japanese carriers in a number of films and TV productions (including the aforementioned *Midway*), and for its role in *War and Remembrance* it was fitted with a number of working WW2 vintage 20mm Oerlikon and 40mm Bofors anti-aircraft guns. These included quad 40mm Bofors mounts, which weren't used by the US Navy until much later in the war.

A total of 38 flyable aircraft were used in the Midway sequences, including two genuine airworthy Douglas SBD-Dauntless dive bombers, N670AM and N54532. The latter was actually an A-24B Banshee, which was the land-based version of the aircraft. As mentioned earlier, N670AM had been used for cockpit shots in *Midway* in 1976. To increase the numbers of aircraft on screen, four T-6 Harvards were painted in 1942 US Navy colours and used in background shots. Thus in scenes which apparently show three Dauntlesses in formation, the rearmost aircraft is a T-6. This trick of keeping the least authentic aircraft in the background has been used in many aviation films, including *Appointment in London* (1953), *633 Squadron*, *The Blue Max* (1966), *Battle of Britain* and *Mosquito Squadron*.

Two Grumman FM-2 Wildcats, N47201 and N5HP, were also used in some aerial scenes, and two of the Vultee BT-13 Valiant-based 'Kate' replicas created for *Tora, Tora, Tora* were repainted in 1942 US Navy markings to represent Douglas TBD Devastators. 16 US Navy turboprop T-34C trainers were also used to flesh out shots of distant formations.

In addition, 12 North American T-6 and SNJ trainers were fitted with twin 0.30 inch Browning machine guns in their rear cockpits and painted in 1942 US Navy colours to resemble SBD Dauntlesses in aerial and carrier deck scenes. All the planes were painted at the Naval Air Station at Pensacola using Spray-Lat, a water-based acrylic paint which can be removed easily by power-washing. Markings were applied using self-adhesive vinyl decals, though individual aircraft numbers were omitted to avoid continuity problems.

One problem with Spray-Lat was that it tended to peel off and so had to be touched up frequently. After the US carrier scenes were completed, the 12 T-6s and SNJs were repainted in Japanese colours for the shots in which Japanese carriers are bombed by US aircraft.

Veteran warbird pilot Steven Hinton – who has done a lot of flying for various aviation movies – was in charge of the aerial filming unit. While the T-6s, SNJs and Wildcats had their engines run up during filming and were taxied on deck, they were not actually flown off the deck of the *Lexington*. However, permission was obtained for the two Dauntlesses to fly off the carrier, provided that a carrier-qualified pilot was on board each time and each aircraft made two take-offs during filming. The first carrier-borne launch of an SBD occurred on 8 September 1987, when John Maloney flew the Planes of Fame aircraft off the *Lexington* with former Blue Angels team leader Bob Aumack sitting in the rear gunner's compartment. A second SBD, owned by the Confederate Air Force (CAF), flew off shortly afterwards with retired US Marine pilot Howard Pardue in the back seat. Unfortunately the Navy wouldn't allow the two SBDs to land back on the carrier, so they then had to fly 40 miles back to the Naval Air Station at Pensacola.

Another stunning shot that was filmed soon afterwards depicted a Dauntless taking off from the carrier deck, and was shot from the rear gunner's compartment with veteran aerial cameraman Frank Holgate manning a hand-held camera in the gunner's compartment. Some simulated deck launches were also shot by getting the Dauntlesses to perform some high-speed taxying followed by a sudden stop.

One of the *Lexington's* cruises into the Gulf of Mexico was an overnighter, to permit shots of the dive-bombers landing at sunset. Another scene shot during this period was one in which the *Lexington* switches on its landing lights at night to allow its aircraft to get back down on the deck. One of the 33 convincing T-6-based SBD mock-ups created by Bruce Orriss for the Goldie Hawn movie *Swing Shift* (1984) was re-used to depict a battle-damaged Dauntless. These T-6s were sourced from a US Navy boneyard in Florida. Two other ex-*Swing Shift* T-6/SBD mock-ups were also used in the production to depict Douglas Dauntlesses in carrier deck scenes, and all three were subsequently given a repaint in Japanese colours and then blown up for the shots in which Japanese carriers were hit by American bombs. The actual carrier touchdowns were filmed on the shore at the Naval Air Station at Pensacola and at the Choctaw Auxiliary Field to the east, with the runway dressed to look like a carrier deck.

The 12 T-6s and SNJs which appeared in the flight deck sequences were used mainly for run-up and taxi scenes on the carrier itself. Most of the aerial scenes were filmed over the Gulf of Mexico using the two SBD Dauntlesses, the two Wildcats, two TBD-Devastators (actually ex-*Tora, Tora, Tora* Kates in US markings), and two SNJs standing in for Dauntlesses. The aerial camera ships for the production comprised a Bell Jet Ranger helicopter and a T-28 camera ship with cameras in underwing hardpoints and in the rear cockpit.

The pilots for the Midway segment were Bob Aumack, Tom Friedkin, Tom Gregory, Steve Hinton, Craig Hosking, John Maloney, John Muszala, Howard Pardue, Chuck Wentworth and Bruce Ellis.

Part of the plot involved 'Pug' Henry's son Warren 'buzzing' his father's cruiser USS *Northampton* to let him know he has survived his mission. To achieve this shot, the superstructure of a WW2 cruiser was mocked up on a barge which was towed by another ship.

The climactic dive bombing attack by Warren Henry's Dauntless was shot at Choctaw Field using three more of the SBD/T-6 replicas built by Bruce Orriss for the movie *Swing Shift* painted in Japanese markings. After this achievement, his aircraft is pursued by a lone Zero, played by one of the T-6-based replicas created for *Tora, Tora, Tora*. Eventually, his gunner Cornett severely damages the Zero with his twin thirty-calibre machine guns. These sequences were filmed at the Navarre Beach Pier on the Gulf Breeze shore, just outside Pensacola. John Muszala flew the Dauntless, while Chuck Wentworth piloted the Zero.

The Midway segment ends when 'Pug' Henry's aviator son Warren dies after his Dauntless is shot down after attacking a Japanese cruiser. The large and highly realistic Dauntless miniature used in this shot was later acquired for display in the Planet Hollywood restaurant in Las Vegas.

Aircraft carriers also played an important role in the Korean War, which lasted from 1950 to 1953, and one film which depicted strikes by naval aircraft was *The Bridges at Toko-Ri* (1954), an American war film – based on a novel by James Michener – which was directed and Mark Robson and which starred William Holden, Mickey Rooney, Fredric March, Grace Kelly and Robert Strauss.

The plot was relatively simple, and involved an attack by US Navy carrier planes from the USS *Savo Island* on key bridges at Toko-Ri. The mission is especially dangerous because of the heavy anti-aircraft defences around the target.

Michener's novel was based on his own experiences when he reported missions flown against railway bridges at Majon-ni and Samdong-ni, North Korea, during the winter of

1951-52 when he was a news reporter on the aircraft carriers USS *Essex* and USS *Oriskany*. Michener based the character of Harry Brubaker (played by William Holden in the film) on Lieutenant Donald S. Brubaker, who was a Naval Reservist recalled to active duty aboard USS *Valley Forge*.

Incidentally, the USS *Valley Forge* has itself appeared in a number of films. It was the derelict aircraft carrier tied up at San Francisco which plays a key part in the plot of the second *Dirty Harry* film, *Magnum Force* (1973), and its interior also played the inside of the spaceship – also called *Valley Forge* – in the science fiction movie *Silent Running* (1971), which starred Bruce Dern and was directed by Douglas Trumbull.

In Michener's original novel, Brubaker's squadron flew McDonnell F2H Banshees, but in the film Grumman F9F-2 Panthers were used – although these were still correct for the period. The film was highly praised for its very realistic special effects, particularly the climactic attack on the bridge which was achieved using miniatures flown on wires. These are noticeably more lifelike than similar sequences in *633 Squadron*, made a decade later.

The movie also has a scene where Chief Petty Officer Mike Forney (Mickey Rooney) and Airman Nestor Gamidge (Earl Holliman) arrive in a Sikorsky HO3S-1 helicopter in a futile attempt to rescue Brubaker, who has been shot down by anti-aircraft fire. Korea was the first conflict in which helicopters were widely used in various roles including casualty evacuation and rescuing downed aircrew, and this was the first cinematic depiction of the use of rotary-winged aircraft for this purpose. The film was well received on its release, making $4.7m at the US box office and winning an Academy Award for its Special Effects.

Carrier operations played an important part in the Vietnam War, which lasted from 1965 to 1975 (with most US Forces pulling out in 1973 after the signing of a 'peace agreement' with North Vietnam), and one notable film about the air campaign over North Vietnam was *Flight of the Intruder* (1991). Although unpopular with the general public and critics at the time of its release, it has since become a cult classic with aviation enthusiasts, and remains the only film about carrier operations during the Vietnam War.

The film was based on a novel by Stephen Coonts, a Denver lawyer who had served as a US Navy pilot during the Vietnam War, flying 1,600 hours in Grumman A-6 Intruder aircraft. Coonts sent the manuscript to 36 publishers. 30 refused to even look at it, and four rejected it outright. Coonts was waiting to hear from the remaining two publishers when the book was accepted for publication by the Naval Institute Arm, which had previously published Tom Clancy's book *The Hunt for Red October*, the first novel that the Institute had published in its 122-year history. Coonts has since written a large number of novels with military themes, including a direct sequel to *Flight of the Intruder* called *The Final Flight*.

The rights were bought by producer Mace Neufeld, and the original director assigned to the project was John McTiernan, who had helmed three previous hit movies, *Predator* (1987), *Die Hard* (1988) and *The Hunt for Red October* (1990). Eventually McTiernan dropped out and was replaced by John Milius, best-known for his Cold War paranoia movie *Red Dawn* (1984).

The plot of *Flight of the Intruder* centred around a US Navy carrier pilot, Lieutenant Jake 'Cool Hand' Grafton (Brad Johnson), who teams up with Lieutenant Commander William Cole (Willem Dafoe) to carry out an unauthorised mission against a missile depot (which they dub 'SAM City') in the centre of Hanoi. This part of the plot was fictional, and reflected Stephen Coonts' own concerns about the Vietnam War which – he felt – had been lost because of interference from American politicians who would often prevent US forces from doing what had to be done.

The mission is successful, but when the pair return to their carrier their commanding officer, Commander Frank Camparelli (Danny Glover), informs them that they are to be court-martialled. The charges are dropped the next day when Operation Linebacker II is ordered by President Richard Nixon, and the unauthorized mission is covered up. However, the pair are grounded while the rest of the squadron carries out air strikes to attack anti-aircraft sites in North Vietnam.

During the mission, Camparelli's A-6 is shot down by a North Vietnamese ZSU-23-4 *Shilka* anti-aircraft tank (a weapon never used in the Vietnam War) and crash lands, his bombardier dead. Jake and Cole, despite being officially grounded, fly to Camparelli's aid. They manage to destroy the *Shilka*, but are forced to eject from their damaged aircraft. Jake finds Camparelli, while a mortally-wounded Cole calls in air support in the form of two Douglas A-1 Skyraiders which use their four 20mm cannon and napalm bombs to hold off advancing North Vietnamese troops until Camparelli and Grafton can be picked up by a Sikorsky HH-53 'Jolly Green Giant' rescue helicopter.

Filming began in November 1989 on location in Hawaii. The US Navy cooperated fully with the producers and the carrier USS *Independence* (CV-62) was made available for two weeks of filming in November 1989 using A-6E Intruders from the VA-165 'Boomers' Squadron. All the A-6Es used in the film were cosmetically modified and painted to resemble the earlier A-6A and A-6B versions used in the Vietnam War. A number of older US Navy types which were still in service in 1989 also appeared in the movie, including the North American RA-5C Vigilante, the Vought A-7 Corsair II, the Grumman C-2 Greyhound, and the McDonnell Douglas Phantom II. Two privately-owned Douglas A-1 Skyraiders were obtained and painted in Vietnam War markings for the sequence at the end. The film was released in January 1991 but did not do well, making only $15m against its budget of $30m.

Another more successful film which depicted modern carrier action was *Top Gun* (1986), which was directed by Ridley Scott's late brother, Tony Scott. This proved to be one of the great box-office hits of 1986, and was the film which made Tom Cruise into a superstar. Its unique combination of stunning aerial scenes and a rock music soundtrack proved very popular with audiences, and led to a number of less successful imitations such as the *Iron Eagle* series of films.

The inspiration for the film was an article, *Top Guns*, by Ehud Yonay which was published in the May 1983 edition of *California* magazine, and which described the lives of fighter pilots at the Naval Air Station in San Diego, nicknamed 'Fightertown, USA'. This led to film producers Jerry Bruckheimer and Don Simpson commissioning a screenplay from Jim Cash and Jack Epps Jr.

Matthew Modine, who went on to star in two other war films – *Full Metal Jacket* (1987) and *Memphis Belle* (1990) – was offered the role of Maverick, but turned it down because he objected to the film's pro-military stance. Interestingly, both of these movies would be regarded as 'anti-war' films, and producer David Puttnam allegedly got the idea to make *Memphis Belle* after being annoyed by *Top Gun's* jingoistic tone.

Tom Cruise greatly enjoyed making *Top Gun*, and this should come as no surprise because the actor has a pilot's licence and owns and flies his own P-51 Mustang. He was also linked to two proposed WW2 flying films – *The Few*, and another about the American Volunteer Group (AVG), the famous 'Flying Tigers' – neither of which have been made.

Top Gun opens with scenes set aboard the carrier USS *Enterprise* (CVN-65). Lieutenant Pete 'Maverick' Mitchell (Tom Cruise) and his Radar Intercept Officer (RIO), Nick 'Goose' Bradshaw (Anthony Edwards), are catapulted off the deck of the carrier with another F-14 Tomcat fighter to intercept two hostile aircraft, fictional MiG-28s (actually American F-5Es). During the ensuing encounter, one of the MiG-28s gets a missile lock on Maverick's wingman, 'Cougar' (John Stockwell). 'Cougar' is not attacked, but is still shaken up by the encounter and has to be shepherded back to the carrier (against orders) by Maverick.

Maverick is reprimanded for his recklessness and is sent with his RIO, 'Goose', to the Top Gun school of combat flying at the Naval Air Station at Mirimar. While there, Maverick starts a relationship with Charlotte 'Charlie' Blackwood (Kelly McGillis), a civilian scientist and Top Gun instructor. Maverick performs well at the Top Gun school, but then suffers an accident when he flies into another F-14's jet wash. Maverick's aircraft goes into a flat spin and – although he ejects safely – Goose hits the F-14s canopy while ejecting and is killed.

Maverick is exonerated of all blame for the accident at a subsequent inquiry, but still feels remorse over what has happened. The incident affects his confidence, and he appears to have lost his mojo. Although he graduates from Top Gun, it is Iceman (Val Kilmer) who collects the Top Gun trophy.

Maverick doesn't have long to ponder over what has happened, because at the graduation party all the aviators receive orders to return to their carrier as they are needed urgently to assist an American ship that has broken down and drifted into hostile waters. Maverick subsequently becomes involved in an air battle with hostile MiG-28s. At first, he appears to have lost his confidence, but he gets it back and shoots down three enemy aircraft with AIM-9M Sidewinder missiles while Iceman bags another. He returns to his carrier a hero, where he is congratulated by Iceman who tells him he can be his wingman any day.

Filming of *Top Gun* took place with the assistance of the US Navy, although they insisted on a number of changes to the screenplay. The climactic dogfight was to have taken place off Cuba, but this was changed to 'international waters'. Maverick's love interest, 'Charlie', was originally to have been an aerobics instructor, then a female US Navy Officer, and finally became a civilian contractor attached to the Navy.

All carrier scenes were filmed aboard the USS *Enterprise* using F-14 Tomcats from the VF-114 and VF-213 Squadrons. Director Tony Scott was keen to get as many shots as possible with aircraft back-lit by the sun for greater artistic effect. When told that the carrier had changed course and it would cost $25,000 to put it back on its original heading, Scott promptly wrote the captain a cheque for this amount from his own private bank account!

Most of the sequences of aircraft flying over land were shot at the naval air station at Fallon, Nevada using ground-mounted cameras. Air-to-air footage was achieved using a Learjet camera plane and with specially-created camera pods attached to an F-14 which could shoot forwards or backwards. Some point-of-view shots were also obtained by stunt pilot Art Scholl using his Pitts Special biplane. During filming, Scholl's biplane entered an uncontrollable spin and crashed into the Pacific Ocean. Scholl's body was never found, and the film's end titles include a dedication to him.

The shots of missiles leaving their launch rails were real, but for cost reasons the US Navy would only permit a single Sidewinder to be fired. In order to use the same shot repeatedly, the film was sometimes flipped over during editing; a familiar cinematic trick. As the movie was made in the pre-CGI era, extensive use was made of miniatures, and some of these were nothing more than readily-available 1/32 scale plastic kits of F-14s. One very impressive shot of Maverick's fighter in a flat spin was achieved very simply by siting the camera on the ground, looking vertically upwards, and then dropping a spinning model onto it from a great height.

The film was a great success, making about £357 million at the worldwide box office, set against a budget of $15 million. As well as inspiring a number of cheap imitations, the film inspired a spoof movie – *Hot Shots* (1991) – starring Charlie Sheen and Lloyd Bridges, which used small, ex-RAF Folland Gnat trainers instead of F-14s.

A sequel to *Top Gun* has been mooted for decades, and at the time of writing a trailer has just been released on the internet. The new film is entitled *Top Gun: Maverick*, and reports have suggested that Tom Cruise's character will be the chief instructor at the Top Gun Fighter School. The plot features drones and the new F-35 carrier fighters, and Joseph Kosinski is rumoured to be the director of the new feature.

7
AMPHIBIOUS OPERATIONS

ONE of the many reasons the Allies won the Second World War was because they developed a vast amphibious capability, creating a large range of landing craft and specialised vessels which could deliver troops and heavy equipment directly onto enemy beaches. For example, they had the small LCVP (Landing Craft Vehicle Personnel) which could carry troops and/or a Jeep with trailer, the LCM (Landing Craft Mechanised) which could hold a medium tank – such as an M-4 Sherman – and the larger LCT (Landing Craft Tank). The first LCTs were built by the British and could only carry three tanks, but further improved versions were built, culminating in the Mark 4 which could carry nine M-4 Shermans. Even the earlier versions proved their worth as they were able to evacuate tanks from Greece and Crete, enabling them to be used again in North Africa. This was something that had proved impossible at Dunkirk, as at that time the Royal Navy had limited amphibious capability.

The ultimate amphibious vessel was the LST (Landing Ship Tank) with a displacement of about 5,000 tons, fully loaded. Various marks of LST were made, with most able to carry 20 medium tanks plus vehicles and troops. All these vessels were flat-bottomed, which meant that they could be driven up onto a beach and bow doors opened, rather like a modern roll on/roll off car ferry. The only downside was that the flat bottom made the ships roll heavily in anything but a dead calm, and seasickness amongst crews and embarked soldiers was a problem – particularly on D-Day.

As well as a huge family of landing craft, the Allies also developed a range of amphibious vehicles. Prominent amongst these was the DUKW ('Duck'), which was an amphibious version of the GMC 'Deuce-and-a-Half' two-and-a-half ton truck. This vehicle was first used during Operation Husky, the Allied invasion of Sicily in July 1943, where it proved its worth taking supplies between ships and shore. The Americans also developed a range of 'Amtrack' vehicles, which were used in both the European and Pacific theatres. These were based on tracked amphibious vehicles which had been created before the war for use in the swamps of Florida. The best-known of these was the famous 'Buffalo', which was like a cross between a landing craft and a tracked armoured personnel carrier as it featured a drop-down ramp which gave access to an inner open-topped compartment which could hold a Jeep and trailer or a squad of troops. Buffalos were used extensively in the Pacific War, and also saw some action during the Rhine Crossings in March 1945.

The main advantage of amphibious vehicles like the DUKW and Buffalo was that they could swim ashore and then drive on land like a normal wheeled or tracked vehicle, and descendants of these craft are still used today. The initial Argentine assault on the Falkland Islands in April 1982 was carried out by Marines using LVTP-7 Amtracks, vehicles which were modern versions of the Buffalos used in WW2.

The Axis powers never developed any great amphibious capability, and the Germans were particularly weak in this area. Their plans for invading Britain in September 1940 (Operation Sealion) involved hundreds of converted river and canal barges which had been purloined from across Europe. Some of these were modified with drop-down ramps, and many were unpowered with the intention being that they would be towed across the channel by other vessels. Some craft were fitted with outboard motors, and others were powered by aircraft engines and airscrews mounted on a framework towards the rear of the vessel. This is illustrated by a scene in *Battle of Britain* (1969), when a damaged Heinkel He-III flies low over a French port with one engine smoking. The spectacle is witnessed by the crew of a barge which is powered by an aircraft engine and propeller. This is a good example of how the makers of this epic went to great lengths to get the details right, even in relatively short scenes.

The British used their rapidly expanding amphibious capabilities in various raids in the first three years of the war – particularly the disastrous Dieppe Raid on 19 August 1942 (Operation Jubilee) – and this is described in detail earlier in the book. The next major amphibious assault was Operation Torch – the invasion of French North Africa – which took place between 8-10 November 1942. A few months later, Sicily was invaded (Operation Husky) in a campaign which lasted between 9 July and 17 August 1943. Soon after this, on 3 September 1943, the Allies landed on mainland Italy at Salerno (Operation Avalanche), Calabria (Operation Baytown) and Taranto (Operation Slapstick).

No feature film has ever been made about any of these operations, but the subsequent landings at Anzio on the west coast of Italy on 22 January 1944 (Operation Shingle) were the subject of a film, *Anzio*, which was released in 1968. After the initial invasions of southern Italy in September 1943 the Allies expected to knock Italy out of the war, allowing them to advance north and attack Germany from the south. This had always been Churchill's intention, as he was fearful that an invasion of France might fail and he persistently referred to Italy and the Balkans as 'the soft underbelly of Europe', which would be easy to attack.

Things didn't work out as planned, however, because although the Italians did capitulate soon after the Allied landings, the Germans did not react as expected. Although Germany's best general, Field Marshal Erwin Rommel, had recommended that Germany simply withdraw from Italy, Hitler thought otherwise and gave orders that his former Axis partner should be massively reinforced. The Italian military could have bought time for the Allies by blowing railway lines, bridges, roads and tunnels in northern Italy to prevent reinforcements being sent from Germany, but this did not happen and the Nazis soon took control of much of the country.

The Allies slowly advanced north, but found the going tough since the terrain favoured the defender as Italy had a mountainous spine. In the early 1940s it had also had few roads, and those that existed were of poor quality. There was also a lot of rainfall in autumn, winter and early spring, which turned roads into a quagmire. Instead of being the 'soft underbelly of Europe', Italy became known as the 'tough old gut'.

As a result of all these factors, the Allied advance was slow, and in an effort to break the stalemate an amphibious operation was launched behind enemy lines at the coastal town of Anzio, south west of Rome, on 22 January 1944. The landing was successful, but what happened next was beyond belief. Even though motorized reconnaissance patrols had shown that there were no German forces between Anzio and Rome, the Allies made no attempt to take the capital and simply dug in and waited for the German forces to attack. Had they gone for hell for leather for Rome (as General Patton or his German counterpart, Rommel, would have done in the same situation) then the war might have ended a few months earlier. Unfortunately the American generals in Italy were not of a sufficiently high calibre. Major General John P. Lucas was excessively cautious, and Lieutenant General Mark W. Clark, Commander of the Fifth Army, was a vain egotist who cultivated publicity. Had the American forces at Anzio been commanded by General Patton then there would probably have been a different outcome, but Patton was in Allied Supreme Commander General Eisenhower's bad books because of the two 'slapping incidents' in Sicily in August 1943 when he verbally and physically abused two soldiers who were suffering from 'battle fatigue'.

Some of these issues were mentioned in the 1968 film *Anzio*, which was directed by Edward Dmytryk and Duilio Coletti and produced by Dino De Laurentiis. Coletti, it will be recalled, was also responsible for *Submarine Raider* (1954) which is discussed elsewhere in this book. De Laurentiis, who died in 2010, was a prolific Italian producer who was also involved in two other war films, *Battle of the Bulge* (1965) and *U-571* (2000).

The screenplay was by H.A.L. Craig, based on the 1961 novel *Anzio* by former British war correspondent Wynford Vaughan-Thomas. As was common practice at the time, the names of certain individuals were changed for legal reasons. The timid General John P. Lucas became Major General Jack Lesley (Arthur Kennedy), and Lieutenant General Mark

Clark became Lieutenant General Carson (Robert Ryan). The lead, Robert Mitchum, played a character called Dick Ennis who was based on the real-life war correspondent Ernie Pyle, while Peter Falk (in his pre-*Columbo* days) was Corporal Jack Rabinoff, who was inspired by the real-life Jake Wallenstein who had run a brothel from the back of an ambulance (though this detail was not mentioned in the film).

The film was made entirely in Italy, with vehicles and equipment supplied by that country's armed forces. This did mean, though, that much of it was wrong for the period, so Korean War-era M-47 Patton tanks represented both American and German tanks in the film.

The film opens with American war correspondent Dick Ennis being assigned to cover the Anzio landings, which are designed to outflank the Germans. The landings are unopposed, but the incompetent American General Jack Lesley is too afraid to make a push for Rome and simply digs in, awaiting the inevitable German counter-attack. Meanwhile, Ennis and a US Ranger drive to Rome in a Jeep and confirm that there are few German forces between Anzio and Rome, but this information is simply ignored. As a result, Field Marshal Kesselring is able to bring up massive reinforcements and launches a counter-attack. In the real battle, radio-controlled glider-bombs launched from Dornier 217s and a huge railway gun known as 'Anzio Annie' were deployed against the Allied forces, but these details were omitted from the film.

Much of the remainder of the film deals with the Battle of Cisterna, when US Rangers were ambushed by German troops, and the fallout from this battle as a group of American survivors make their way back to Allied lines. The men take shelter in a house occupied by three Italian women.

A German patrol subsequently arrives, and the Americans are forced to kill them. Over the next few days most of the US troops are killed in battles with German snipers. Eventually the war correspondent Ennis is forced to defend himself using Rabinoff's gun. Only Ennis, Technical Sergeant Stimmler (Earl Holliman) and Private Movie (Reni Santoni) survive and make it back to Allied lines.

The film ends with a recreation of the Allied capture of Rome on 5 June, but avoids dealing with the controversial events which led to this outcome. Lieutenant General Mark Clark's superior, General Harold Alexander, had ordered Clark to use his forces to block the retreat of the German Army. Clark – who was a publicity-seeking egotist – deliberately ignored these orders so that he would have the glory of capturing Rome instead. As a result of this ego-driven blunder, a huge number of German troops escaped north to fight another day, and an opportunity to end the Italian campaign in the summer of 1944 was missed.

In his book about his wartime experiences, *Whicker's War*, journalist Alan Whicker claimed that this was the biggest mistake of the war and pointed out that right up until his death in 1984, Mark Clark had repeatedly attempted to justify his crass decision. As Whicker pointed out, if Mark Clark had been a general in the German Army he would have been shot. Churchill commented on the initial failure of the Anzio landings in his usual eloquent fashion: 'I had hoped that we were hurling a wildcat onto the shore, but all we got was a stranded whale'.

Anzio premiered in the USA on 24 July 1968 and received generally negative reviews. *The New York Times* film review was typical, describing it as an 'ordinary war movie with an epic title'.

The greatest amphibious operation in history was of course Operation Overlord, the Allied invasion of Normandy, and this was recounted in *The Longest Day* (1962) which was based on a best-selling book by former war correspondent Cornelius Ryan.

It was not the first film to be made about D-Day, though. An earlier production, *D-Day: Sixth of June* (1956), had dealt with the invasion but – in my opinion – was not a true war film. There was little action, and the storyline centred around a love triangle involving Captain Brad Parker (Robert Taylor), Lt. Col. John Wynter (Richard Todd) and Valerie Russell (Dana Wynter). At the end of the film Lt. Col. Wynter solves his personal crisis by deliberately stepping on a landmine. Love triangles have featured in a number of war movies, including *Mosquito Squadron* (1968) and *Pearl Harbor* (2001). *The Longest Day* was a completely different type of film, though, as it was a documentary account of the Normandy landings, based on a 1959 book by Cornelius Ryan who was a war correspondent in WW2 and later wrote *A Bridge Too Far*, which was also turned into a film in 1976 and is covered elsewhere in this book.

Work on bringing *The Longest Day* to the big screen started in 1960, when French producer Raoul Levy signed a deal with Simon & Schuster to purchase the filming rights to Cornelius Ryan's book. At this point the film was to be made at the Associated British Picture Corporation's studios at Elstree, with Michael Anderson directing. Unfortunately it proved impossible to raise the required $6 million budget, and the rights were eventually purchased from Levy by former 20th Century Fox mogul Darryl F. Zanuck for $175,000. The screenplay was written by Cornelius Ryan, but – as is often the case in the world of moviemaking – other writers were brought in to polish the script including James Jones and Romain Gary, with some input from Zanuck himself.

Bearing in mind the scale of the production and the number of battle scenes that would be required, Zanuck considered that four directors would be needed, so Ken Annakin, Andrew Marton, Gerd Oswald and Bernhard Wicki were all employed on the production. Annakin directed the British scenes and Marton helmed the shots involving Americans, while Oswald and Wicki directed the German segments of the film. In addition, Darryl F. Zanuck is rumoured to have directed a few scenes on an uncredited basis. At any one time, between two and four units were filming simultaneously to ensure the film was completed within a reasonable time span.

One of the biggest problems facing the filmmakers was acquiring a sufficient number of period vehicles, equipment and weapons. Fortunately the armed forces of Britain, France, the United States and Germany were able to help out. One thing that kept costs down was the fact that in 1961, just sixteen years after the war had ended, much WW2 equipment was still being used by the armed forces of many nations. The French Army, for example, still owned a number of Sherman tanks, M3 halftracks, DUKWs, Dodge weapons carriers and Jeeps. Furthermore, the French Hotchkiss company was still producing its own version of the wartime American Jeep called the M201 and, incredibly, this remained in service with the French Army until the early 2000s. The British War Office (now called the Ministry of Defence) also helped out with the provision of British vehicles and equipment.

One scene that might have been very expensive to shoot was that involving the US landings at Omaha Beach, but Zanuck solved the problem by obtaining permission to film 1,600 US Marines landing on Corsica as part of a US

Sixth Fleet exercise between 21-30 June 1961. With the addition of some special effects explosions and beach obstacles, this became Omaha Beach in 1944. Zanuck also shot footage of 22 US Navy ships of the Sixth Fleet at sea, though the aircraft carriers had to be kept out of shot as there were none present at D-Day. Some footage of 1,000 British paratroopers dropping over Cyprus was also shot for use in the film, though this ended up on the cutting room floor.

Many period weapons were still required, though, and the Imperial War Museum in London supplied a PIAT (Projector Infantry Anti-Tank). No ammunition could be found for the PIAT, so replica shells had to be cast in plastic. Several German guns of various calibres were obtained from French sources and used as part of the beach defences in various scenes.

Six aircraft were acquired for use in the production, comprising four Supermarine Spitfire Mark LF IXs (MH434, MH415, MK297 and MK923) and two French Nord 1002 Pingouin IIs (F-BFYX and F-BGVU), licence-built versions of the wartime Messerschmitt Bf108. The Spitfires were all supplied by COGEA, a Belgian target-towing firm based in Ostend, and were fitted with new Rolls-Royce Merlin engines and painted in Free French markings. No genuine wartime gliders could be found, so wooden replicas of an RAF Airspeed Horsa and a US Army CG4A Waco glider were built for ground sequences. Rather oddly, no effort was made to obtain C-47 Skytrain aircraft for the parachuting scenes, and the finished film has no shots showing paratroopers boarding their aircraft. This can only have done to keep costs down, as in 1961 the C-47 (and its civil counterpart the DC-3) was still in use with many of the world's air forces and airlines. British

European Airlines (BEA), for example, only retired its last DC-3s in 1962.

50 international stars took part in the film, although some – such as Sean Connery and Richard Burton – only had cameo roles, with these two actors only doing one day's filming each. Many of the actors were much older than the characters they played. For example, John Wayne – then aged 55 – played the 27-year-old Lt. Colonel Benjamin Vandervoort, while Robert Ryan, 51, portrayed the 37-year-old General James Gavin. Even Richard Todd at 42 was really too old to portray the 31-year-old Major John Howard. Todd, incidentally, was a paratrooper in WW2 and took part in the real-life assault on Pegasus Bridge, and at one point consideration was given to the idea of letting Todd play himself in the film. In the end Todd was cast as Major John Howard, who led the initial glider-borne attack which preceded the assault by paratroopers.

To portray the huge number of soldiers in various scenes, 2,000 extras were used, who were all serving soldiers in the French and US Armies. 60 Frenchmen were also used to portray German soldiers, and these received three weeks of training by Johnny Jendrich, a former German paratrooper.

Music plays an important part in most war films, but *The Longest Day* was quite unusual in that there was very little of it. The striking theme tune was composed by singer Paul Anka (who also appears in the film as a US Army Ranger, as does Fabian – another contemporary pop star), and is re-used at the end of the film and also in a couple of scenes where it is played on a harmonica and a piano. But, apart from this, there is very little incidental music.

Unlike in most war films, the Germans speak German and the French speak French with subtitles used so that English audiences can understand what is going on. However, all scenes were also shot a second time in English to enable the film to be screened without subtitles.

The film was made entirely in mainland France and Corsica. The original locations were used wherever possible, but in some cases filming had to be conducted elsewhere. For example, it was not possible to film on the actual Omaha Beach because of the huge memorial on the site. Thus the Omaha Beach sequences were filmed in Corsica and at Ile De Re (an island off the west coast of France), while the Ouistreham casino segment was lensed at Port-en-Bessin.

The Longest Day was one of the first films to make extensive use of helicopter shots, which were made possible by the flying skills of Gilbert Chomat, who many regarded as the best helicopter pilot in the world. Chomat's usual mount was the Sud-Aviation SA318 Alouette II helicopter, which proved ideal as a camera ship. Chomat worked on a number of 1960s productions with aerial camera work, including *The Blue Max* (1966) and *You Only Live Twice* (1967), but was killed when his Alouette collided with a replica SE.5A during the filming of *Zeppelin* in Ireland in 1970.

At an early stage, the decision was made to make the film in black-and-white for three reasons – to give it a documentary feel, to enable archive film to be used, and to make the relatively old stars look younger. Thus *The Longest Day* became one of the last major features to be shot in monochrome, and was the most expensive black-and-white film to be made until *Schindler's List* (1993).

Personally I think this was a mistake, as very little newsreel footage was used in the production (which could easily have been omitted) and the film would have been much more spectacular in colour. The fact that a colourized version was made in 1994 would support my contention.

The Longest Day premiered in France on 25 September 1962, followed by the USA premiere on 4 October and the UK premiere on 23 October. The film made $30 million in worldwide rentals against a final budget of $10 million, and effectively saved 20th Century Fox after the financially disastrous *Cleopatra*. The film attracted favourable reviews and won five Academy Awards for Art Direction, Cinematography, Editing, Special Effects and Best Picture. It has had several cinema releases up to the early seventies, including a 70mm version in 1969.

The next major production about D-Day was *Saving Private Ryan*, an epic war film set during the invasion of Normandy in June 1944. Unlike the earlier movie *The Longest Day* (1962), it does not attempt to be a comprehensive account of Operation Overlord. Instead, the first 27 minutes of the film deals with the landings on Omaha Beach, an operation which nearly ended in disaster for the US Forces involved. The middle section of the film deals with an American patrol's search for the elusive Private Ryan, whose three brothers have all died in action, and the last part of the film is a bit like *The Alamo* (1960) and *Sahara* (1943) in which a group of soldiers hold a position against overwhelming odds. The film is best remembered for its highly realistic battle scenes and its unflinching depiction of violence, which influenced many subsequent productions such as *Black Hawk Down* and *Pearl Harbor* (both 2001). It was also one of the first movies to use 'washed out' colour, a stylistic trend which has even been employed in other genres, including recent Bond movies such as *Spectre* (2015).

The film started life in 1994 as a script by Robert Rodat. The plot concerned Private James Francis Ryan being removed from combat duties in Normandy when his three brothers die in action. The storyline was based on a number of true incidents – including that of the Niland brothers – and followed a ruling by US President Franklin D. Roosevelt that, if a family lost more than two sons in combat, any remaining siblings should be brought home. Roosevelt's decision was a result of the case involving the five Sullivan brothers, all serving on the cruiser USS *Juneau*, who were lost in action off Guadalcanal in November 1942. Incidentally, this true story was itself made into a film *The Sullivans* (aka *The Fighting Sullivans*) in 1944.

Rodat's script was sent to producer Mark Gordon who passed it on to Steven Spielberg, regarded as one of the world's greatest film directors. Spielberg had a lifelong fascination with WW2 which was at least in part due to his father Arnold's experiences during the war when he had served as a radio operator in USAAF North American B-25 aircraft in Burma and India. At age 16, the young Spielberg had made his first war movie, *Escape to Nowhere*, in the Californian desert. Another of his early amateur productions was *Fighter Squadron* which used abandoned WW2 fighters at Sky Harbor Airport in Phoenix, plus stock gun camera footage which the teenage Spielberg purchased at his local drugstore.

Spielberg decided that the film was to be as authentic as possible, and so shooting it in the USA was not an option. It was also impossible to use the real Omaha Beach because of the huge memorial at the site, plus a lot of modern redevelopment which included a power station, so another location had to be found.

Spielberg originally intended to film the Omaha Beach sequences in Sheringham, Norfolk, but that was ruled out as well after John Major's Government and the Ministry of Defence proved uncooperative – particularly regarding the provision of extras from the Regular and Territorial Armies.

Eventually the producers opted to film the Omaha Beach sequences in the Republic of Ireland, which offered a number of incentives for filmmakers. A number of major film productions had been shot there, including Mel Gibson's historical drama *Braveheart* (1995) and two war movies, *The Blue Max* (1966) and *The McKenzie Break* (1970). The Irish Army was more than happy to assist the film-makers, and 850 reservists plus civilian battle re-enactors played American and German soldiers.

The location chosen to represent Omaha was Ballinesker Beach, Curracloe Strand, Ballinesker – just east of Curracloe, County Wexford, Ireland. The topography was similar to that at Omaha, as the wide sandy beach was overlooked by grassy high ground on which German pillboxes could be built. Replica beach defences were installed along the waterline plus acres of fake barbed wire, which was made from rubber to avoid causing injuries to the actors.

A large bunker made out of wood and plaster was built on the site, based on an accurate model built by Tom Sanders in Hollywood, and various machine guns and artillery pieces were installed as part of the beach defences. These were supplied by Steve Lamonby of Plus Film Services and included a Skoda 105mm artillery piece, MG 42 machine guns, and a German 20mm Flak 38 weapon.

One problem was finding enough period landing craft. At one point the producers considered building new vessels for the film, but suitable boats were eventually found. Two

British LCMs (Landing Craft Mechanised) were discovered in the Boston Boatyard in Oreston, Plymouth, and were restored to correct WW2 configuration by former Royal Marine James Wakefield. For the film these wore the codes PA30-10 and PA30-31, indicating they were from the US troopship APA 30, the *Thomas Jefferson*. Ten of the smaller LCVP (Landing Craft Vehicle/Personnel) were located sitting in the desert in Palm Springs, and were shipped to the UK where they were reconditioned for use in the film by Robin Davies' team from Square Sail in St Austell, Cornwall. In addition, a derelict landing craft was patched up so it could be blown up in certain scenes, while a section of one was constructed for use in underwater sequences shot in a water tank. A Russian civilian vessel based in Scotland was also acquired specifically to land tanks on the beach, although this ship doesn't appear in the final cut of the film.

A large number of period military vehicles were employed in the production, including Willis MB Jeeps, M3 halftracks, GMC 'Deuce-and-a-half' trucks and Dodge weapons carriers. Two genuine M4 Sherman tanks were sourced and fitted with mock-up deep wading snorkels for a scene where American armour lands on Omaha Beach, but this footage was deleted from the final cut of the film which only includes a brief glimpse of a single Sherman at the end of the movie.

Various German military vehicles were also sourced for the film, including an Opel Blitz truck, a Horch staff car, five motorcycle-sidecar combinations, three Kettenrad motorcycle-halftracks and an Sd.Kfz. 251 halftrack.

As had been the case with *A Bridge Too Far* (1977), it proved impossible to find any genuine wartime German tanks in running condition. However, the script called for a tank assault on Captain Miller's squad in the final section of the movie. The solution was to build replicas of German armoured vehicles using readily available types.

Art Director Alan Tomkins, who had previously worked on many classic British war films including *The Heroes of Telemark* (1965), *Battle of Britain* (1969), *A Bridge Too Far* (1977) and *Memphis Belle* (1990), had designed a replica Russian T-54 tank – using a British Alvis Saracen armoured car – for the James Bond film *Goldeneye* (1995). Tomkins originally thought that a T-55 could be used to create a reproduction of a German Tiger I tank, but was informed that the earlier T34/85 would be a better base vehicle as it had the same barrel height as a Tiger and its all-round dimensions were slightly smaller than the German vehicle, making it ideal for conversion.

Eventually, Steve Lamonby and his team from Plus Film Services – working from drawings made by Tomkins – built two replica Tiger Is over a wooden framework applied to the Russian tanks. Much assistance was provided by the Tank Museum at Bovington in Dorset, who allowed detailed photos and measurements to be taken of their preserved example, Tiger 131, which had been captured by British forces after being disabled by a British Churchill tank in Tunisia in 1943.

As a result, the two mock Tigers were near-perfect in every detail. The only feature of the Tiger which couldn't be replicated were the roadwheels. A real Tiger has interleaved, overlapping road wheels, while the film reproductions had the spaced road wheels of a T34.

If you have read the chapter on *Kelly's Heroes* (1970) in my book *Battles on Screen: World War II Action Movies* (Extremis Publishing, 2017), you will know that the three

Tigers used in that film were also created using T34/85 tanks resulting incorrect reports on the internet that the Tiger replicas in *Saving Private Ryan* were the same ones used in the earlier film. This is not true, and the fate of the three *Kelly's Heroes* Tigers is unknown.

The screenplay also called for two Marder III self-propelled guns. One was built specially for the film by Steve Lamonby using the chassis of a Panzer 38 (t) found in Czechoslovakia, while the second was a cosmetically-modified Swedish SAVM/43 self-propelled 105mm gun which also used the Panzer 38 (t) chassis. The Panzer 38 (t) was a German adaptation of a pre-war Czech tank manufactured by Skoda. Large numbers were captured when the Germans invaded Czechoslovakia in 1939, and were used by the *Wehrmacht* during the Blitzkrieg in 1940. Although the tank soon became obsolete, the chassis was used in a number of German self-propelled guns, including the Marder III.

About 2,000 historically accurate firearms were used in the production including M1 Garand rifles, M1 carbines, and Thompson submachine guns and BAR (Browning Automatic Rifles). 500 of them could fire blanks, while the remaining 1,500 were lightweight rubber replicas which could be carried by extras. As few original uniforms from the 1940s existed, thousands of new ones were created by various manufacturers and then artificially aged to give a correct worn-in look.

The musical score for the film was composed by Spielberg's long-time collaborator John Williams, and at the director's request there was no music during the battle scenes which make up a considerable portion of the movie. This makes an interesting comparison with *The Guns of Navarone* (1961), in which only ten minutes of screen time lack music.

Tom Hanks was cast in the key role of Captain Miller. Oher actors who were considered for the role were Harrison Ford and Mel Gibson. Private Ryan was played by Matt Damon, who at that time was relatively unknown. Later, Damon was to achieve worldwide fame through the series of Jason Bourne movies starting with *The Bourne Identity* (2002). The other seven members of Miller's rescue squad consisted of Sergeant Horvath (Tom Sizemore), Corporal Upham (Jeremy Davies), Tech/4 Wade (Giovanni Ribisi), Private Caparzo (Vin Diesel), Private Jackson (Barry Pepper), Private Mellish (Adam Goldberg), and Private Reiben (Edward Burns).

All the actors playing Miller's eight-man rescue team attended a ten day 'boot camp' prior to the start of filming, run by former US Marine Dale Dye who also appears in the film as an officer in the War Department casualty section. Dye ran a company called Warriors Inc. and forced the actors to live under canvas, eat army rations and do intensive training including weapons handling. Matt Damon was deliberately excluded from this course so that the other actors would feel resentment towards him (which they did).

Apart from the Omaha Beach sequences, most of the film was made in a huge outdoor set which had been created at the former British Aerospace factory and airfield at Hatfield. During WW2 the facility had been owned by the De Havilland Company, which built the famous wooden Mosquito bomber. Hatfield's large grounds were also the location for Dale Dye's 'boot camp'. This outdoor set, which included a fake river and bridge, was used to depict two different ruined French villages – Ramelle and Neuville.

The former British Aerospace offices at Hatfield appear in the film as the War Department casualty section in Washington, while the director's suite on the first floor became

General Marshall's office. The huge building at Hatfield became a temporary studio, with the former aircraft hangars in particular being used to store vehicles and equipment.

The budget was set at $70m, with $11m set aside for the Omaha Beach sequences. The film was shot in just 59 days in the summer of 1997, which was a remarkably short time compared with other epics such as *Battle of Britain* (1969) and *A Bridge Too Far* (1977) which both took about six months to film.

Saving Private Ryan was released on 24 July 1998 and was a critical and commercial success, making $491.8m at the box office with another $44m from various home entertainment releases. The film was nominated for eleven Academy Awards and won five for Best Cinematography, Best Sound Mixing, Best Sound Effects Editing, Best Film Editing and Best Director.

It was widely praised for the realism of its battle scenes, and many war veterans who saw it were quite shaken by the experience. The film influenced many subsequent war movies, and also started the trend for 'washed out' colour which – in my personal opinion – has now become an over-used cliché. Would films such as *Goldfinger* (1964) and *You Only Live Twice* (1967) have made such an impact if they had been filmed in muted colour rather than Technicolor? Indeed, when *Saving Private Ryan* was first broadcast on satellite television in the USA, many viewers 'phoned in to say there was something wrong with the colour, resulting in the broadcasters turning up the colour saturation to produce a 'normal' looking picture.

Apart from the muted colour and the technical and historical errors in *Saving Private Ryan*, it suffers (like most of Spielberg's films) from an excess of sentimentality and emotional manipulation of the audience. Indeed, one of the staunchest critics of the film has been respected Oscar-winning American screenwriter William Goldman, who wrote the script for *A Bridge Too Far* (1977). In his 2001 book *The Big Picture: Who Killed Hollywood?*, Goldman criticizes the film, particularly the last hour which he describes as 'fifty plus minutes of phoney, manipulative shit'. Goldman also disliked the opening and closing scenes with the aged Ryan. How could this individual have a 'flashback' to the landings at Omaha Beach since he wasn't there? If you are interested in reading Goldman's views on the film, his essay has also been reproduced in full on a number of websites.

Quite apart from Goldman's concerns, the film also implies that D-Day (and the Second World War in general) was won by the Americans alone without any help from the British, as had been suggested before in Hollywood films like *Objective Burma* (1945) and *Patton* (1970). Despite these qualms, *Saving Private Ryan* remains an impressive technical achievement and a landmark in the history of war movies.

Amphibious operations played a key role in the Pacific theatre as well. After the Japanese had been defeated at the Battle of Midway in June 1942, the Americans felt sufficiently confident in their growing strength to start retaking island chains which had been captured by the Japanese. In this way they would start moving towards the Japanese home islands; something that became known as the 'island hopping' campaign.

The first island to be recaptured in this fashion was Guadalcanal, which was subjected to an amphibious assault in August 1942. US Marines swiftly took over a partially-completed airstrip which was renamed 'Henderson Field', and US Navy and Army planes were flown in. Unfortunately the island was stubbornly defended by the Japanese, and the US Navy in particular took heavy losses in keeping the troops supplied. Both sides attempted to send in reinforcements, and a battle of attrition developed. After six months of bitter fighting the Japanese withdrew from the island in February 1943, giving the Americans their first major land victory against the Japanese in WW2.

These dramatic events were the subject of a book by James Jones, *The Thin Red Line*, which was published in 1962 and has been filmed twice. The first version, made in 1964, was directed by Andrew Marton who had previously been one of the directors of *The Longest Day* and also had a lot of experience as a second unit director, supervising the chariot race scenes in *Ben-Hur* (1959) and the climactic tank battle in *Kelly's Heroes* (1970).

This original version was filmed in monochrome Cinemascope on location near Madrid in Spain. The village of Boola Boola which the US Marines capture was an outdoor set at Embalse De Santillana at Manzanares El Real. The main subplot concerned Private Doll (Keir Dullea), who had married Judy (Merlyn Yordan) just before leaving for action and was relentlessly bullied by First Sergeant Welsh (Jack Warden). The title of the novel and film comes from a line of dialogue by Captain Stone (Ray Daley): 'There's only a thin red line between the sane and the mad'.

A remake, written and directed by Terrence Malick, was released in 1998 and was inevitably compared with *Saving Private Ryan* which had premiered just a few months before. The problem with this version of *The Thin Red Line* was that it had the look of an art house movie, with little action. It was also lacking in spectacle.

One thing that was conspicuously lacking in the film were shots of large numbers of ships at sea or planes in the air. The entire US transport fleet was represent by a single vessel, the SS *Lane Victory* (which was also used in *Flags of Our Fathers* a decade later). Similarly, only a single warship – a modern minesweeper supplied by the Royal Australian Navy – appears in the film, and the large air fleet which covered the landings was represented by a single, rare Australian-built CAC Wirraway fighter supplied by the Temora Aviation Museum, which was painted to represent a US Navy Douglas Dauntless dive-bomber.

One piece of authenticity in the film was the replica American aircraft seen sitting on Henderson Field, which were authentic-looking Bell P-39 Airacobras. The P-39 was one of the most revolutionary fighter designs of WW2, as it had a modern tricycle undercarriage like a modern jet. It was powered by an Allison V-1710 V12 engine which was mounted behind the cockpit, with the propeller being driven by a long shaft which passed beneath the pilot's seat. This meant the front fuselage between the cockpit and the propeller could be used to mount a heavy armament of one 37mm cannon and two Browning M2 fifty-calibre machine guns. In addition, four thirty-calibre Brownings were mounted in the wings, giving the aircraft a good punch. It could also carry a small bomb load, and in later versions the four thirty-calibre wing guns were replaced by two M2 fifty-calibre weapons.

Though it had many excellent design features, it was a failure as a combat aircraft in both the European and Pacific theatres. The main problem was the Allison V-1710 engine which only had a single-stage supercharger, resulting in the aircraft having poor performance above 10,000 feet. It was thus unsuitable for combat against Japanese Zeros or German

Messerschmitt Bf109s, and it was rejected by the RAF after they deployed a single squadron in combat. It did, though, prove very popular with the Soviet air force whose operations were largely conducted at low-level, and most P-39s were used by the USSR who received thousands of them, with many Russian pilots becoming aces on the type.

This new version of *The Thin Red Line* was inevitably compared with *Saving Private Ryan*, but it offered a very different experience. While *Saving Private Ryan* had a strong anti-war message, it had well-staged action scenes. *The Thin Red Line* was very talky by comparison, and was more of a character drama with cameos from many established Hollywood stars such as George Clooney, Sean Penn, Nick Nolte and Adrien Brody. Brody was reportedly unhappy that many of his scenes ended up on the cutting room floor. *The Thin Red Line* was nominated for several Oscars, namely Best Picture, Best Director, Best Adapted Screenplay and Best Score, but ultimately won none of them.

The battle for Guadalcanal also featured in the first two episodes of *The Pacific* (2010), a 10-part HBO miniseries by HBO which was a follow-up to the previous miniseries *Band of Brothers* (2001), which was itself inspired by the success of *Saving Private Ryan*.

The series explored the exploits of a group of US Marines including PFC Robert Leckie (James Badge Dale), Corporal Eugene Sledge (Joe Mazzello), and Sergeant John Basilone (Jon Seda) as they participated in the US Navy's 'island-hopping' campaign against Guadalcanal and other Japanese islands. Unlike *The Thin Red Line*, the series gave a very good impression of the scale of US amphibious operations against the Japanese through its effective use of CGI. The series was popular with the general public and well-received by critics, and at time of writing a third HBO WW2 miniseries (about the USAAF), *The Mighty Eighth*, is currently in production.

One of the hardest fought battles the US Marines fought in WW2 was the capture of the strategically-important island of Iwo Jima. In June 1944 the US Navy had captured the Marianas Islands (comprising Guam, Saipan and Tinian), and speedily built huge airfields on them from which giant B-29 Superfortress bombers could mount raids on Japan. By February 1945 the US Navy was in a position to take Iwo Jima, a small volcanic island between the Marianas and Japan which already had three airfields on it.

The capture of Iwo Jima would allow squadrons of long-range North American P-51D Mustangs to be based there and escort the B-29s to and from the target, cutting their losses from Japanese fighters. In addition, damaged B-29s returning from missions could make emergency landings on the island. The Japanese High Command was aware of the strategic importance of these islands, and was determined to defend them at any cost. In any case, the ancient Japanese warrior of code of *Bushido* forbade surrender to the enemy, which meant that a fight to the death was in prospect.

The first film to be made about the Iwo Jima campaign was *The Sands of Iwo Jima* (1949), which was directed by Allan Dwan and starred John Wayne as Marine Sergeant John M. Stryker. The film opens not long after the Guadalcanal campaign has concluded, and begins with Stryker whipping his squad of Marines into shape. This is a familiar theme in both British and American war movies – an unpopular commander is hard on his men during training, but they later thank him for it when they face the reality of combat.

After a period of intense training in New Zealand, the Marines are sent off to fight, first of all on Tarawa and later on Iwo Jima. The film was made by Republic Pictures and was shot mainly in California, using a combination of original and newsreel footage. It also features unique shots of LVT2 tracked amphibious landing vehicles in action.

After successfully capturing Tarawa, the Marines are sent to Hawaii to recuperate before being shipped out to assault the volcanic island of Iwo Jima. This proves to be a hard-fought battle, and the Marines bring in Sherman tanks equipped with flamethrowers (probably the only time a flamethrower Sherman has ever appeared in a war movie). Towards the end of the movie, Stryker is shot by a sniper; one of only five times John Wayne died on screen.

The climax of the film depicts the raising of the US flag on the summit of Mount Suribachi, which is officially recorded as happening on 23 February 1945. In fact, this raising of the flag was actually the second time this happened, as it had to be staged a second time for the cameras. This may seem like a small point, but it forms the entire focus of the plot of a second, more recent movie about the capture of Iwo Jima – *Flags of Our Fathers* (2006) – which was directed by Clint Eastwood, based on a 2000 book by James Bradley and Ron Powers.

Flags of Our Fathers concentrates on the story of three survivors, 'Doc' Bradley (Ryan Phillipe), Rene Gagnon (Jesse Bradford) and Ira Haynes (Adam Beach), who were involved in the staged flag-raising and subsequently took part in a publicity tour of the USA to promote the sale of War Bonds. This is one of the main faults of the film, as it makes a big issue over something (the fact that the flag-raising was staged) that most people outside the USA are probably unaware of, and care little about.

As Iwo Jima is now a war grave and access to the island is limited, director Clint Eastwood chose to make most of the film in Iceland, which has similar black volcanic sand. Using the same 'washed out colour' and staccato shutter effects as *Saving Private Ryan*, the film made extensive use of CGI to depict explosions, ships and aircraft. This gave the production a very unrealistic feel. For example, the shot of F4U Corsair fighters flying over the US fleet followed by a subjective view from inside the cockpit – all done by CGI – looks very much like an excerpt from the *Dogfights* documentary series, which was largely created by computer.

The rest of the film was lensed in the USA, with Los Angeles, Texas and Chicago being used for scenes during the War Bonds tour. The genuine WW2 troop transport SS *Lane Victory* – which was previously used in *The Thin Red Line* – also makes an appearance.

The same year, Eastwood also directed *Letters from Iwo Jima*, which presented the same events from the Japanese perspective. This used battle scenes from *Flags of Our Fathers* with additional new footage, supposedly set in Japan but actually filmed in California. This time the screenplay was based on a book, *Picture Letters from Commander in Chief* by Tadamichi Kuribayashi (published in 1992), who was the general in charge of forces on the island.

Letters from Iwo Jima was filmed entirely in Japanese with Japanese actors, and portrays the Nipponese forces as the underdogs, being forced to fight a battle against the technologically and numerically superior Americans.

The next major amphibious operation occurred during the Korean War in 1950, when United Nations forces (mainly

American) conducted a daring landing behind enemy lines to prevent South Korea from being overrun by Communist North Korean troops.

At the end of WW2, Korea was divided into two separate countries: North Korea, which had a hard-line Communist regime, and the democratic South Korea which was supported by the West. Some US troops were stationed in the South to deter North Korean forces from attacking. By 1950 North Korea was well-stocked with the latest Soviet weapons, particularly T34/85 medium tanks which had proved very effective in WW2 against the Germans, and on 25 June they launched an invasion of the South. American and South Korean troops fought bravely, but the country was soon in danger of being overrun. The South Korean capital of Seoul was captured, and UN forces were left holding only a small area of the country around Pusan. A Dunkirk-style evacuation seemed likely.

General Douglas MacArthur – who had led US Forces to victory in the Pacific in WW2 – travelled from Japan to South Korea to assess the situation and came up with a master plan. He would launch a huge amphibious invasion at the harbour town of Inchon (aka Incheon) which was Seoul's port, outflank the invaders, cut their supply lines and then invade the north. The plan was risky but ultimately successful, and United Nations forces led by MacArthur took over most of North Korea. At this point it looked as though the war would be won with Korea re-united as part of the free world but unfortunately MacArthur's forces approached close to the Chinese border, provoking an attack from that nation across the Yalu River. Millions of Chinese troops poured south over the border and drove back the UN troops. Although the Chinese soldiers were not as well-equipped or trained as the UN troops, they won many battles through sheer weight of numbers.

General MacArthur hoped to reverse the situation by bombing Chinese airfields and possibly even using nuclear weapons, but President Harry Truman was worried about escalating the conflict as he feared it could trigger a Third World War and the possibility of an atomic holocaust. The USSR was already involved, as it had supplied North Korea and China with weaponry including T34/85 tanks. The Chinese were also using the latest Soviet fighter, the MiG-15, and it is now known that many of these were flown by Russian pilots keen to get combat experience.

Seven months after the Inchon landings, President Harry Truman relieved General MacArthur of his command. The war continued until 1953 when a ceasefire was agreed, leaving the Communists in control in the North and a pro-western regime in the South; a stalemate that has continued to this day.

Despite this rather unsatisfactory outcome to the war, the Battle of Inchon is still regarded as a national victory in South Korea in the same way that British people honour their famous battles such as Trafalgar, Waterloo and the Battle of Britain, and General MacArthur is regarded as a national hero in that country.

For that reason, the historic victory has been the subject of not one but two major motion pictures made in South Korea. The first of those was *Inchon* (1981), a multinational production made in South Korea, Ireland, Italy and England by One-Way Productions. The film has always been very controversial because of its huge budget overruns and lack of profitability. It also received a limited release and has never been issued on any home entertainment format. At the time of writing, the film can be viewed in its entirety on YouTube and this version appears to an off-air recording made on VHS during its broadcast on the Good Life TV network in the USA.

The film is also very contentious as it was largely funded by the founder of the Unification Church, Sun Myung Moon, who was extremely wealthy and had lots of money to burn. Another person who put up cash for the production was the Japanese newspaper publisher Mitsuharu Ishii. Although Ishii was officially the film's producer, Moon was credited as 'Special Advisor on Korean Matters' and contributed $30million to Ishii's film production company. Additional funding was also provided by Robert Standard, the associate producer and a member of the Unification Church of the United States.

Prior to production, Moon and Ishii had considered making biopics of Jesus or Elvis Presley, but in 1978 they consulted a psychic, Jeane Dixon, about the possibility of making an Inchon film. Dixon apparently got in touch with the spirit of the deceased General MacArthur, who approved the film. Dixon also chose the director of the project, Terence Young, who is best-known for directing three Bond films: *Dr No* (1962), *From Russia with Love* (1963) and *Thunderball* (1965). In the end the film cost $46 million, a staggering sum in 1980.

The main writer working on the film was Robin Moore, who had penned the novels on which the films *The Green Berets* (1968) and *The French Connection* (1971) were based. Moore had a rather unique working technique as he liked to strip off and use his typewriter while standing naked, as he considered even a wristwatch to be an impediment to creativity.

For the all-important role of General MacArthur, the producers chose English actor Laurence Olivier who, at that point in his career, was willing to take on almost any role provided that it paid well. Olivier was paid £1 million plus $2,500 per week expenses to play the General. To portray him, Olivier spent hours watching films and listening to tapes to get the voice and mannerisms right. One of MacArthur's subordinates, Lieutenant Al Haig (who later became a general and a key member of the Reagan administration), told Olivier that MacArthur sounded a bit like the late actor and comedian W.C. Fields, so Olivier's voice in the film is like that person with a bit of Jimmy Durante thrown in.

Considerable make-up was applied to Olivier to make him more closely resemble the late General, and this included a false nose, mascara, lipstick and brown hair dye. The real MacArthur was a vain egotist who, by 1950, wore a corset and lipstick and dyed his hair, so this was entirely accurate. This meant that Olivier had to endure a two-and-a-half-hour makeup session before shooting began each day. One feature of MacArthur's personality which did come over well in the film was his deep religious conviction and his belief that God was on his side, a trait which MacArthur shared with his WW2 contemporary General George Patton.

An all-star cast was assembled for the production including Ben Gazzara, Jacqueline Bisset, Toshiro Mifune, Richard Roundtree and David Janssen. One of the subplots concerned an American officer, Colonel Haldsworth (Ben Gazzara), who is having an affair with a young South Korean girl (Karen Kahn). Meanwhile, his wife Barbara (Jacqueline Bisset) flees south in a car with five South Korean children. On their way their car breaks down, but they are helped by an US Army Sergeant named August Henderson (Richard

Roundtree). Born in Weybridge, England, Jacqueline Bisset had a prolific career encompassing many Hollywood epics, including *Bullitt* (1968) and *Airline* (1969). She got the role in *Inchon* as a direct result of her glamorous appearance in *The Deep* (1977), in which she wore a wet T-shirt for much of the production. *Inchon* is one of the few films Bisset made in which she spoke in her natural English accent, as she usually played Americans.

David Janssen (in his last film), who is best known for portraying Dr Richard Kimble in *The Fugitive* TV series (1963-67), plays a war correspondent named David Feld. Gabrielle Ferzetti – who played Draco in *On Her Majesty's Secret Service* (1969) – appears as a Turkish Brigadier, while Anthony Dawson (who was Dent in *Dr No* in 1962) is General Collins. The musical score was by respected and prolific composer Jerry Goldsmith.

Filming was carried out in the summer of 1980 in South Korea with the assistance of US and South Korean forces. Equipment loaned to the producers by the armed forces of these two countries included several M-47 and M-48 tanks, six North American F-86 Sabre fighters, six destroyers and numerous Jeeps, trucks, field guns and period cars. An authentic Douglas C-54 Skymaster appears as MacArthur's personal transport. As no genuine T-34/85 tanks were available in South Korea at the time of shooting, these were represented by American M-47 and M-48 Patton tanks covered with foliage and fake external fuel tanks.

There were problems with the shooting schedule, caused by the inhospitable climate. At times the crew had to endure baking heat, while there were also frequent heavy rainstorms including two actual typhoons which destroyed outdoor film sets. Jacqueline Bisset developed severe laryngitis which meant that shooting had to be stopped for a week.

As a result, the film went wildly over budget and only made $2 million at the box office against a production cost of $46 million ($124 million in today's money). It did not receive a widespread release, and has never been issued on any home entertainment format. In their book *The Hollywood Hall of Shame: The Most Expensive Flops in Movie History* film historians Harry and Michael Medved have declared *Inchon* to be the biggest flop of all time, and possibly the worst movie ever made. Having seen the film in its entirety fairly recently, I cannot concur with this view. While agreeing that it was a financial disaster, I don't think it is really that bad. It is no worse than *Anzio* or any number of Italian 'macaroni combats'. What it true is that it doesn't *look* as though a lot of money was spent on it, and it is no more visually impressive than any of the Oakmont Films productions of the late sixties which each cost no more than $1 million. The last 15 minutes of the film, depicting the landings at Inchon, are quite spectacular and reminiscent of similar scenes in *The Longest Day*, but the rest of the film is quite talky.

Bearing in mind the financial failure of *Inchon*, it is surprising that a film company would consider making another film about the same subject. Yet that is what happened in 2015 when the South Korean film industry made another epic, *Operation Chromite*, which covered much the same ground as the Terence Young picture. One difference, though, was that much of the film featured a subplot in which a force of South Korean soldiers infiltrates the North Korean forces in a clandestine operation known as 'X-Ray'. Their mission is to obtain information about the positioning of defences such as mines and artillery and secure a vital lighthouse (the Palomino lighthouse) overlooking the harbour, which can be used to assist the invading American forces. The lighthouse also features in a similar capacity in the earlier film.

The cast was mainly South Korean, with General Douglas MacArthur being played by Northern Irish actor Liam Neeson – who, with the addition of a peaked cap, aviator sunglasses and a corncob pipe, looked very much like the famous General. The film was made on a relatively small budget of just $12.7 million (which, allowing for inflation, was just one-tenth of *Inchon's* budget), and many sequences (such as the fleet at sea) were created using CGI.

Uniforms, weapons and equipment were more accurate than in the earlier *Inchon* film, and this was largely because in the post-Cold War era it is now possible to obtain genuine Soviet tanks and equipment for use in war films. In *Inchon* the North Koreans drive American Willys MB Jeeps and M47 and M48 tanks, but in *Operation Chromite* they travel in Russian GAZ Jeeps and have T34 tanks. The film proved very popular in South Korea and made $50million at the worldwide box-office, proving that films about Inchon (and war movies in general) don't need to be box-office disasters!

8
COLD WAR OPERATIONS

THE period between 1947 and 1991 is one which historians now refer to as the 'Cold War', but the origins of this era go back to the last few months of the Second World War. Just prior to WW2, on 23 August 1939, the Foreign Ministers of Germany and Russia had signed a non-aggression pact (The Molotov-Ribbentrop Pact), and one result of this was that the USSR took control of the eastern part of Poland after war broke out in September 1939. Stalin also supplied the Germans with oil and grain.

All that changed on 22 June 1941 when Germany invaded Russia. Taken by surprise (and having disregarded warnings of the impending attack from Churchill), Stalin was desperate for help from Britain and the United States. Despite Britain's perilous supply situation, vast quantities of munitions, tanks, aircraft, food and other war supplies were shipped to the Soviet Union via the Arctic convoy route; something that Churchill called the 'worst journey in the world'. Enormous amounts of American equipment – including P-39 and P-40 fighters, A-20 light bombers, Lee and Sherman tanks, and military trucks – were also supplied to Russia.

This aid was given at a time when the British Army and RAF were desperately short of modern equipment. For example, 3,000 Hawker Hurricane fighters – almost a quarter of total wartime production – were supplied to the Soviet Air Force. Had they been sent to the Middle East and the Far East instead, then they might have had a significant effect on the course of the war. The sinking of HMS *Prince of Wales* and HMS *Repulse,* and the fall of Singapore, might have been prevented if a large force of modern fighters had been based in Malaya and Singapore, backed up by radar stations and observation posts.

Stalin expressed little gratitude for the efforts made by his Allies, and even complained to Churchill that they had been sent old Hurricanes and not the latest Spitfires. 'Our pilots think little of them,' he said. In response to this criticism, Churchill later sent 1,000 Mark IX Spitfires to Russia.

Stalin, Churchill and the American President Franklin D. Roosevelt met a few times during the war to discuss strategic issues, but in the last few months of his life (he died on 12 April 1945) Roosevelt behaved very badly towards Churchill, excluding him from discussions about the future of post-war Europe. Strange though it may seem now, Roosevelt was quite happy for Stalin to be given control of large swathes of Eastern Europe, including Poland, Czechoslovakia, Bulgaria, Hungary and the eastern half of Germany. He was also allowed to capture Berlin and – through Supreme Commander General Eisenhower – Roosevelt gave the order that the US Third Army should halt at the River Elbe to allow the Russians to take Berlin.

One person who warned of the dangers of this policy was none other than America's greatest general, George S. Patton, who wanted the US Third Army to advance as far east as possible and take Berlin before the Russians got there. After the war had ended, Patton even suggested that the Germans should be re-armed and a combined Allied and German force should push the Russians back to their original borders. Patton's views were unpopular and out of step with contemporary thinking, which was that the Russians were valued allies, and it has been suggested that his death following a car accident on December 1945 was actually a carefully planned assassination. The conspiracy theories about Patton's death have been the subject of a novel and a film, *Brass Target* (1978), in which the General was supposedly killed by a special bullet manufactured to look like a piece of a car.

In the immediate post-war period, the Russians were looked on as friendly Allies, and one result was that the British gave them their latest technology including 55 examples of their new high-performance jet engine, the Rolls-Royce Nene. This was promptly copied by the Russians (as the Klimov RD-45) and installed in their latest fighter, the MiG-15, which gave UN forces a lot of trouble during the Korean War (1950-53).

The first major event of the Cold War occurred in 1948 when the Russians attempted a blockade of Berlin. At that point, Germany had been divided into West Germany (controlled by the Allies) and East Germany (dominated by the Russians). The former German capital, Berlin, lay deep inside East Germany but was divided into West Berlin (controlled by the British, French and Americans) and Soviet-governed East Berlin. West Berlin was connected to West Germany by a rail and road corridor, but in 1948 the Soviets closed the route in an attempt to show their authority. The Western allies mounted a massive re-supply operation to feed the population and supply them with coal using hundreds of transport aircraft. After several months the Soviets backed down, and the rail and road corridor was re-opened.

The so-called 'Berlin Airlift' would appear to be the ideal subject for a feature film, but – surprisingly – one has never been made. About a decade ago there were plans to make such a film, and two Douglas C-54 Skymaster aircraft were sourced and flown to North Weald airfield, north of London, to take part in filming. But unfortunately the movie never happened, and the aircraft were eventually scrapped. The Berlin Airlift did feature, though, in the final episode of Yorkshire Television's 1982 series *Airline*, which dealt with the activities of Ruskin Air Services in the years following WW2. Starring Roy Marsden as Jack Ruskin, the series was created by Wilfrid Greatorex, who had co-scripted *Battle of Britain* (1969). The storyline was apparently inspired by the exploits of the real-life Freddie Laker, who established the world's first low-cost, 'no frills' airline – Laker Airways – in 1966. Several series were planned to take the timeline up to the present day but the series was scrapped after just nine episodes, allegedly because of a dispute between Greatorex and Yorkshire Television. Most episodes employed only two Dakota aircraft supplied by North Weald-based film aviation specialists Aces High, but several were used in the final instalment – dealing with the Berlin Airlift – which was filmed on Malta.

One of the earliest naval films to deal with Cold War tensions was *Hell and High Water* (1954), which was directed by Samuel Fuller and starred Richard Widmark as US submarine commander Adam Jones. This movie reflected contemporary anxieties about nuclear weapons being used by Russia or China against the USA. In late July 1945, during the Potsdam Conference, US President Harry Truman had taken Stalin to one side and privately told him that the USA was going to hit Japan with nuclear weapons. Stalin was apparently pleased at the news and feigned surprise at learning about the atomic bomb. In fact, Stalin had known about the Manhattan Project to build a nuclear bomb for years, as his intelligence agency – the NKVD (a forerunner of the KGB) – had been spying on Britain and the USA all through WW2. Truman's revelation had a secondary purpose – by revealing to Stalin that America had the atom bomb and a plane to deliver it (the B-29 Superfortress), he hoped to deter the Soviet dictator from invading Western Europe once Germany had been defeated. Unfortunately, by 1949 the USSR had developed its own atomic weapons.

Hell and High Water, though, did not feature Soviet forces but dealt with the possible implications of China developing a nuclear capability (which it eventually did). The film opens with respected French scientist Professor Montel (Victor Francen) apparently defecting to the USSR along with four other scientists. Meanwhile, former submarine commander Adam Jones (Richard Widmark) arrives in Tokyo after receiving a package containing $5,000.

He subsequently meets Professor Montel and his colleagues, who have apparently not defected at all but are concerned that the Communist Chinese are building a secret base on an island north of Japan. Montel offers Jones another $45,000 if he will command an old WW2 Japanese submarine and follow the Japanese freighter *Kiang Ghing*, which has been making deliveries to the island base. Jones puts together a crew and follows the freighter. During the journey they are harassed by a Chinese submarine, but cannot sink it as their torpedo tubes are faulty. When the Chinese submarine surfaces, Jones rams it.

The US-manned submarine follows the *Kiang Ching* to the island. A boarding party lands on the island and is involved in a firefight with Chinese soldiers. One prisoner, a pilot named Ho-Chin, is taken back to the submarine and reveals the existence of a second island base with an airstrip. The submarine travels to the second island and, while lying offshore, Jones sees a Boeing B-29 Superfortress bomber sitting on the airstrip. His prisoner reveals that the Communist plan is to use the B-29 to drop an atomic bomb on Korea or Manchuria and then blame it on the Americans.

It may seem odd for the Communists to be using a B-29, but this is factually correct. During WW2, three Boeing B-29 Superfortresses returning from bombing missions over Japan landed on Soviet territory. On the orders of Stalin, they were not returned to the USAAF and were impounded. One was completely dismantled and used to reverse-engineer a Soviet copy of the B-29 known as the Tupolev Tu-4 Bull, in a process which took years. The design was actually improved, with the original's defensive fifty-calibre Browning M2 machine guns being replaced with harder-hitting Soviet NS-23 23mm cannon. Some of these Bulls were eventually supplied to the Chinese Air Force, and a version was even produced with modern turboprop engines. Even today, many Russian transport and bomber aircraft have a tail gun position which is similar to the rear turret of a B-29.

Jones surfaces the submarine, and the crew stand on deck carrying every machine gun they can find. As the B-29 takes off, they riddle it with bullets. It crashes on the island, detonating the atomic bomb and killing Montel who had previously sneaked ashore.

China was another hot-spot during the early days of the Cold War. In the years following WW2, a civil war broke out in China between the Nationalists lead by Chiang Kai-shek and the Communists under Mao Tse Tung (aka Mao Zedong). The outcome was that the entirety of mainland China came under the control of the Communists while the island of Formosa (now called Taiwan) became what is known as Nationalist China – a situation which has remained unchanged to the present day.

Britain did not want to become involved in the conflict, but in 1949 a British sloop – HMS *Amethyst* – became trapped on the Yangtse River after coming under fire from Communist forces, and this episode in British naval history was the subject of a film, *The Yangtse Incident* (1957). Regarded as one of the most classic British war movies of all time, which has been shown many times on television, the film starred Richard Todd as Lieutenant Commander John Kerans and was directed by Michael Anderson.

Stars Richard Todd and Richard Leech, director Michael Anderson and composer Leighton Lucas had all previously been involved in another classic war movie, *The Dambusters* (1955). Another notable cast member was future *Doctor Who* William Hartnell, who played Leading Seaman (Quartermaster) Lesley Frank. At that point in his career, Hartnell specialised in playing military types such as drill sergeants.

The film begins on 19 April 1949 as the Royal Navy frigate HMS *Amethyst* sails up the Yangtse River on her way to Nanking, the Chinese capital, to deliver supplies to the British embassy. Suddenly she comes under attack from shore batteries operated by the Communist Peoples Liberation Army (PLA). The warship returns fire but is badly hit, and fifty-four of her crew are dead or wounded. Among the casualties is the Captain, who is killed in the exchange. An attempt to evacuate the wounded is unsuccessful, and two of the crew are captured by the PLA and held at a nearby hospital.

Lieutenant Commander Kerans (Richard Todd) arrives to take command of the ship and resolve the situation. Initially, an attempt is made to tow the *Amethyst* off the mud bank where she lies stranded, using HMS *Consort*, but this fails due to enemy fire. Kerans has a meeting with the local Chinese Communist official, Colonel Peng (Akim Tamiroff), who seems determined to humiliate the British. Unless the British Government releases a grovelling apology and admits responsibility for what has happened, the *Amethyst* and her crew will not be allowed to leave. However, Kerans does manage to negotiate the release of two captured Petty Officers.

As talks continue, Kerans makes plans for the vessel to escape. The ship is repaired and, using rope and canvas painted black, the outline of the vessel is changed. As night falls, the *Amethyst* makes its way downriver following a Chinese merchant ship. She has to navigate around several sunken vessels, and is eventually discovered by the PLA who open fire with their shore batteries. *Amethyst* returns fire with her own 4-inch and 40mm guns. Eventually she reaches the open seas where she meets up with HMS *Concord*, having freed herself from captivity.

Filming of *The Yangtse Incident* took place in the autumn of 1956. The real HMS *Amethyst* received a temporary reprieve from scrapping to participate in the production but, as her engines no longer worked, shots of her moving employed her sister ship – another *Black Swan*-class sloop, HMS *Magpie*. Other shots employed HMS *Essex*, which was called away to take part in the Suez Operation while filming was in progress.

The destroyer HMS *Teazer* stood in for both HMS *Consort* and HMS *Concord*, and Commander John Kerans served as a technical advisor during filming. Although set in China, the film was made entirely in England with the rivers Orwell and Stour becoming the Yangtse River. The Chinese PLA gun batteries were depicted by old Royal Navy field guns mounted on land carriages which were deployed on the sloping banks of the Boys' Training Establishment at HMS *Ganges* at Shotley Gate, facing Felixstowe, on the Orwell. A genuine RAF Short Sunderland V flying boat appeared in a brief scene in which it landed to drop off an RAF doctor, Flight Lieutenant Michael Edward Fearnley (Robert Urquhart). At the time the RAF still operated Sunderlands, with the last squadron (based in Singapore) being retired in 1959.

Tensions between the superpowers continued throughout the fifties and sixties, and were reflected in a number of films. *Fail Safe* (1964) described a fictional scenario in which a US Convair B-58 Hustler bomber is accidentally ordered to drop a nuclear bomb on Moscow. All attempts to recall it or shoot it down fail. Eventually the President (Henry Fonda) realises the only way to prevent a Third World War is for the Americans to drop a second nuclear bomb on New York. The film didn't do very well at the box-office, largely because it was competing with Stanley Kubrick's *Dr Strangelove, or How I Learned to Stop Worrying and Love the Bomb* (1964). This had essentially the same plot as *Fail Safe* but dealt with matters in a more satirical (and at times humorous) way. The film is best remembered for Peter Sellers' multiple roles in which he displayed his unique talent for funny voices and complex characterizations.

Neither of these films dealt with naval matters, but one film which did was *The Bedford Incident* (1965) starring Richard Widmark and Sidney Poitier, which showed how a cat-and-mouse game between a destroyer and submarine could escalate into a nuclear battle in the modern age.

The Bedford Incident was unusual, as it looked like an American film but was actually made entirely in the UK at Shepperton Studios with a largely American cast. All shots of naval vessels in the film were either miniatures or current Royal Navy frigates. By this point in his career, Richard Widmark specialized in playing unpopular commanders, and *The Bedford Incident* was a typical role as he plays a character called Captain Eric Finlander who becomes obsessed with a Soviet submarine in the same way that Captain Ahab is preoccupied with the mighty whale in the film and book, *Moby Dick*. In fact, some critics have described *The Bedford Incident* as an alternative, modern version of *Moby Dick* in which the submarine replaces the whale.

The film opens with the USS *Bedford* (DLG-113) discovering a diesel-electric Soviet submarine in the GIUK (Greenland Iceland UK) gap near the Greenland coast. Although hostilities have not broken out with the USSR, Captain Finlander harasses the sub continuously, much to the concern of NATO naval advisor and former U-Boat commander Commodore Wolfgang Schrepke (Eric Portman) and journalist Ben Munceford (Sidney Poitier). Also among the crew is Ensign Ralston (James MacArthur), a young, inexperienced sailor prone to making mistakes. The same year, MacArthur played a similar character in *Battle of the Bulge*.

Munceford becomes concerned at Finlander's increasing anxiety and aggression over the situation, which is putting great strain on the crew. Eventually, Finlander locates the sub but it ignores his demands for it to surface and identify itself, at which point the US Navy Captain escalates the situation by destroying the submarine's schnorkel (breathing tube) which will force it to surface eventually. (A modern nuclear submarine can remain underwater for up to three months, but diesel-electric subs of the early sixties could only remain underwater for a few hours unless they used their schnorkel).

Finlander waits patiently for the submarine to surface, and orders all weapons to be readied for action. He reassures Schrepke that he is in control of the situation and tells him that 'If he fires one, I'll fire one'. Unfortunately the nervous Ensign Ralston thinks he has given the command to 'fire one', and releases a RUR-5 ASROC anti-submarine missile at the submerged vessel. The destroyer crew quickly realise the mistake and attempt to disarm the missile, but they are too late and the Soviet submarine is hit and destroyed.

Just as they are recovering from this shock, the destroyer's sonar picks up four nuclear-tipped torpedoes heading towards them. The Soviet submarine had launched them as soon as it detected the launch of the ASROC. The *Bedford* is hit and consumed by a large nuclear explosion.

The Royal Navy cooperated fully in the production of this film. Although most shots of the *Bedford* used a large miniature of a *Farragut*-class guided missile destroyer, interior shots were filmed on board the Royal Navy Type 15 frigate HMS *Trourbridge*. Munceford's arrival on board the vessel was shot using another Type 15 frigate, HMS *Wakeful*, and a Royal Navy Westland Whirlwind helicopter. The Whirlwind was a British-built version of the American Sikorsky S-55 which was used by US Forces.

The cast included a number of Americans and Canadians who were at that time resident in the UK, including Ed

Bishop and Donald Sutherland. Bishop had appeared in the WW2 aviation movie *The War Lover* (1962), and later had small roles in two James Bond pictures, *You Only Live Twice* (1976) and *Diamonds Are Forever* (1971). He is also well-known for his involvement in two Gerry Anderson productions, *Captain Scarlet and the Mysterons* (1967) – in which he provided the voice of Captain Blue – and *UFO* (1969-70), in which he played Colonel Straker. Canadian actor Donald Sutherland spent a few years in London in the mid-sixties, during which time he appeared in *The Dirty Dozen* (1966) and *The Avengers* (1967). His son (future *24* star Kiefer Sutherland) was born in London in 1966, which makes him technically British.

Ice Station Zebra (1968), directed by John Sturges and starring Rock Hudson and Patrick McGoohan, was based on a 1963 novel by Alistair MacLean and – like *The Bedford Incident* – had a plot which relied on the tensions and misunderstandings of the Cold War.

The film opens with a top-secret satellite ejecting a capsule which lands in the Arctic. The captain of the USS *Tigerfish*, Commander James Farraday (Rock Hudson), is ordered by Admiral Garvey to rescue the personnel of Drift Ice Station Zebra, a British civilian scientific weather station located in the moving Arctic ice pack. However, this is merely a cover for the real mission, which is the retrieval of the satellite's capsule.

A platoon of Marines led by Captain Anders (Jim Brown) is embarked on the *Tigerfish,* plus several additional personnel including British intelligence agent David Jones (Patrick McGoohan) and Russian defector Boris Vaslov (Ernest Borgnine). McGoohan was a good choice to play a British spy, as he was at that time identified with the role of espionage operative John Drake in the long-running *Danger Man* TV series (1960-62 and 1964-68). At the time of the filming of *Ice Station Zebra*, McGoohan was in the middle of filming *The Prisoner* at MGM Borehamwood Studios and, to enable him to participate in both productions, one episode of *The Prisoner* (*Do Not Forsake Me, Oh My Darling*) was rewritten to include a mind transfer plot so that Nigel Stock could play the lead role of Number 6. The other episode of *The Prisoner* filmed around this time was *The Girl Who Was Death* and, to minimize McGoohan's need to be on set, his character wore a deerstalker and cape for much of the episode, allowing a double to be used in most scenes. Incidentally, *Do Not Forsake Me, Oh My Darling* was the original title of the Western-themed episode of *The Prisoner*, which later became *Living in Harmony*. As film buffs may know, the words *Do Not Forsake Me, Oh My Darling* come from the lyrics of composer Dimitri Tiomkin's title song to the classic Western *High Noon* (1952).

The *Tigerfish* makes her way to the Arctic to *Zebra's* position and attempts to break through the ice with her conning tower. When this fails, Captain Ferraday attempts to use a torpedo to blast a hole in the ice. But this nearly causes the loss of the submarine as water pours inside when the inner door is opened due to the fact that the outer doors had been left open, even though indicators had shown them to be closed. (This plot point may be have been inspired by a real-life incident in 1939, when HMS *Thetis* sunk in Liverpool Bay after both inner and outer torpedo tube doors were opened. This incident led to an additional safety lock being fitted to the inner door of torpedo tubes in RN submarines.)

Jones and Ferraday manage to close the tube and save the vessel from sinking, but the Captain is puzzled as to how the accident could have happened as an indicator should have revealed that the outer door was open. Ferraday investigates further and finds that epoxy glue was used to sabotage the indicator. (Again, this may have been inspired by the *Thetis* incident in which the culprit was found to be some bitumen paint jamming up a crucial indicator.)

Jones and Ferraday conclude there is a saboteur on board (again, a common theme in most Alistair MacLean novels, in which one or more characters is either a traitor or a saboteur). Ferraday suspects Vaslov, while Jones is suspicious of Anders. Jones then demands that Ferraday fires off another torpedo to blast a hole in the ice, but Ferraday refuses to comply until he is told the purpose of the mission. At that point an area of thin ice is found, and the submarine breaks through using its conning tower.

Ferraday, Vaslov, Jones and the Marines set off for Ice Station Zebra, which is found to be partially destroyed by fire. Jones reveals what the mission is all about. An advanced British space camera using high-tech American film had been stolen by the Soviets. After photographing American missile silos it had malfunctioned, filming Soviet missile bases as well, before landing in in the Arctic. The missing satellite capsule is located frozen beneath the ice, and Ferraday's crew use a welding torch to melt their way through to it. Meanwhile, Vaslov is revealed to be a double agent and saboteur, but tricks Jones into shooting Anders.

The *Tigerfish's* radar shows a force of Soviet aircraft heading towards them – consisting of Tupolev Tu-96 *Bear* four-engined planes carrying paratroops, escorted by MiG -21 fighters. The shots of the planes were created using miniatures, and looked quite phoney. In addition, the choice of aircraft was wrong, as the *Bear* was a maritime reconnaissance aircraft, not a parachute-dropping aircraft.

Soviet paratroopers led by Commander Ostrovsky (Alf Kjellin) drop from the skies just at the American marines extract the satellite. A stand-off develops as the Russians demand the film. Ostrovsky shows Ferraday a radio-controlled detonator in his hand which can be used to explode the capsule. Eventually, Ferraday lets the Russians have the film but then explodes it using another remote detonator which he had recovered earlier from Vaslov. In the process he destroys a MiG-21, which had been attempting to pick up the film using a balloon recovery system (similar to the Fulton 'Skyhook' system seen at the end of the James Bond film *Thunderball*). The jet fighter which is briefly glimpsed in this scene is actually stock footage of an American F-4 Phantom. The film ends with a teletype news story which tells how US and Soviet forces had cooperated in a humanitarian mission to save scientists at an Arctic base.

The film was moderately successful, making $15.7 million against a production budget of $8million. Some of the miniature work, namely the submarine sequences and the depiction of the ice cap, was widely praised. The submarine shots were considered so realistic that they were re-used in *Never Say Never Again* (1983) and *Gray Lady Down* (1976). Some footage of the conning tower breaking through the Arctic ice also featured in the Clint Eastwood movie *Firefox* (1982).

Nautical matters also featured in *When Eight Bells Toll* (1971), a thriller scripted by Alistair MacLean which starred Anthony Hopkins as Philip Calvert, a Royal Naval officer turned spy. The film was made by Winkast Productions as a follow-up to their hugely successful WW2 spy thriller *Where Eagles Dare* (1968), and was directed by Belgian Etienne Perier.

Producer Elliott Kastner originally intended *When Eight Bells Toll* to be part of a 14-picture deal, including *Where Eagles Dare*, with Anthony Hopkins starring as Philip Calvert in a series of spy adventures to rival Bond. In fact, there are a number of connections between the Bond series of films and *When Eight Bells Toll*. Both Calvert and Bond are Royal Navy officers, and are expert frogmen and marksmen. Both the Bond films and *When Eight Bells Toll* were shot at Pinewood Studios, and used the talents of Australian stunt arranger Bob Simmons. It was Simmons (and not Sean Connery) who appeared in the 'looking through the gunbarrel' sequence at the beginning of the first three James Bond films. From *Thunderball* onwards, Connery (and subsequent Bond actors) performed this role. Another actor who was considered for the role of Calvert was Michael Jayston, who later played the title role in the BBC series *Quiller* (1975) and voiced Bond in the 1990 BBC radio adaptation of *You Only Live Twice*.

The movie opens with a shot of Calvert in scuba gear (or, to be more precise, his stunt double Bob Simmons) climbing up the anchor chain of a cargo vessel, the *Nantesville*. Calvert has been sent by the Admiralty to investigate the disappearance of five cargo ships off the coast of North West Scotland. Calvert discovers another spy (Prentis Hancock) who has been hiding on board with a radio along with a colleague, but they are both dead. There is then a flashback to how it all began, with Calvert arriving at Naval Intelligence HQ in a helicopter.

The HQ building is actually Heatherden Hall (aka Pinewood House), which was the mansion around which the

Pinewood Studio complex was built. Heatherden Hall has itself served as a location in various films and TV series. The scene where Rosa Klebb meets 'Red' Grant for the first time in *From Russia with Love* (1963) was filmed on the lawns in front of the building. It also served as the 'American Ambassador's Residence' in *Who Dares Wins* (1982), and as a nursing home in *Doppelganger* (1969). The helicopter in this scene was a French Aerospatiale Alouette II, civil registration G-AWAP – with fake Royal Navy markings – which was also the camera helicopter for the production. This particular aircraft had been used in a large number of film and TV productions in the sixties, and had also appeared in some of them. At the time of the shooting of the film it was owned by Film Flight Ltd., but was later bought by pilot John Crewdson who had flown helicopters and fixed-wing aircraft in a number of sixties films. Crewdson had flown a B-17 at ultra-low level at RAF Bovingdon in *The War Lover* (1962), and had performed a simulated belly landing of a Mosquito at the same location for *633 Squadron* (1964). He was also Draco's helicopter pilot in *On Her Majesty's Secret Service* (1969). Crewdson eventually died in a fatal helicopter crash involving G-AWAP on 26 June 1983.

After this flashback sequence, the action resumes aboard the *Nantesville* when Calvert gets into a fight with a group of villains who have hijacked the ship. He escapes back to his yacht, the *Firecrest*, where he confers with his colleague Hunslett (Corin Redgrave). Later, they receive a visit from some Customs Officers, and Calvert recognizes one of them – Quinn (Oliver MacGreevey), a thug he fought with on the *Nantesville* the previous night.

A helicopter (an old Royal Navy Westland Widgeon) arrives to take Calvert back to England, but the agent persuades the pilot (Maurice Roeves) to instead do an air search of the surrounding area in the hope that this will reveal the villain's lair. One place they stop at is a nearby castle, and Calvert finds the owner's daughter to be hostile and uncooperative. Having completed the search without discovering anything, the helicopter returns to Torbay. As the ground is damp, Calvert jumps off the hovering helicopter, and at that precise moment they come under attack from three thugs armed with FN automatic rifles. The helicopter is hit, but Calvert grabs onto the skid and tries to pull himself up into the cabin as the aircraft moves higher into the air and further away. Just as it looks as though they have escaped, the pilot is fatally wounded by gunfire and the helicopter spins out of control. It crashes onto rocks, bursting into flames, and then falls into the ocean.

Making this stunt proved a memorable experience for Bob Simmons, as he recalled in his autobiography *Nobody Does It Better* (1987). The original plan was that he was to hang onto the skid and then pull himself up into the cabin of the chopper, but things didn't go as planned and he fell off as the helicopter gained height. As a result, he fell a considerable distance into the freezing waters. All this was captured on film and looked spectacular, and consideration was given to keeping this shot in the film. But this would have required a major rewrite, so the shot was deleted. In the final cut of the film, Calvert remains within the cabin of the helicopter as it sinks to the ocean floor. He then looks up and sees the bottom of the boat containing the villains, who assume he has drowned. In fact, Calvert has survived by breathing from the pilot's oxygen mask. This was a neat idea, but technically incorrect as helicopters don't carry oxygen masks due to the fact that they don't fly high enough to need them.

The helicopter used in these scenes was a civilian Westland Widgeon, G-ANLW, which was painted in fake Royal Navy markings. Based on the earlier Westland WS-51 Dragonfly, itself based on the Sikorsky S-51 (which first flew in 1943), only 15 were made. Powered by a 520 hp Alvis Leonides piston engine, it had a top speed of 109 mph and a service ceiling of 11,800 feet. It was never used by the Royal Navy, so its appearance in the film is an inaccuracy. The example used in the film was provided by Film Flight Ltd.

After the villains have left, Calvert swims ashore and returns to the *Firecrest*, but Hunslett is nowhere to be found. However, he has been joined by his boss, Arthur Arnford-Jones (Robert Morley). Together they repel boarders, and when Calvert raises the anchor he discovers Hunslett's body tied to it. Soon after this, he gets his revenge when a speedboat full of baddies launches an attack on the *Firecrest*. Calvert rams the boat, shoots the occupants, and then blows up the vessel with a well-aimed shot to the petrol tank.

By this point, Calvert has been joined by Skouras's wife Charlotte (Nathalie Delon), and he seeks some assistance from a group of shark fishermen led by Tim Hutchinson (Leon Collins). Calvert dives into the bay in scuba gear and discovers that the *Nantesville* has been sunk and is slowly being stripped off its gold. In an exciting underwater sequence he battles Quinn, who is clad in a heavy, old fashioned diving suit with a brass helmet in a nod to the underwater fights in *Thunderball*.

Later, he infiltrates Lord Kirkside's castle and discovers that Skouras is actually innocent and his real wife is being held hostage along with several other local people. An underground dock is being used to ship out the gold bars. At midnight (the eight bells of the title), Hutchinson's men burst into the dock using their fishing boat. But they have been betrayed by Charlotte Skouras, who is a traitor (a familiar theme in Alistair MacLean's writings), and the gang of villains is ready for them. They are held at gunpoint, but Calvert instigates a firefight and the baddies are wiped out. Calvert takes pity on Charlotte and lets her escape in a dinghy with a single gold bar.

The film has an excellent musical score by Walter Stott. In 1972, Stott had transgender surgery and changed his name to Angela Morley. All his compositions after this date were released under this new name.

The film was poorly received by both the general public and critics, and the proposed series of spy films featuring the Calvert character was shelved. Another factor was that Kastner had thought that the Bond series might end with *On Her Majesty's Secret Service* (1969), but as things happened Sean Connery returned to make *Diamonds Are Forever* (1971) and Roger Moore then took over in the role, meaning that a series of Calvert spy thrillers would have been competing with a glossier and more expensive product.

Cold War issues also featured in the BBC TV series *Warship* (1973-77) which ran to 45 episodes over four seasons and dealt with life on board the Royal Navy *Leander*-class frigate HMS *Hero*. The series was created by Ian Mackintosh and Anthony Coburn, and was hugely popular. Mackintosh was a serving Royal Navy officer with a great knowledge of Intelligence matters. He later created and wrote the highly acclaimed Yorkshire TV spy drama *The Sandbaggers* (1978-80), which starred Roy Marsden and presented a more intellectual view of intelligence operations than the Bond series of films, and may be regarded as the predecessor of the BBC's popular *Spooks* series (2002-2011). Anthony Coburn was a veteran writer who had actually written the very first *Doctor Who* story, *100,000 BC*, in 1963. The theme music by Anthony Isaacs was played by the band of the Royal Marines conducted by Lieutenant Colonel Paul Neville, MVO, FRAM, RM, and even today is popular with military bands.

In the first two series of *Warship*, the Captain of HMS *Hero* was Commander Mark Nialls, played by Donald Burton. In series three he was replaced by Commander Allan Glenn, played by Bryan Marshall (who also played the Captain of HMS *Ranger* in *The Spy Who Loved Me*). For the final season Captain Edward Holt, a former nuclear submariner, was played by Derek Godfrey.

The *Hero*'s First Lieutenant, Derek 'Porky' Beaumont, was played by David Savile in the first three series. Savile specialised in playing military roles, having played Lieutenant Carstairs in the *Doctor Who* story *The War Games* (1969), and Brigadier Lethbridge-Stewart's replacement – Colonel Crichton – in a later *Doctor Who* story, *The Five Doctors* (1983). He also played an Army officer in the BBC TV production *The Man Who Hunted Himself* (1972), which starred Donald Burton.

The series was made with the full cooperation of the Royal Navy. Seven different *Leander*-class frigates were used to play the *Hero*, namely HMS *Phoebe*, HMS *Danae*, HMS *Dido*, HMS *Diomede*, HMS *Hermione*, HMS *Juno*, and HMS *Jupiter*. All were repainted with *Phoebe's* pennant number (F42) for continuity reasons. HMAS *Derwent*, a *River*-class destroyer of the Australian Navy, also portrayed the *Hero* in some scenes filmed in 1976 in Hong Kong and Singapore.

All the crews of these vessels were give *Hero* cap tallies for filming purposes, and the ships' single Westland Wasp helicopters (from the Fleet Air Arm's 829 Squadron) were repainted with the identification HMS *Hero*, the code 471, and the nickname 'the fighting forty-two'. Among the Wasps used in the fictional '*Hero* flight' were XT419 from HMS *Phoebe*, XV625, and XV626. XV625 is still painted in the 471 code, and is preserved at HMS *Sultan* in the Royal Navy Engineering and Survival School.

The series gives a fascinating glimpse into the Royal Navy in the early seventies, and vessels which can be seen in various episodes include the aircraft carrier HMS *Ark Royal*, the helicopter cruiser HMS *Blake*, the commando carrier HMS *Bulwark*, and the submarine HMS *Andrew*.

One episode, *A Matter of History*, depicted HMS *Hero* visiting a fictional British Overseas Territory – Eddowes Island – which was being handed over to an unnamed Latin American country. The citizens were offered the choice of remaining British citizens and leaving the island, or else staying and becoming citizens of the South American country. The parallels with the Falkland Islands were obvious, and around that time James Callaghan's Labour government sent some warships to the South Atlantic to deter Argentine aggression. Another episode, *Away Seaboat's Crew* (1974), featured one of the earliest screen appearances by Lewis Collins, who later starred as Philip Bodie in LWT's *The Professionals* (1977-83).

Naval warfare and Cold War intrigue were also featured in *The Hunt for Red October* (1990), a thriller directed by John McTiernan who had previously made *Predator* (1987) and *Die Hard* (1988). The film was based on a 1984 novel by Tom Clancy who specialized in techno-thrillers which involved an enormous amount of research. His books have been very well received, and critics and readers alike have particularly appreciated the level of detail in them. They have also influenced many other authors such as Patrick Robinson, who has written a series of excellent modern-day naval thrillers.

The Hunt for Red October featured the first screen appearance of the Jack Ryan character, a CIA analyst who on this occasion was played by Alec Baldwin. In the next two films featuring the character, the part was recast with Harrison Ford playing the role. This is something that has always rankled Alec Baldwin, who felt he should have been given the opportunity to play the part again as he has related in his recent autobiography *Nevertheless: A Memoir* (2017).

Producer Mace Neufeld took out an option on Tom Clancy's novel after reading the galley proofs in February 1985. At that point no Hollywood studio was interested in the story (even though it was a best-seller), as they felt the plot was too complicated. Eventually Paramount Pictures, who had a great success with *Top Gun* (1986), agreed to develop the project, and screenwriters Larry Ferguson and Donald Stewart worked on the script, simplifying Clancy's rather complex story.

The US Navy cooperated fully in the production, and several *Los Angeles*-class attack submarines were used in the production. The USS *Louisville* was used for the scene where Ryan is dropped onto the deck of a submarine, though in most scenes the USS *Dallas* was portrayed by the USS *Houston*.

The all-important role of Captain Ramius was played by Sean Connery, who had actually served in the Royal Navy as a young man. He had trained as an anti-aircraft gunner before being invalided out with ulcers. His co-star in *Never Say Never Again* (1983), Klaus Maria Brandauer, had originally been cast as Ramius but had to quit after two weeks due to other commitments. Scott Glenn had served in the US Marine Corps, and his co-star James Earl Jones had been in the US Army. Many of the extras were actually serving submariners, as it was easier to use them than to train up lay people to work the controls of a submarine correctly.

John Milius rewrote some of the screenplay. Although it was originally intended that he would write the whole film, in the end he only redrafted the Russian sequences.

As real submarines were too cramped for filming, two 50-foot square platforms housing mock-ups of the *Red October* and the *Dallas* were built in sound stages on the Paramount lot. These were fitted with gimbals to simulate the movement of a submarine. A near full-size floatable replica of the *Red October* was built over two barges, and was used for ocean scenes. As the film was made when CGI was still in its infancy, large miniatures of the *Red October*, *Dallas* and the *Konovalov* were constructed for the underwater scenes. As was normal practice in the film industry, these model scenes were filmed 'dry' with added smoke to simulate a murky ocean. Some CGI was used for bubble effects.

The Hunt for Red October was set in 1984, before Mikhail Gorbachev came to power and when the Cold War was still very much a fact of life. Soviet submarine captain Marko Ramius (Sean Connery) is in command of the *Red October*, a *Typhoon*-class nuclear submarine with an extra-quiet propulsion system, the caterpillar drive. The *Red October* is to conduct exercises with the attack submarine V.K. *Konovalov*, but once at sea Ramius kills the on-board political officer Ivan Putin (Peter Firth) and heads for the USA.

The US military takes these developments very seriously, and CIA analyst and former Marine Jack Ryan (Alec Baldwin) becomes involved. The US Government fears that

Ramius has gone rogue and is planning to attack the USA with nuclear missiles, but Ryan thinks he may be instead be intending to defect to the USA. He is ordered to meet up with the submarine USS *Dallas* and attempt to contact Ramius. Meanwhile, the Soviet fleet – led by Tupolev (Stellan Skarsgard), who regards Ramius as his mentor – has been mobilized and ordered to sink the errant submarine commander.

Red October's caterpillar drive fails, and a sonar technician aboard the *Dallas* finds a way to plot the Soviet sub using underwater acoustics. Ryan is put on board the *Dallas* by helicopter and persuades its Captain, Commander Bart Mancuso (Scott Glenn), to contact Ramius.

The Soviet Ambassador informs the US Government that Ramius has gone rogue and asks for their assistance in sinking the *Red October*. But Ryan knows the truth, and convinces Mancuso to offer assistance. Ramius fakes a nuclear reactor emergency to make his crew abandon ship. When a US frigate is spotted, Ramius submerges, but Ryan, Petty Officer Jones and Mancuso board the *Red October* using a rescue sub. Ramius then requests political asylum in the USA for himself and his officers.

Suddenly the *Red October* is attacked by the *Konovalov*, which has followed them across the Atlantic. As the battle is in progress, one of *Red October's* cooks – Loginov (Tomas Arana), who is an undercover agent – opens fire and fatally wounds First Officer Vasily Borodin (Sam Neill) before seeking refuge in the missile bay, where he is pursued by Ryan and Ramius. Loginov shoots Ramius, wounding him, but is then shot by Ryan before he can detonate a missile.

An underwater battle ensues between the *Red October* and the *Konovalov*, during which Ramius demonstrates his tactical skills. Eventually Ramius uses clever manoeuvring to make the *Konovalov* destroy itself with one of its own torpedoes. The crew of the *Red October* watch the explosion from the deck of the US frigate and think that Ramius has sacrificed himself and scuttled his own sub.

Ryan and Ramius sail the *Red October* to Maine in the USA, and the Russian Captain admits that the reason he defected was because the submarine was a nuclear war first strike weapon and he had moral objections to such a system.

The film premiered on 12 June 1990, two months after the Communist Party lost power in the Soviet Union, so a caption had to be added at the start of the film explaining that its events took place in 1984 before Gorbachev took power, laying the seeds for the collapse of Communism. The film proved a hit, making $200 million against a budget of $36 million, and won an Oscar for Best Sound Editing.

The success of *The Hunt for Red October* led to a number of other Jack Ryan pictures being greenlighted, starting with *Patriot Games* (1992) with Harrison Ford replacing Alec Baldwin. However, as Baldwin noted in his autobiography, this film was not as financially successful as its predecessor. Ford played Jack Ryan a second time in *Clear and Present Danger* (1994), but was replaced by Ben Affleck in *The Sum of All Fears* (2002). The latter is of great interest to naval weapons enthusiasts, as it features a scene where a US Navy carrier group is attacked by missiles. Many of them are shot down by Vulcan Phalanx 20mm automatic gun turrets, but some of the missiles get through and severely damage the American force.

Jack Ryan appeared again in the film *Jack Ryan: Shadow Recruit* (2014), this time played by Chris Pine, and a TV series featuring the character is planned.

Crimson Tide (1995) was another submarine movie which dealt with the impact of political tensions in Russia following the end of the Cold War. It was directed by Tony Scott and produced by Don Simpson and Jerry Bruckheimer, who were the team behind Top Gun.

In post-war Russia, civil war erupts as a result of the ongoing conflict in Chechnya. Vladimir Radchenko and his troops take over a Russian missile base and threaten to start a nuclear war. The American nuclear submarine USS *Alabama* is ordered out on patrol, and is told to launch its missiles on a pre-emptive strike if Radchenko attempts to carry out his threat. The sub is commanded by Captain Frank Ramsey (Gene Hackman), and his thoughtful executive officer is Lieutenant Commander Ron Hunter (Denzel Washington). Tensions soon break out between the two men, and then the *Alabama* receives orders to launch its missiles followed by a second incomplete message which is cut off as a Russian *Akula*-class submarine is attacking.

Ramsey wants to fire his missiles but Hunter is more cautious, arguing that the second message may be a retraction. Much of the rest of the movie then deals with the conflict between the two men as a mutiny ensues. Eventually the crew manage to get their radio working again and they are able to establish that the second message was indeed a retraction, and nuclear war is averted. The two men subsequently face a naval tribunal which concludes that neither was at fault and they should not face disciplinary action.

The film had to be made without any assistance from the US military. Although the US Navy was consulted at an early stage and some video filming was carried out aboard the submarine USS *Florida* for research purposes, the US military establishment eventually withdrew all cooperation as they had concerns about the plot, which involved a mutiny to prevent a missile launch.

The French Navy (*Marine Nationale*) eventually stepped in, and made the carrier *Foch* and one *Triomphant*-class submarine available for filming. The former USS *Barbel* (which was in the process of being scrapped) was fitted with a dummy plywood conning tower for a dockside scene featuring the *Alabama*. The film was a critical and commercial success, making $163.7 million against a budget of $53 million.

K-19: The Widowmaker (2002) is the most recent big-budget submarine movie to be made to date, and chronicles the series of disasters which befell the Soviet Union's first ballistic missile submarine, which was launched in 1961. The film starred Harrison Ford as Captain Alexei Vostrikov and Liam Neeson as his executive officer Mikhail Polenin, and was directed by Kathryn Bigelow. It was mainly made in Canada, with that country's armed forces providing vessels for use in the production. HMCSO *Jibwa* portrayed the Soviet *Whiskey*-class *S-270*, HMCS *Terra Nova* played USS *Decatur*, while the *Hotel*-class submarine *K-19* was played by an actual Russian submarine, the *Juliett*-class *K-77*. The shipyards in Halifax, Canada stood in for their Russian equivalents.

The film was not a success, making only $65.7 million at the box office set against a budget of $90 million.

The Last Ship (2014-present) is a TV series which has so far run to 56 episodes over five seasons (with the fifth season still to be broadcast at the time of writing). The plot is very similar to many zombie movies, *The Walking Dead* TV series (2010-present), *The Day of the Triffids* (1963), and the TV series *Survivors* (1975-77 and 2008-09), as it depicts a world in which 80% of the population has been wiped out by a virus, and anarchy reigns. The American frigate USS *Na-*

than James is at sea at the time of the outbreak, and the crew battle to survive in this new world while trying to find a cure for the disease and obtain basic essentials such as fuel, food, medical supplies and munitions.

Their adversaries include a hostile Russian warship and a British nuclear submarine which has gone rogue (and is also apparently crewed entirely by cockneys!). The series starred Eric Dane as Admiral Chandler, Adam Baldwin as Admiral Mike Slattery, and Rhona Mitra as scientist Dr Rachel Scott who is desperately seeking a cure for the pandemic.

The series also has some similarities with *On the Beach* (1959). Based on Nevil Shute's 1959 novel, it tells the story of the crew of a US submarine, the USS *Sawfish*, who are in Australia in 1964 when a nuclear war devastates the Northern Hemisphere. The film starred Gregory Peck as Commander Dwight Lionel Towers, Captain of the USS *Sawfish*, and Ava Gardner as his love interest Moira Davidson.

A strange Morse Code message is detected which appears to be originating from the West Coast of America. The *Sawfish* makes its way to San Diego, where communications officer Lieutenant Sunderstrom goes ashore in a radiation suit to investigate. Eventually he discovers that the Morse signals are being sent by a Coke bottle dangling from a window cord which is bumping up against a radio transmitter's morse key. The *Sawfish* returns to Australia to find the cloud of radiation is heading towards the country. Various characters commit suicide by various means, and the *Sawfish* heads back to a radioactive America and certain death for all its crew. The film ends on a bleak note, with a shot of a Salvation Army banner proclaiming that: 'There is still time... Brother. Nuclear war and the end of humanity can still be prevented'.

9
ACTION IN THE SOUTH ATLANTIC

THE Falklands War – which lasted from 2 April to 14 June 1982 – had an impact which has lasted to this day. Prior to the campaign, British leader Mrs Margaret Thatcher was one of the most unpopular Prime Ministers in history. Yet her determination to recover the islands, whatever the cost in lives and equipment, led to a surge in her popularity and resulted in her winning a landslide victory at the next General Election the following year. This outcome may even have influenced Prime Minister Tony Blair when he ordered British forces into action in Iraq alongside the American military in 2003.

The Falklands War also had an effect on navies throughout the world, as it emphasised the importance of carrier-based air power, airborne early-warning (AEW) aircraft, effective shipborne surface-to-air missile defences and close-in weapons systems (CIWS), including short-range missiles, radar-directed, computer-controlled quick-firing guns plus more modern, manually-aimed weapons.

The Falklands conflict started with an incident on 19 March 1982 when a group of scrap merchants employed by the Argentine government landed illegally on the British-owned island of South Georgia in the South Atlantic, with the intention of dismantling a disused whaling station. This squad of men then hoisted the Argentine national flag and claimed that the territory now belonged to Argentina. The British government responded by ordering the Royal Navy's ice patrol ship HMS *Endurance* – with a detachment of Royal Marines on board – to sail to South Georgia and reclaim the territory. From then on, things escalated rapidly. On 2 April, Argentine Marines and special forces launched an invasion of the Falkland Islands (Operation Rosario). Despite being heavily out-numbered, the garrison of about 80 Royal Marines plus Falkland Island Defence Forces (FIDF) volunteers put up stiff resistance, sinking a landing craft, destroying an LVTP-7 Amtrack (amphibious armoured personnel carrier) and damaging another, and killing several Argentine soldiers. On the island of South Georgia, another small party of Royal Marines led by Lieutenant Keith Mills also resisted an Argentine attack.

Mills' men riddled the *Drummond*-class Argentine corvette ARA *Guerrico* with small-arms fire, and blew a hole in its side using an 84mm Carl Gustav recoilless anti-tank weapon. They also shot down an Argentine Puma helicopter before surrendering.

For propaganda purposes, the fascist Argentine government of dictator General Galtieri released photos of captured British Marines lying face down on the ground in the Falklands capital, Port Stanley. Intended to humiliate Britain, these photos had the reverse effect as they led to a public outcry in the UK against the Argentine invasion and demands for military action to retake the islands.

Opinion polls taken at the time showed that the majority of the British public supported military action to liberate the islands and even the Labour Party supported the campaign, though there were some dissenters, including the 'usual suspects' such as the left-wing MPs Tony Benn and Tam Dalyell who were very much against sending the Royal Navy into battle.

Recapturing the islands posed a number of problems to the British. They were 8,000 miles away, the longest supply line in military history, and every bullet, bomb, missile and can of beans used by the Task Force would have to be shipped this vast distance. Eventually the British solved the problem by using over 100 requisitioned merchant vessels, known as STUFT (Ships Taken Up From Trade), to back up the warships and Royal Fleet Auxiliaries. These civilian vessels included the liners S.S. *Canberra* and the *Queen Elizabeth II* (*QE2*), which were used as troopships, with the school cruise ship *Uganda* becoming a floating hospital.

Another problem facing the Royal Navy was a lack of suitable warships. At the start of the Second World War the Royal Navy was the largest in the world, with several hundred vessels. Even in 1962 – twenty years before the Falklands War – it had 363 ships, including six aircraft carriers.

In the mid-1960s the Labour government's Defence Secretary Denis Healey made the decision to cancel a proposed new class of aircraft carrier (the 63,000 ton CVA-01), and all the existing 'flat-tops' were gradually withdrawn from service. Britain's last large aircraft carrier for some decades, HMS *Ark Royal* (R09), was scrapped in 1979.

By 1982, only two small carriers were left in service: the elderly *Hermes* and the modern *Illustrious*. But the primary role of these vessels was as anti-submarine vessels, designed to hunt down Soviet submarines as part of a task group. The only fixed-wing aircraft they could carry was the British Aerospace Sea Harrier FRS.1, a naval version of the RAF's successful 'jump jet'. Excellent fighter though it was, the Sea Harrier had a limited range, a basic Blue Fox radar, was subsonic, and carried just two heat-seeking Sidewinder missiles.

Furthermore, in peacetime HMS *Invincible* normally carried just five of these fighters, while HMS *Hermes* had eight. For the Falklands operation, *Invincible* took eight Sea Harriers on board while *Hermes* had twelve, and eventually 20 additional Sea Harriers and RAF Harrier GR.3s were sent to the South Atlantic with many of them travelling on board the requisitioned container ship *Atlantic Conveyor*.

The earlier *Ark Royal* fielded supersonic McDonnell-Douglas F-4 Phantom fighters, each carrying four heat-seeking Sidewinders and a quartet of medium-range, radar-guided Sparrow missiles plus a deadly 20mm Vulcan cannon. In addition she carried Blackburn Buccaneer bombers, regarded as one of the most effective low-level strike aircraft in the world. Most importantly, it also had some Fairey Gannet airborne early warning (AEW) aircraft, each mounting a powerful AN/APS 20 search radar which could detect low-flying aircraft at a considerable distance. *Invincible* and *Hermes* lacked this capability, as they did not have the steam catapults that were required to launch the Gannet.

In 1982 the Royal Navy only had 50 frigates and destroyers, some of which were being refitted or on essential duties, so only 23 could be sent to the South Atlantic initially. (It is a sobering thought that in 2018 the Royal Navy only has 13 frigates and six destroyers; something that has greatly alarmed former Sea Lord Alan West, who commanded the Type 21 frigate HMS *Ardent* during the Falklands War.)

The Task Force was also hampered by recent and ongoing defence cuts. Defence Minister John Nott had recently announced a series of savage cuts affecting the Royal Navy. Among other things, he planned to sell the nearly-new carrier HMS *Invincible* to Australia and the Royal Fleet Auxiliary (RFA) tanker *Tidepool* to Chile. He also planned to scrap the Antarctic ice patrol ship HMS *Endurance*, a move which may have given the Argentine government the impression that Britain was not interested in defending the Falklands. These decisions were immediately reversed when the war broke out. Defence Secretary John Nott offered Mrs Thatcher his resignation when the conflict started, but this was refused.

Another vessel that would have been useful to the Task Force was the specialised aircraft detection frigate HMS *Salisbury*, which could detect planes at great range and direct Royal Navy fighters onto hostile contacts, but she had been decommissioned in 1980. Consideration was also given to reactivating HMS *Bulwark*, an elderly aircraft carrier which was tied up awaiting disposal, but a survey showed that it would take too long to put her back into working order, particularly as her aircraft catapults had already been removed.

Despite all these problems – especially a lack of suitable ships and equipment – a large Task Force was quickly put together and sailed south to do battle with Argentine forces. The first British forces to arrive in the Falklands were British nuclear hunter-killer submarines, and this prompted the British government to declare a Total Exclusion Zone of 200 miles radius around the Falklands Islands on 30 April 1982. The terms of this declaration stated that any Argentine ship or aircraft found within this zone would be attacked without warning.

Two days later, on 2 May 1982, the British nuclear submarine HMS *Conqueror* attacked and sank the Argentine cruiser *General Belgrano* using two torpedoes, with considerable loss of life. The large death toll (323) was largely a result of the fact that the two escorting Argentine destroyers made no attempt to pick up survivors, and left the area rapidly to avoid being attacked. *Conqueror's* action proved highly controversial, as opponents of the Falklands War claimed that Mrs Thatcher had deliberately ordered an attack on the vessel to scupper any peace proposals as the *Belgrano* was sailing outside the Exclusion Zone at the time of the attack.

In fact, Thatcher only gave permission for the attack after receiving a request for this to happen from the top brass in the Royal Navy and the Captain of the *Conqueror*. The fact that the *Belgrano* was sailing outside the Total Exclusion Zone was irrelevant. Even if she had been tied up at the quayside in Rio De Janeiro she would have been a legitimate target, and it should be noted that both the captain of the *Belgrano*, Hector Bonzo, and the Argentine government have since admitted that the sinking was justified. One person who disagreed with this assessment was the late Labour MP Tam Dalyell, who became obsessed with the sinking of the *Belgrano* – considering it a 'war crime' – and even wrote a book about it called *One Man's Falklands*. Interestingly, in recent years some evidence has emerged that the Argentine government had a plan to sink Royal Navy ships at anchor in Gibraltar (Operation Algeciras) as early as April 1982 in order to weaken the military operation, and only refrained from doing do when the plot was discovered. If the attack had gone ahead, Italian-made limpet mines would have been attached to the hulls of warships, and fuel and ammunition dumps would have been targeted along with the runway at RAF Gibraltar.

Regardless of the rights and wrongs of the sinking of the *Belgrano*, it had a great effect on the Argentine Navy as it subsequently retreated to its home ports and took no further part in the war, making the Royal Navy's job much easier.

Two days after the loss of the *Belgrano*, on 4 May 1982, two Argentine Super Etendard aircraft attacked and sank HMS *Sheffield*, a Type 42 air-defence destroyer, using two air-launched MM39 Exocet missiles. One of the missiles was successfully deflected by HMS *Yarmouth* using chaff and fell into the sea, but the other scored a direct hit on *Sheffield* which caught fire and eventually sank.

One of the reasons that *Sheffield* was hit was that she was not at Action Stations at the time and was taken by surprise. Had she manoeuvred to face the missile head-on (to present a smaller target) and fired off chaff rockets then she might have survived. *Sheffield* was armed with Sea Dart surface-to-air missiles, but this system – which used 1960s valve-era electronics – had a fatal weakness, as it was not very effective at engaging targets flying at less than 1,000 feet. The Argentines were aware of this limitation, as they had two British-built Type 42 destroyers in their own navy – the ARA *Hercules* and the ARA *Santisima Trinidad* – and had discovered through practice sorties against these vessels that their own jets could avoid being shot down by Sea Dart by flying at a very low altitude. In theory, a Type 42 destroyer could engage a Super Etendard at 20-30 miles range with Sea Dart provided the aircraft flew above 1,000 feet. However, Sea Dart was not effective against sea-skimming Exocet missiles as they flew too low. An upgrade to the Sea Dart system which would have enabled them to engage sea-skimmers had been cancelled by the government some years before to save money.

The only weapon the Royal Navy possessed which could theoretically destroy an Exocet was the excellent Sea Wolf missile system which was fitted to just two ships in the

Task Force, the Type 22 frigates HMS *Broadsword* and HMS *Brilliant*. However, Sea Wolf was a point-defence system which was designed to protect only the ship to which it was fitted. The only way a Type 22 frigate could defend another ship was to get between an incoming missile (or aircraft) and the vessel it was guarding, making itself the target. HMS *Sheffield* might also have been saved if it had been fitted with a Close In Weapons System (CWIS) such as the American 20mm Vulcan Phalanx or the Dutch 30mm Goalkeeper. These were both fully automatic, fast-firing, radar-directed, computer-controlled gun turrets which would shoot down any missile or aircraft which came within range. Having said that, such weapons are only effective if they are switched on, and it must be noted that in 1987 the US frigate USS *Stark* – which *was* fitted with the Vulcan Phalanx CIWS system – was hit and badly damaged by an Exocet missile fired in error by an Iraqi aircraft. The Phalanx could have engaged the missile and destroyed it, but did not do so because it was not turned on at the time as the vessel was not at Action Stations.

On 21 May, British forces landed in the Falklands at Port San Carlos while a group of Royal Navy frigates and destroyers took up positions in Falkland Sound to defend the landing force. Initially the two Seawolf-equipped vessels, HMS *Broadsword* and HMS *Brilliant,* were deployed in Falkland Sound as it was expected that their missile systems would take a heavy toll of attacking Argentine aircraft. In practice it was found that Sea Wolf didn't perform well close to land, as its missile tracking radar was badly affected by 'clutter'. In addition, the Sea Wolf system's computers (which were the size of a small house) had been programmed to engage only targets which were considered an immediate threat

– namely missiles or aircraft heading directly towards the ship. Thus the automatic system tended to ignore high-speed crossing targets, such as Argentine Skyhawks and Mirages. In radar-guided mode, Sea Wolf had some difficulty engaging low-level targets because of 'clutter' from sea and land, and the missile operators were sometimes forced to switch to a backup camera-guided mode in which they had to keep the target centred on the crosshairs of a CCTV monitor using a joystick. HMS *Broadsword* subsequently shot down two Argentine aircraft using this method, but battle damage to her and her sister ship HMS *Brilliant* led to them being eventually withdrawn from Falkland Sound for repairs.

The most common naval surface-to-air missile used in what became known as 'The Battle of Bomb Alley', though, was actually the elderly Seacat missile, which was fitted to the majority of the frigates used in the conflict, plus the assault ships HMS *Fearless* and HMS *Intrepid*, the carrier HMS *Hermes*, and the *County*-class guided-missile destroyers HMS *Antrim* and HMS *Glamorgan*. Designed in the 1950s by Short of Belfast and based on the earlier wire-guided Malkara anti-tank missile, the Seacat entered service with the Royal Navy in 1961 and was only ever fired in action in the Falklands War. Unfortunately, the system was found wanting during the conflict. The main problem was that the missile was subsonic with a top speed of Mach 0.8 and had a limited range. It was thus too slow to have much chance of engaging a fast jet, particularly if it presented as a high-speed crossing target. In addition, early versions of the missile (the GWS-20) fitted to HMS *Fearless*, HMS *Intrepid*, HMS *Plymouth* and HMS *Yarmouth* employed an optical tracking system, so the operator had to keep the target centred on crosshairs in a pair of binoculars while he steered the missile onto the target using a joystick. A later version of the Seacat system, the GWS-24 – fitted to the Type 21 frigates – employed a TV monitor and semi-automatic tracking similar to that used in the early Sea Wolf mountings, but overall Seacat proved largely ineffective in the Falklands War. Although an MoD Defence White Paper published some months after the conflict credited the system with six 'kills', independent researchers Jeffrey Ethell and Alfred Price (in their book *Air War South Atlantic*, 1983) have suggested that only one Argentine aircraft was shot down by Seacat during the entire conflict.

Another problem facing the Royal Navy was that too much faith had been placed in their missile systems, and they had neglected to provide their ships with modern fast-firing weapons for close-in air defence. Frigates and destroyers normally carried a pair of WW2-vintage 40mm Bofors L40/60 or 20mm Oerlikon guns which were usually ineffective against modern jets, although Bofors fire from HMS *Intrepid* did destroy one Argentine A-4 Skyhawk on 27 May.

There were similar problems ashore with the Army's much-vaunted Rapier surface-to-air missile system, which had been in service for many years and had replaced the earlier Bofors guns. A battery of Rapiers had been sent to the Falklands, but it was clear that there were problems with the system as it was designed to be towed into battle behind a forward control Land Rover and not shipped 8,000 miles and dumped onto the battlefield as an underslung load beneath a helicopter. Sensitive equipment, it took a full day to set up and was thus not available on the first day of the landings, Friday 21 May. In addition, the system was plagued with technical failures and a shortage of spare parts which was aggravated by the loss of the *Atlantic Conveyor* on 25 May as she was carrying a large quantity of Rapier spares.

The siting of each Rapier fire unit had been determined by computers at the Radar Research Institute at Malvern in order to give the best possible air defence coverage to the ground troops and Royal Navy ships lying in Falkland Sound, but it was soon found that the system was not performing as well as expected. In exercises on the flat West German plains, Rapier had proved highly effective against low-flying aircraft, but it had problems coping with the hilly terrain of the Falklands. Enemy jets would appear from behind a hill and only be in view for a few seconds, leaving the operators with insufficient time to launch and track a missile.

Contrary to some news reports at the time, Rapier was not a 'fire and forget' system. Instead, the operator had to acquire the target in an optical sight similar to a telescope, fire a missile, and then keep the hostile aircraft centred in a set of crosshairs until the missile was steered automatically to a 'kill' by a computer in the tracker unit which viewed flares in the tailfins of each Rapier missile via a small CCTV camera.

The version of Rapier initially deployed to the Falklands only had a basic surveillance radar for the detection of target bearings and guidance of the missile was optical, using small flares in the tailfins. This was a system known as Semi-Automatic Command to Line of Sight (SACLOS) guidance. A more advanced version of Rapier, employing 'Blindfire' radar which could engage targets at night, arrived in the islands towards the end of the conflict.

Unlike most surface-to-air missiles, Rapier actually struck its target with a relatively small warhead and lacked a proximity fuse which would allow it to destroy an aircraft through the blast effect of a near miss. Former Rapier operator Tony McNally described the problems with the system in his book *Watching Men Burn* (2007). On 8 June 1982,

McNally was sitting at the controls of a single Rapier unit which had been deployed to Fitzroy to defend the two RFA landing ships, *Sir Galahad* and *Sir Percival*. As Argentine A-4 Skyhawks swooped in to bomb the vessels, McNally acquired one of the jets in the crosshairs of his missile tracker and attempted to fire a missile, but nothing happened. In his book, McNally has claimed that that particular fire unit had an intermittent fault and it was unfortunate that that particular unit was used to defend these ships.

The Ministry of Defence White Paper on the Falklands operation, which was published a few months after the war, concluded that 14 Argentine aircraft were shot down by Rapier missiles. But independent research by authors Jeffrey Ethell and Alfred Price for the book *Air War South Atlantic* (1983) suggested that only one Argentine jet was brought down by this weapon during the entire Falklands War (with four others being shot down by 'multiple weapons', including Rapier).

Another British air defence weapon which underperformed during the conflict was the Blowpipe shoulder-launched surface-to-air missile. Manufactured by Short of Belfast, the Blowpipe launcher was a heavy and cumbersome device which looked like a larger and fatter version of the wartime bazooka. After firing the missile, the operator had to keep the target aircraft in his optical sight and then steer the missile towards it using a thumb-operated joystick. Only one Argentine aircraft – a Macchi MB.339, which was attacking British troops at Goose Green – was brought down by the missile, and after the war the subsonic Blowpipe was replaced by the more effective Short Javelin which itself has since been succeeded by the even more sophisticated Starstreak system.

Largely as a result of these problems with various surface-to-air missile systems, two British frigates – HMS *Ardent* and HMS *Antelope* – were sunk during the Battle of San Carlos Water, and several more damaged. On the other hand, a large number of Argentine aircraft were shot down by patrolling Sea Harriers, ships' missiles and guns, and by the end of the conflict the Argentine Air Force had been decimated.

There were further setbacks for the British, namely the sinking of HMS *Coventry* and the cargo ship *Atlantic Conveyor* on 25 May, plus the aforementioned disaster at Fitzroy on 8 June when two Royal Fleet Auxiliaries *Sir Galahad* and *Sir Tristram* were bombed by Argentine A-4 Skyhawks. There were a huge number of casualties amongst the Welsh Guardsmen on board, including Simon Weston who suffered severe burns in the attack. Despite this tragedy, the British Forces ashore advanced on the capital of the Falklands Island, Port Stanley, and on 14 June the Argentines surrendered.

Despite overwhelming odds, minimal air cover, no airborne early-warning radar, an 8,000 mile supply line and inadequate air-defence weapons, the British forces triumphed. What is not often appreciated is that the British forces were at breaking point just before the Argentine surrender, as they were running low on food and ammunition and most of the ships were showing signs of wear and tear with the barrels of most of the 4.5 inch guns of the warships needing replacement. 16 out of 23 escort vessels had been damaged, and four of these (HMS *Sheffield*, HMS *Ardent*, HMS *Antelope* and HMS *Coventry*) had been sunk, in addition to the loss of *Atlantic Conveyor* and *Sir Galahad*. As the commander of the British task force – Admiral Sandy Woodward – later admitted, it was 'a close-run thing'.

Why has there never been a feature film about the Falklands War?

The Falklands War, then, would seem to form the ideal subject for a big-budget movie, as it had all the elements for an interesting screenplay – powerful human dramas, political intrigue, military victories against all the odds, fascinating technological problems, and an ending in which good triumphs over evil. Yet almost 40 years after the event, no movie has ever appeared, though there have been a few serious attempts to make such a film.

Back in 1982, actor Lewis Collins (who had achieved stardom in *The Professionals*) starred as SAS Captain Peter Skellen in *Who Dares Wins*. With a screenplay by Reginald Rose and George Markstein (which was turned into a novel *The Tiptoe Boys* by James Follett), the film dealt with an anarchist anti-nuclear terrorist group called The People's Lobby, led by deluded American activist Frankie Leith (Judy Davis). After taking over the American ambassador's residence in London, the People's Lobby threaten to execute all their hostages unless a nuclear weapon is detonated at the US Navy Holy Loch base in Scotland. The plot is thwarted by an SAS attack on the building, closely resembling the real-life SAS assault on the Iranian Embassy in London in 1980. (A detailed analysis of *Who Dares Wins* can be found in another of my books, *Dying Harder: Action Movies of the 1980s*, Extremis Publishing, 2017). The film was hugely popular – particularly in the UK – and in late 1982 producer Euan Lloyd announced that he intended to make at least three more films with his new star, Lewis Collins.

One of these proposed productions was *Task Force South* (aka *Battle of the Falklands*), which dealt with SAS and SBS (Special Boat Service) operations in the Falklands. The movie would have seen Collins reprising his role of Captain Peter Skellen, and filming was to take place in both the Falkland Islands themselves and Scotland. As things transpired, *Task Force South* was never made. The two reasons that were given at the time were difficulties obtaining suitable funding – the budget was £10 million – and the fact that other film companies were planning similar projects (although none of these subsequently appeared).

The only other serious attempt to make a film about the Falklands War has been the movie *Destroyer*, which was announced several years ago. Based on Captain David Hart-Dyke's book *25 Days in May* (2007), the story dealt with the exploits of the Type 42 Destroyer HMS *Coventry* during the Falklands War and its tragic sinking on 25 May 1982.

By that point in the war, the Royal Navy was using a new tactic to defeat Argentine air attacks; namely the use of a Type 22 Frigate and Type 42 Destroyer in combination, something that became known as a 'Type 64'. On 25 May 1982, HMS *Coventry* and the Type 22 Frigate HMS *Broadsword* were positioned well out to sea near Pebble Island to the north west of the main Falkland Islands. The theory was that this location would provide ideal operating conditions for HMS *Coventry*'s Sea Dart missile system, and the warship could thus shoot down Argentine aircraft which were returning from strike missions against targets in the San Carlos area. If the Argentines tried to attack the two British ships, then HMS *Broadsword* could defend both vessels with her Sea Wolf close range missiles.

Initially the plan seemed to be working, as HMS *Coventry* shot down two Argentine A-4 Skyhawks with her Sea Dart system. Unfortunately, Argentine observers on Pebble

Island saw the smoke trails of the missiles and called in an airstrike to destroy the two British vessels; accordingly, two pairs of Skyhawks were despatched to deal with the troublesome warships. The first two skimmed low over the sea and headed towards HMS *Broadsword*, which achieved a radar lock with its Sea Wolf missile system. Aboard the British warship the crew waited for the system to blast the two aircraft out the sky as soon as they came within effective range. It was at that point that *Broadsword's* Sea Wolf 'sulked'. Faced with two targets flying very close together and unable to decide which to fire at first, the system's computers cancelled the engagement. One solution would have been to switch Sea Wolf to the alternative CCTV and joystick-guided mode, but there wasn't time to do this and one 1,000-pound bomb struck *Broadsword* aft, travelling up through the flight deck and destroying the vessel's Lynx helicopter before landing in the sea. At this point *Broadsword* had been damaged – but not fatally – and *Coventry* was unharmed, but a second pair of Skyhawks was on its way.

In an effort to save his ship, Captain Hart-Dyke manoeuvred his vessel dramatically, but in doing so he accidentally got between *Broadsword* and the attacking aircraft, preventing the Type 22 frigate from firing its Sea Wolf. Although *Coventry* managed to achieve a radar lock on the Skyhawks with its Type 909 missile tracking radar, this subsequently failed and the ship was hit by bombs and sunk.

This tragedy was one of the most controversial episodes of the entire conflict. In recent years, former Sea Harrier pilot Dave Morgan in his book *Hostile Skies* (2007) has pointed out that *Coventry* could probably have been saved if the patrolling Sea Harriers – which were in the area at the time – had been given the job of intercepting the Skyhawks. Instead, a decision was made to deal with the attacking aircraft using Sea Dart and Sea Wolf – systems which had been shown to be prone to failure earlier in the conflict. Indeed, the Type 22 frigate HMS *Brilliant* had experienced a similar glitch on 3 May off Port Stanley. After shooting down two Skyhawks with Sea Wolf, and causing a third to crash into the sea, she was attacked by a second wave of aircraft. This time the Sea Wolf 'sulked', and HMS *Glasgow* was hit by a bomb which passed through her hull without exploding. Although she was not sunk, she sustained serious damage and had to be withdrawn for repairs and then sent back to the UK.

The loss of HMS *Coventry* could also have been prevented if she had been fitted with a modern Close-in Weapons System (CIWS) such as the Dutch 30mm Goalkeeper or the American 20mm Vulcan Phalanx. Soon after the conflict had concluded, all the surviving Type 42 Destroyers were fitted with two twin 30mm and two single 20mm BMARC guns as a stopgap measure, and the 30mm weapons were subsequently replaced with 20mm Vulcan Phalanx CWIS units.

As can be seen, the story of HMS *Coventry*'s exploits in the Falklands War would make an excellent feature film, and the movie *Destroyer* has been in development for several years. Colin Firth was originally to have played Captain Hart-Dyke, but has since withdrawn from the project. Although some filming was carried out with HMS *Edinburgh* (the last operational Type 42 Destroyer) in 2013, and other scenes were due to be filmed on Malta (where there is a huge water tank next to the sea at Malta Film Facilities), nothing has been heard about this production for years. When the author contacted the HMS *Coventry* Association during the writing of this book, he was told that there had been no news of this film for years. It is unclear if the film has been cancelled or whether it will eventually be made some years from now.

However, although no cinematic feature films have yet been made about the Falklands conflict, it has been the subject of the three different TV productions. *Tumbledown* (1988) was a BBC TV movie which dealt with the story of Lieutenant Robert Lawrence, a British soldier who suffered severe brain injuries during the battle for Mount Tumbledown during the Falklands War. Lawrence was played by Colin Firth who (as mentioned earlier) was the original choice to play Captain David Hart-Dyke in *Destroyer*.

An Ungentlemanly Act (1992) was another BBC TV movie, which this time focused on the events of 2 April 1982 when a force of Argentine Marines and Special Forces captured Port Stanley. Ian Richardson played the Falklands Governor Rex Hunt, while Bob Peck (best-known for his role in the original 1985 BBC TV version of *Edge of Darkness*) played Major Mike Norman, who commanded the small Royal Marines garrison on the islands. The film was fairly accurate, with some scenes being shot in the Falklands Islands.

The most controversial TV production about the Falklands War was *The Falklands Play*, a 1987 production written by Ian Curteis and starring Patricia Hodge as Margaret Thatcher. Originally to have been broadcast in 1986, the programme was shelved on the orders of the Controller of BBC 1, Michael Grade, who allegedly disliked the production because of its pro-Thatcher stance and jingoistic tone. One scene which particularly upset BBC bosses was one in Mrs Thatcher shed tears when hearing about the deaths of British sailors.

Although the BBC was once a patriotic organisation which supported our armed forces, this had all changed by the

1980s and its anti-war, anti-Conservative and pro-Labour stance was well-known and continues to this day. In the mid-1980s there was still considerable resentment in the Armed Forces about the way the BBC had reported the Falklands War. One thing which particularly annoyed them was that the BBC World Service reported that most Argentine bombs were not exploding. The Argentinians heard this on the radio and altered their bomb fusings, making their attacks more effective. (Something similar happened in WW2 when an American Congressman publicly announced that the Japanese were setting their fuses on depth charges to explode at too shallow a depth, thus saving many US submarines from destruction. The Japanese heard this on the radio and altered their fuse settings accordingly.) The BBC also reported that the Parachute Regiment was going to attack Goose Green, although fortunately this revelation did not affect the outcome of the battle.

Although the broadcast of the play was blocked by BBC bosses, it was eventually released on DVD by the BBC in 2007. An entirely studio-bound production, it dealt with all the political intrigues before and during the Falklands War.

In summary then, what are the reasons why there has never been a feature film or TV mini-series about the Falklands War? I think there are a number of possible explanations which are legal, financial, practical, political and cultural.

Legal Issues

A lot of proposed films and TV series are never made because of objections from people who are to be depicted in these productions. Sometimes there can even be issues with the estate of deceased persons. For example, two proposed TV series and a cinema film based on deceased RAF pilot Richard Hillary's book *The Last Enemy* were mooted in the late eighties but never went ahead, allegedly because of objections from Hillary's family. Instead, all that appeared was a LWT miniseries – *Perfect Hero* (1991) – which starred Nigel Havers as a Richard Hillary-like character. Similarly, *Battle of Britain* (1969) came about after producer Benjamin Fisz was unable to secure the rights to make a film about the life of Major-General Orde Wingate (leader and creator of the Chindits), allegedly because of a lack of permission from his surviving relatives. With most members of the 1982 Task Force still being alive (and many of the politicians too) there are obviously a lot of people who might object to such a production and take legal action over the way they might be depicted on screen.

Financial Issues

Any film or TV series about the Falklands War would be enormously expensive. A huge cast and crew would be required, and big stars would have to be included to make the film successful. Some filming would have to be carried out in the Falkland Islands, which are 8,000 miles from Britain. It should be noted that two of the biggest British war epics, *Battle of Britain* (1969) and *A Bridge Too Far* (1977), were also among the most expensive films ever made. *Battle of Britain* originally flopped at the box-office. Although it was the Number 1 film in Britain and was also very popular in West Germany and the Commonwealth countries, it never made any impact on the all-important American market and has only very recently gone into profit because of DVD and Blu-Ray sales and TV screening fees. *A Bridge Too Far* did make a small profit, but again was not popular in the USA – possibly because of its rather bleak tone.

Practical Issues

At the time of writing, 36 years have elapsed since the Falklands War and – as a result – much of the equipment used in the conflict no longer exists. The assault ships HMS *Fearless* and HMS *Intrepid* were scrapped a long time ago, as was the Falklands flagship HMS *Invincible*. HMS *Hermes* was sold to the Indian Navy, becoming the *Vikrant*, and was recently decommissioned with discussions currently ongoing about her future. The Type 21 Frigates HMS *Ardent* and HMS *Antelope* were sunk during the Falklands War, but their six sister vessels were sold to Pakistan in 1994 and are still in service. The Type 22 Frigates HMS *Broadsword* and HMS *Brilliant* were sold to Brazil and remain in service, while the *County* class guided-missile destroyers HMS *Antrim* and HMS *Glamorgan* (which were sold to Chile) have been decommissioned only recently. All the other warships which participated in the Falklands War have been scrapped – including the last surviving Type 42 Destroyer, HMS *Edinburgh*, which went to the breaker's yard in 2015 – as have most of the civilian vessels which participated in the conflict. The S.S. *Canberra* was scrapped in 1997. The *QE2* still exists in Port Rashid, Dubai, having been converted to a floating hotel.

Most of the aircraft which took part in the conflict have also been scrapped. The RAF disposed of its last Harriers in 2010, and the Royal Navy no longer has any Sea Harriers. The last airworthy RAF Avro Vulcan bomber XH558 – a type which took part in long-range bombing missions from Ascension Island during the war – has now been grounded.

So it can be seen that there would be serious practical difficulties in making a film about the Falklands War as all the hardware would have to be recreated using miniatures, CGI, and mock-ups. CGI technology is improving all the time – for example, the realistic Royal Navy aircraft carrier (apparently HMS *Hermes*) which appears in *The Man From UNCLE* (2015) was created with this method – but it can be very expensive, and this would have an impact on the cost of the production. Another possibility might be to do some filming with ex-Falklands War vessels which are now owned by foreign navies, for example the Type 21 frigates owned by Pakistan or the Type 22s operated by Brazil. There is a precedent for this, as the Turkish Navy supplied a submarine and patrol boat for *The McKenzie Break* (1970), the Yugoslavian Army provided the tanks and vehicles used in *Kelly's Heroes* (1970), the Dutch and Belgian Armies loaned out tanks for *A Bridge Too Far* (1977), and of course *Battle of the Bulge* (1965), *Battle of Britain* (1969) and *Patton* (1970) were all made with the help of the Spanish Armed Forces.

Political Issues

It would be impossible to make a film about the Falklands War which did not show Mrs Thatcher in a positive light, and this would not sit well with many people in the film and television industry who – for many decades – have tended to have left-wing, anti-war views and would not approve of a production which glorified conflict and depicted a former colonial power triumphing over a small South American country. One has only to take the case of the late film producer Euan Lloyd to see what I mean. Lloyd received a lot of abuse from left-wing critics for his film *The Wild Geese* (1978), simply because it was made in South Africa before apartheid ended and was partly financed by South African companies. Claims were made that the film supported apartheid, though in fact the screenplay had a strong anti-apartheid message as the 'hero', deposed President Julius Limbani, was clearly based on Nelson Mandela. Even more venom was directed at one of Lloyd's subsequent productions, the aforementioned *Who Dares Wins* (1982), with its implied criticism of the CND, anti-war activists and left-wingers. Lloyd was often accused of being right-wing, although I would consider him 'centrist', and it is interesting that he has been one of only a few British film producers who have seriously considered making a film about the Falklands War. One of the reasons that *Who Dares Wins* was not a great financial success outwith the UK was that Ronald Reagan liked it, and once word got out that it was a 'Reagan film' no distributor wanted to touch it.

In summary then, the institutional left-wing bias of the BBC and both the British and American film industries means that it is highly unlikely that anyone will ever make a film about the Falklands War, since any honest account of the conflict would be perceived by critics as being right-wing and pro-war.

Cultural Issues

Another factor militating against a film or TV series about the Falklands War is this simple fact — no Americans were involved in the conflict. President Reagan could have intervened decisively in the war by sending a modern carrier battle group to the Falklands, which would have probably destroyed the entire Argentine Air Force in 72 hours. He chose not to become involved, largely because he saw General Galtieri's fascist regime as being an important ally in the fight against Communism. The Americans did eventually help the British by supplying the latest version of the Sidewinder missile – the AIM-9L – which proved a decisive weapon in the conflict. At the time of the Argentine surrender, they were also planning to send the British HAWK and Stinger surface-to-air missiles, which were much more effective than British Rapiers and Blowpipes. Thus the Americans helped out with supplies of weapons, but were not directly involved in the fighting.

Historically, American cinema audiences are not keen on British war movies and those that have triumphed at the all-important US box office have tended to have Americans in the cast. Thus *The Guns of Navarone* (1961) featured Gregory Peck, James Darren and Anthony Quinn; *633 Squadron* (1964) starred Cliff Robertson and George Chakiris, while *Operation Crossbow* (1965) included George Peppard in its cast. The American involvement in Operation Market Garden was greatly emphasised in *A Bridge Too Far* in an attempt to make the film a success.

Thus any Falklands movie would only be a success at the US box office if it included American actors in the cast. It is matter of historical record that many British actors have managed convincing American accents, but the reverse is not usually true. Good examples would be Marlon Brando's mumbling attempt at an English accent in *Mutiny on The Bounty* (1962), and Anthony Perkins' variable efforts in the TV movie *The Glory Boys* (1984). In a more recent production, *Allied* (2016), the problem was solved by making Brad Pitt's character Canadian instead of British. So in conclusion, there are a number of different factors which would prevent a movie ever being made about the Falklands War and I think it is highly unlikely that one will ever see the light of day.

10
OTHER GENRES

NAVAL warfare and Cold War tensions have influenced films and TV series in other genres. The feature film *Voyage to the Bottom of the Sea* (1961) reflected anxieties about nuclear weapons, atomic power, the Cold War and the impact of new technologies. It also incorporated a number of tropes found in WW2 submarine films (with a nod to the works of Jules Verne as well), and led to a long-running TV series.

The film was directed and co-written by Irwin Allen, whose career went through a series of distinct phases. In the 1950s he was well-known for making documentaries such as *The Sea Around Us* (1953). In the 1960s, after the success of the original *Voyage to the Bottom of the Sea* film, Allen made a TV series based on the film, which ran for four seasons from 1964 to 1968. He also produced three other science-fiction TV series, namely *Lost in Space* (1965-68), *The Time Tunnel* (1966-67), and *Land of the Giants* (1968-70).

The next phase of his career was in the seventies, when he made several disaster movies starting with *The Poseidon Adventure* (1972) and concluding with *When Time Ran Out* (1980). One notable success during this period was *The Tow-

ering Inferno (1974), which had an all-star cast including Paul Newman and Steve McQueen. At the time Allen said he produced the film to highlight the dangers of fires breaking out in tower blocks – a problem that is still with us, as shown by the recent Grenfell Tower tragedy in London.

Writer Roderick Thorpe apparently got the inspiration for the book *Nothing Lasts Forever* (which later became the 1988 film *Die Hard*) from a dream he had after watching *The Towering Inferno*, so Allen's 1974 film indirectly led to that very successful movie, plus its many sequels and imitations.

The original *Voyage to the Bottom of the Sea* movie, though, was very much a product of its time. In 1958 the world's first nuclear-powered submarine, the USS *Nautilus* (SSN-571), was the first vessel to travel under the Arctic ice cap, and also the first to travel from the Pacific to the Atlantic via the North Pole. On 17 March 1959, the nuclear submarine USS *Skate* under the command of Commander James F. Calvert became the first craft to break through the ice and surface at the North Pole.

There was also great public anxiety at the time about the effects of nuclear power, as shown by a number of science fiction movies like *Them* (1954) and *Tarantula* (1955) in which monsters were accidentally created as a result of scientific experiments. The Japanese movie *Godzilla* (1955) – in which a dinosaur-like monster rampages through Tokyo – reflected popular concerns about radiation and the trauma suffered by the Japanese nation as a result of the atomic bombings of Hiroshima and Nagasaki in 1945.

Voyage to the Bottom of the Sea opens with the brand-new nuclear submarine, the *Seaview*, being tested in the Arctic Ocean by its designer – scientist and engineering genius Admiral Harriman Nelson (Walter Pidgeon). Pidgeon had previously played the scientist Morbius in the MGM science-fiction classic *Forbidden Planet* (1956).

During the diving trials, the crew notice that the Arctic ice cap is cracking and melting, and when they surface they discover a fire burning in the sky. It appears that the Van Allen Belts (areas of radiation lying hundreds of miles above the Earth) have caught fire. Nelson orders Captain Lee Crane (Robert Sterling) to sail the *Seaview* back to New York as quickly as possible. Incidentally 'Robert Sterling' is the marine biologist alias adopted by Roger Moore's James Bond in the highly nautical 007 picture *The Spy Who Loved Me* (1977) when he initially infiltrates Stromberg's headquarters.

Nelson and his friend Commodore Emery (Peter Lorre) attend a meeting at the United Nations to discuss the crisis. It appears that the fire has been caused by a meteor shower piercing the Van Allen belt and igniting it. Nelson believes the solution is to fire a nuclear missile at the belt, snuffing out the flames, but other scientists disagree and insist that the fire will burn itself out.

Nelson decides to carry out the mission anyway, although he hopes to tap into an undersea telephone cable to get authorization from the President. Nelson and Crane also realise that a saboteur is on board the submarine (an idea pinched by Alistair MacLean for his book *Ice Station Zebra* in 1966 and the subsequent film adaptation). Towards the end of the film, the identity of the saboteur is revealed to be Dr Susan Hiller (Joan Fontaine).

Eventually the *Seaview* reaches its destination, the deep Marianas Trench in the Pacific Ocean. Admiral Nelson orders a missile to be fired at the Van Allen Belt, the flames are extinguished, and the world is saved.

The film was moderately successful, making $7 million at the US and Canadian box office set against a budget of $1.6 million, and three years later Irwin Allen turned it into a TV series which ran to 110 episodes over four series, from 1964 to 1968. The series re-used footage, props, sets and ideas from the feature film, which greatly reduced costs. As was common in the USA in the mid-sixties, the first series was made in black-and-white but subsequent series were in colour. Although the American NTSC colour system dated back to 1953, few people in the USA had colour TV sets until the late sixties and this was the reason that many new American TV shows continued to be made in black-and-white until 1966.

All the parts were re-cast, with Richard Basehart now playing Admiral Nelson and David Hedison (formerly Al Hedison) as Captain Lee Crane. The first three seasons were set in the 1970s, while the last season supposedly took place in the eighties.

The first season stories tended to reflect contemporary Cold War tensions and the anxieties and problems of submarine warfare, but from the second season onwards another formula emerged in which some kind of monster got on board the *Seaview* and had to be defeated by the crew. For example there was an episode, *The Mummy*, in which an Egyptian mummy came to life on board the sub and had to be destroyed.

This tendency towards cheesiness was a feature of all Irwin Allen's TV series, particularly *Lost in Space* which started out as a dark and serious production, but eventually became a cliché-ridden parody of itself with its principal villain – Dr Jonathan Smith – becoming something of a comedy act. All Irwin Allen's TV productions did benefit, though, from excellent special effects, and *Voyage to the Bottom of the Sea* was no exception. As well as the very convincing submarine sequences, there was the 'Flying Sub' which featured in later episodes. All these miniature shots were produced by top effects experts such as Howard Lydecker and L.B. Abbott, who also worked on many major motion pictures.

The influence of the war at sea on *Doctor Who*

The popular BBC TV science-fiction series *Doctor Who* (1963-89 and 2005-present) featured a naval-themed adventure in 1972, and the story behind its origins is very interesting. For the first three years of its run, *Doctor Who* alternated between sci-fi stories set in the future (usually on alien planets) and historical dramas which were supposed to be educational. The latter proved unpopular with viewers, and when new producer Innes Lloyd and script editor Gerry Davis took over the reins of the programme in 1966 they made many changes to the format.

The historical stories were phased out (with the last being *The Highlanders* in 1966/67), a new younger Doctor (Patrick Troughton) replaced actor William Hartnell, and there was a move towards more realistic, science-based stories with some even being set on present-day Earth, or the near future. Towards the end of William Hartnell's tenure in the summer of 1966, *The War Machines* had shown what future *Doctor Who* stories could be like. Scripted by Ian Stuart Black from an idea by Dr Kit Pedler (who was a medical doctor and research scientist whose special interest was the structure and function of the retina and the nature of vision), the serial was about a megalomaniac computer called WOTAN (Will Operating Thought Analogue) housed at the top of London's then-uncompleted Post Office Tower, which could take over peoples' minds and had plans for world domination. To achieve this aim, WOTAN directed the construction of mobile tank-like 'War Machines' to patrol the streets of London.

The highlight of this story – the first of four *Doctor Who* serials to be directed by Michael Ferguson – was a scene in which the British Army attempts to destroy a War Machine. Unfortunately their attack fails because the mobile computer is (by technological means which are never explained) able to prevent the soldiers' weapons from firing and grenades from exploding. A neat idea, but it makes for a rather unexciting battle, as there are no explosions or gunshots. Nonetheless, this was the first *Doctor Who* story in which soldiers attempted to fight a monster with firearms.

In February and March 1968 – during the Patrick Troughton era – the BBC screened what is regarded by many fans as the greatest *Doctor Who* story ever made. *The Web of Fear*, scripted by Mervyn Haisman and Henry Lincoln, was a sequel to *The Abominable Snowmen* which had been broadcast just a few months before. In that earlier story, set in 1935, the Doctor had encountered the Yeti but soon found they were really fur-covered robots controlled by The Intelligence, a disembodied alien consciousness floating in space. With the help of his companions Jamie (Frazer Hines) and Victoria (Deborah Watling), plus Professor Travers (Jack Watling), the Doctor thwarted the alien's plans.

In *The Web of Fear*, The Intelligence cocoons the TARDIS (the Doctor's space and time craft) in space and forces it to land in the London Underground in the present day, where the Doctor and his companions soon get into trouble. Some weeks before, The Intelligence had invaded London, filling it with a deadly mist which forced the government to evacuate the capital. The London Underground system was then slowly filled with a suffocating, web-like fungus, and upgraded variants of the robot Yeti (which the Doctor called the 'Mark 2 version') – with a slimmer body and glowing eyes – were patrolling the tunnels, armed with deadly web guns. A small force of British Army troops based in an underground fortress were attempting to stem the Yetis' advance by blowing up tunnels, but were having limited success as the robots kept cocooning explosive charges with web, nullifying their effect.

Bullets from the soldiers' 7.62mm SLR rifles were only marginally effective against the Yeti, and a direct hit between the eyes was required for a 'kill'. Grenades and bazooka shells could stop a Yeti, but these were in short supply.

The highlight of this story was a scene in Episode 4 (broadcast on 24 February 1968) in which Colonel Lethbridge-Stewart (Nicholas Courtney) leads a squad of troops through the streets of London in an effort to rescue the Doctor's TARDIS. Unfortunately they are discovered by the Yeti and cornered in a trader's yard in Covent Garden.

The troops' rifles prove useless against the Yeti, though some of the creatures are destroyed by grenades and bazooka rounds. Eventually the military detachment is overwhelmed by sheer weight of numbers, and a demoralized Colonel Lethbridge-Stewart returns alone to the Army fortress in the Underground. This scene is a landmark in *Doctor Who* history, as it was the first proper 'soldiers versus monsters' battle and was filmed by director Douglas Camfield at T.J. Poupart's Yard, Sheldon Street, Covent Garden, London on 17 December 1967 and 14 January 1968.

All six soldiers in these scenes were played by stuntmen, with one of them being Terry Walsh who did a lot of work for *Doctor Who* in the seventies. Another was portrayed by Derek Martin, who later became an actor in *EastEnders*.

This particular story was junked by the BBC in the early seventies. In the early eighties, a 16mm tele-recording of Episode 1 was returned to the BBC archives, and in October 2013 all the remaining episodes except for Episode 3 were returned to the archives after having been found in Nigeria by archive recovery expert Philip Morris. Morris later claimed that Episode 3 had originally been located by him and was then stolen or purchased by another unnamed individual. At the time of writing it is unclear as to whether this last missing episode of the serial will be recovered.

In November and December 1968, the BBC broadcast *The Invasion*, an eight-part Cyberman story scripted by Derrick Sherwin, based on a story by Kit Pedler. Like *The Web of Fear*, it was directed by Douglas Camfield, who was a former Army officer. This was the first *Doctor Who* story to be made with the cooperation of the Ministry of Defence. In Episode 2, the Doctor and Jamie are reunited with Colonel Lethbridge-Stewart (who they had previously met in *The Web of Fear*). Lethbridge-Stewart is now a Brigadier in charge of the British branch of UNIT (United Nations Intelligence Taskforce). His mobile HQ is inside an RAF Lockheed C-130 Hercules transport plane (the exteriors used a genuine aircraft at RAF Fairford, while the interiors were a studio set).

In Episode 7 the Doctor drives a short-wheelbase Land Rover out of the back of the Hercules (the first time in the series the Doctor ever drove a car), but the fruits of the cooperation with the Ministry of Defence were really apparent in Episode 8 when UNIT forces engaged in a pitched battle with the Cybermen in the grounds of the International Electromatics factory.

For these scenes – which were shot at the disused TCC Condensers factory in Acton, London – a platoon of genuine Coldstream Guards played the part of UNIT soldiers, with a few of the squaddies being portrayed by extras. The genuine British Army soldiers wore their usual black berets with added UNIT badges, while the Army supplied a Bedford RL three-ton truck and two short-wheelbase Land Rovers for these scenes.

The result was one of the most exciting and convincing battle scenes in the history of *Doctor Who*. Only six 'Mark IV' Cybermen costumes were made for this story – with the main suit being a diver's wet suit sprayed silver, and the chest units being lighter than in previous versions – but careful editing made six Cybermen seem like twelve.

The battle follows a tradition established in *Doctor Who*, and most science-fiction movies, as the Cybermen can't be killed by bullets but are vulnerable to grenades and bazooka fire. As in *The Web of Fear*, the soldiers have a bazooka (actually a prop which fires a flash charge), though by 1968 the real British Army wasn't using this weapon – having switched to the Swedish 84mm Carl Gustav recoilless gun – and the *Radio Times* for the week 2-7 November 1968 stated that this story was set in 1975 (which means *The Web of Fear* must have taken place in 1971, as the Brigadier mentions the events of that story as happening four years before).

Unlike in *The Web of Fear*, the soldiers win the battle and all the Cybermen are killed. It is also gratifying to note that in this story all the UNIT troops aim along the barrel of their rifle before firing (as is standard practice in the British

Army) and don't just shoot from the hip, as they did in *The Web of Fear*.

The Invasion was a great success, and proved to be the blueprint for many of the stories in the following Jon Pertwee era in which the Doctor teamed up with the Brigadier and UNIT to defeat an alien menace. Jon Pertwee's first season in the title role in 1970, consisting of just four stories, was very similar to the BBC's 1950s *Quatermass* serials as they were mostly set in futuristic industrial complexes and envisaged a Britain which had a space programme. As the years passed the UNIT stories became less serious, with Brigadier Lethbridge-Stewart eventually becoming a Colonel Blimp-type character.

All the same, there were a few further occasions when the producers obtained cooperation from the Ministry of Defence. *Terror of the Autons* (1971) was originally to have included a spectacular battle scene – made with the help of the Army – in which British troops, tanks and artillery fought the Autons, plastic mannequins animated by the alien Nestene consciousness. Unfortunately the deal fell through, and was replaced with a rather small-scale battle using just a few stuntmen and extras at the end of Episode 4.

However, the next story – *The Mind of Evil* (1971) – was made with the help of the Ministry of Defence. The scene where UNIT troops scale the walls of 'Stangmoor Prison' (actually Dover Castle) was performed by Royal Marines, while the Army supplied a key prop for the production: a 'Thunderbolt Nerve Gas Missile'. This was, in fact, an English Electric Thunderbird 2 surface-to-air missile supplied by the 36th Heavy Air Defence Regiment at Horsehoe Barracks, Shoeburyness, Essex. The Regiment also provided a camouflaged Bedford RL three-ton towing vehicle and a crew of eight soldiers. Some accounts state that the missile used was an RAF Bristol Bloodhound (which did look similar), but this is incorrect.

There was also some Army cooperation in the following story, *The Claws of Axos* (1971), which was filmed in the Dungeness area in early 1971. The Army supplied a long-wheelbase Land Rover and some troops for the scene in Episode 1, where a convoy of UNIT soldiers arrives to investigate the landing of an alien spacecraft. A scene in Episode 2, where the Master jumps from a bridge onto the canvas top of a moving UNIT Bedford RL truck, was filmed at a nearby Army base at St Martin's Plains Camp.

So by 1971 *Doctor Who* had benefited from Army co-operation on a number of occasions, and producer Barry Letts was keen to do a story with the Royal Navy. Letts had himself served in the Senior Service during WW2, and in his previous career as an actor had appeared in two naval epics, *San Demetrio London* (1943) and *The Cruel Sea* (1952). Incidentally, Letts once said that he got wetter making the studio scenes in *San Demetrio London* than he did in all his years in the Royal Navy!

Jon Pertwee also needed little encouragement to do a story set on the sea, as he had been in the Royal Navy himself during WW2. At one point he served on HMS *Hood*, and was transferred off the ship shortly before its battle with the *Bismarck* in 1941 – something which undoubtedly saved his life. He had a lifelong interest in boats and water-sports, and was also well-known for starring in *The Navy Lark*, a long-running BBC radio comedy. Incidentally, his predecessor as *Doctor Who* – Patrick Troughton – was a Royal Navy gunboat (MGB) captain in the English Channel during WW2, although he rarely talked about this chapter in his life.

Filming of this new, nautical-themed adventure took place in the autumn of 1971 at the Royal Navy's Fraser gunnery range near Portsmouth, plus the Isle of Wight. Some shooting also took place on the Royal Navy's specialist diving vessel HMS *Reclaim*, and much stock footage of things like depth charge attacks was provided by the Navy. The story was by prolific screenwriter Malcolm Hulke, and was effectively a sequel to his earlier work *The Silurians* (1970) in which a group of intelligent, humanoid reptiles are awoken from long-term hibernation by the activities of a new nuclear power station in Derbyshire. Believing themselves to be the original and rightful owners of Earth, they proceed with a plan to wipe out mankind with a deadly plague. Eventually the Doctor finds a cure for the disease and tricks the Silurians into returning to their hibernation units. Once they are asleep, the Brigadier blows up their caves.

The sequel, *The Sea Devils* (1972), has a similar plot. This time the Silurians' marine cousins, the Sea Devils, are woken by noisy refurbishment work that is being carried out on an old sea fort which is being converted for use as a sonar testing station by the Royal Navy. The Sea Devils attack and sink some civilian ships in the area, drawing themselves to the attention of the Doctor's old arch-enemy The Master (Roger Delgado), who is currently imprisoned in a castle on a nearby island (actually Norris Castle on the Isle of Wight).

With his hypnotic and manipulative skills, the Master persuades the prisoner's Governor, Colonel Trenchard (Clive Morton), to let him build an electronic communication device. Trenchard is led to believe that the technology will be used to expose foreign saboteurs, but in fact the Master has built the device to communicate with the Sea Devils as he wants to form an alliance with them and help them eradicate mankind and reclaim the planet Earth. Eventually the Master is rescued by the Sea Devils and taken to their underwater base, where he urges them to destroy the human race.

Unfortunately for the Master, the Doctor arrives and persuades the Sea Devils to make peace with the humans, but then – when it appears a settlement has been agreed – a bumptious civil servant, Walker (Martin Boddey), orders the Royal Navy to depth-charge the underwater base. The Sea Devils respond by imprisoning both Time Lords, and the Doctor is forced to double-cross them by sabotaging the machine which awakens them from hibernation (to be precise, he 'reverses the polarity of the neutron flow'). The Doctor and the Master escape the base in submarine escape suits (modern versions of the wartime Davis Escape Apparatus suits) just before it blows up, but the Master gets away in a stolen hovercraft before he can be recaptured.

The story had a highly unusual production design. The guards at the Master's prison wear a uniform of black berets and matching cloaks. All have long hair (as was the fashion in the early seventies) and some have droopy Mexican-style moustaches, making them look like the popular TV character, Jason King. The prison transport consists of two lightweight Citroen Dyane cars with their doors, fabric sunroof, tailgate and rear seat removed to make them look even stranger. (What do they do when it rains?)

The Citroen Dyane, incidentally, was a re-styled version of the famous 2CV. It was introduced in 1967, and was on sale in the UK when *The Sea Devils* was made. In 1974, Citroen re-introduced the original and cheaper 2CV back onto the UK market to replace the Dyane, which was still manufactured in France until 1983. Both of the Dyanes used in the production (and the guards' uniforms) featured a prison logo which appears to be a square version of the famous round Chinese 'Ying and Yang' symbol. Another oddity in the production was the 'experimental' electronic music score by Malcolm Clarke, which even today divides opinion.

The highlight of the story is a spectacular battle in Episode 6 which was broadcast on 1 April 1972. At the end of the previous episode, the Sea Devils invade the naval base and imprison the occupants. Jo Grant (Katy Manning) and Captain Hart (Edwin Richfield) manage to escape in an SR.N5 hovercraft, and later return with a squad of sailors armed with powerful 7.62mm SLR rifles. The hovercraft used in this scene was a Saunders Roe SR.N5A, serial number XT 492, which was one of four such craft used by the Interservice Hovercraft Trials Unit at the Royal Naval Air Station at Lee-on-Solent (HMS *Daedalus*).

A furious battle with the Sea Devils ensues, and Captain Hart kills several of them with a shore-mounted L40/60 40mm Bofors anti-aircraft gun of WW2 vintage. The surviving Sea Devils flee into the sea. Despite the quirkiness of the production design, and the odd music score, the serial proved extremely popular, being repeated twice on 27 December 1972 and 27 May 1974. It was eventually released on DVD in 2008.

Naval references in the James Bond films

The Royal Navy (plus the US and Soviet Navies) have also featured heavily in the series of James Bond films made by Eon Productions from 1962 onwards. In the original series of novels by Ian Fleming, some detail is given about Bond's naval career, particularly in *The Times* obituary which appears in

You Only Live Twice (1967). According to this, Bond joined the Ministry of Defence (then known as the War Office) in 1941, and was given the rank of Lieutenant in the Special Branch of the Royal Navy Volunteer Reserve (RNVR). He was then promoted to Commander, joining MI6 after the war. Thus in the novels, Bond never actually served at sea and his career matched that of his creator, Ian Fleming.

In the films, though, it is made clear that Bond had been a serving member of the Royal Navy, as evidenced by newspaper headlines in both *You Only Live Twice* and *Tomorrow Never Dies* (1997). John Gardner's 1989 Bond novel *Win, Lose or Die* takes things a stage further, as Bond returns to active service aboard the aircraft carrier HMS *Invincible* after gaining promotion to Captain.

In the films, little is revealed about Bond's previous naval career other than the fact that he had served on HMS *Ark Royal*, a fact that is mentioned in *The Spy Who Loved Me* (1977). There have in fact been several *Ark Royals*, with the most likely candidate being the *Audacious*-class aircraft carrier (R09) which was launched in 1950 and scrapped in 1979.

In *You Only Live Twice* and *The Spy Who Loved Me* Bond wears Royal Naval uniform but without any special insignia, which indicates that he is not in any specialist part of the Royal Navy. In *You Only Live Twice*, Bond is wearing ten medal ribbons in three rows, which seems a bit excessive. In *The Spy Who Loved Me* he has just one row of two medals. One of these is the purple and green General Service Medal, which is awarded for service in campaigns for which there are no specific decorations.

In *Tomorrow Never Dies*, Bond wears three rows of medals including the GSM. He also wears the Rhodesia Medal, suggesting he must have been on active service during the transition of power in Zimbabwe in 1979-80. He also wears the Distinguished Service Cross plus the Order of the British Empire (OBE), a major award which is also available to civilians.

Bond also wears a set of HALO (High Altitude Low Opening) wings on his right shoulder, suggesting that he is a former member of the SBS (Special Boat Service), a naval counterpart of the SAS.

Naval vessels in the James Bond films

Several naval vessels have appeared in the Bond movies. Towards the end of *Thunderball* (1965), HMS *Rothesay* (F107) leads the attack on antagonist Emilio Largo's vessel, the *Disco Volante*, and disables it with several rounds from its Mark 6 twin 4.5 inch gun turret. *Rothesay* was the first of the Type 12 frigate class.

In *You Only Live Twice* Bond has a traditional naval burial at sea, with his body wrapped in a sailcloth. This apparently takes place in Hong Kong, but was actually filmed in Gibraltar using HMS *Tenby* (F65), a Type 12 frigate. Incidentally, the fake newspaper obituary which appears in this scene was typeset and pasted onto a real broadsheet; this prop still exists, having been displayed at various James Bond film exhibitions.

Bond's wrapped body sinks into the depths of the ocean (to the accompaniment of some very eerie John Barry music) and is immediately recovered by two divers, who take it to a Royal Navy submarine which is lying on the seabed. This sequence was shot in the Bahamas to take advantage of the very clear water. The submarine in the background was a miniature, while a full-sized hull section was used for the scene where Bond's body is brought on board.

What is supposed to be the same submarine (with the fictitious pennant number 'M1' on the conning tower to indicate it is M's mobile office) appears at the end of the movie in the scene where it surfaces under Bond's rubber dinghy. To achieve this scene, reverse filming had to be used, so the dinghy was placed on the deck of the surfaced submarine which then dived. Once the film was reversed it looked as though the vessel had surfaced directly under the dinghy; something that would be difficult to achieve in reality, as the rubber boat would tend to slide off. The M1 submarine was played by HMS *Aeneas*, an Admiralty A-class diesel-electric boat.

The next Bond movie to feature naval operations was *The Spy Who Loved Me* (1977), which can be thought of as a big-budget remake of *You Only Live Twice* (1967). This time, instead of Ernst Stavro Blofeld capturing American and Russian spacecraft to cause a nuclear war, we had Stromberg stealing American, Russian and British nuclear submarines to bring about an atomic holocaust.

As there were extensive submarine sequences in the film, it was made with full cooperation of the Royal Navy. One sequence early in the movie shows Bond in full naval uniform arriving at the Royal Navy's Faslane submarine base in Scotland by Westland Sea King helicopter.

Three replica nuclear submarines (the HMS *Ranger*, USS *Wayne* and the *Potemkin*) were created for the film by production designer Ken Adam, though these were only 60% of the size of a real Polaris-missile armed boat for reasons of practicality. Also, the Russian submarine *Potemkin* (which is one of three captured vessels in the movie) was depicted by a replica Polaris boat, when in fact a Russian missile sub looked quite different. Additionally, the British and Russian submarines would be much larger than their American equivalent.

The film featured a large submarine dock inside a supertanker, the *Liparus,* and this required the construction of a new studio – the 007 Stage – which was opened by then-Prime Minister Harold Wilson in December 1976. The 007 Stage has been used in many other movies since then, and has burnt down and been rebuilt twice (in 1984 and 2006).

For some scenes, large miniatures of the submarines, the tanker and the dock were filmed by effects maestro Derek Meddings. Some of these were filmed in a tank at Pinewood Studios, while others were lensed in the real ocean in the Bahamas. The tanker *Liparus* was a miniature, 63 feet long, which weighed 20 tons. It was built over a catamaran hull, powered by a hidden Chevrolet V8 outboard motor, and controlled by a single crew member. Stromberg's base, the *Atlantis*, was an eight foot high miniature. The Esprit mini-submarine was a full size-craft using a genuine Lotus body-shell. However, it was actually a 'wet' vessel, controlled by two divers inside it wearing scuba gear – that is the reason the craft suddenly acquired black venetian blinds when it transformed from a car to a submarine. Two quarter-scale miniatures of this car/submarine were also built to depict the transformation of the vessel.

The Royal Navy assault ship HMS *Fearless* (L10) appears at the end of the film in the scene where it picks up the escape pod containing Bond and Anya (Barbara Bach). *Fearless* was commissioned in 1965, and was not taken out of service until 2002. Along with its sister ship HMS *Intrepid,* it played a key part in the Falklands War in 1982. *Fearless* and *Intrepid* both featured internal docks which could be used to operate landing craft and had large flight decks which could carry four Westland Wessex helicopters. They were among the last Royal Navy vessels to be powered by steam turbines, as gas turbine or diesel propulsion had become the norm for Royal Navy surface ships by the 1970s.

For Your Eyes Only (1981) featured a fictitious electronic surveillance ship called the *St Georges* which was sunk by an old WW2 mine, but the next major appearance of the Royal Navy in the Bond films was in *Tomorrow Never Dies* (1997). Curiously, the Royal Navy is never mentioned by name in the film. It is called 'the British Navy' or 'the British fleet'.

A total of three Royal Navy vessels appeared in the film, all of which were supposedly Type 23 frigates. The Type 23 *Duke* class was the standard Royal Navy frigate in the 90s (and some are still in service), and was an advance on the Type 22 which saw action in the 1982 Falklands War. Whereas the original Type 22 vessels had two six-round Seawolf missile launchers – one fore and one aft – and a back-up TV guidance mode, the Type 23 had a much more advanced vertical-launch Seawolf system which could respond much more quickly to air threats. In addition, it had more sophisticated radars and computers, and reinstated the 4.5 inch Mark 7 gun which had been absent from the first batch of Type 22 vessels.

Most of the scenes of frigates in the film were large, realistic models filmed in the large water tank at Baja Studios, Mexico, which had originally been created for James Cameron's *Titanic* (1997). Some footage of the real Type 23 vessel HMS *Somerset* operating off Plymouth was also used. For interior shots, another Type 23 – HMS *Westminster* – was used, while scenes set in the operations rooms of various frigates were filmed in a simulator at HMS *Dryad*, a training facility at Fareham in Hampshire.

Never Say Never Again (1983) was one of two non-Eon Bond films which have been made – with the other being the original, spoof version of *Casino Royale* (1967) – and was produced by Kevin McClory and Jack Schwartzman, with Sean Connery starring as 007. As described in one of my earlier books, *Dying Harder: Action Movies of the 1980s* (Extremis Publishing, 2017), the production of *Never Say Never Again* came about as a result of a 1963 court case resulting from Ian Fleming's 1961 novel *Thunderball*.

Fleming rather unwisely based his book on an aborted 1959 screenplay, *Longitude 78 West* – which was written by himself, Jack Whittingham and Kevin McClory – without first gaining permission from his co-contributors or arranging a deal about royalties.

The outcome of this case was that McClory gained the rights to *Thunderball*, and he subsequently made a deal with Albert Broccoli and Harry Saltzman to co-produce the 1965 film version. The original legal settlement stated that after ten years McClory was entitled to remake *Thunderball*. Although McClory originally hoped to make a new version entitled *Warhead* from 1975 onwards, this project faltered. Eventually media lawyer Jack Schwartzman became involved in the production, and a new Bond film called *Never Say Never Again* was made in 1983.

According to the 1963 legal settlement, McClory was permitted to make a new version of *Thunderball* from 1975 onwards, but was not allowed to produce further Bond adventures. However, anything that was in the original 1959 screenplay and 1961 novel – but was not in the 1965 film – could be used, and that included sequences involving a US

Navy submarine. In Fleming's 1961 novel, the crew of a US Navy submarine launch an underwater attack on SPECTRE frogmen using knives, while in the 1965 film a squad of divers (presumably Navy SEALs) are parachuted into the ocean from a Boeing C-97 Stratofreighter transport aircraft.

In *Never Say Never Again*, the US submarine plays an important part in the plot as it rescues Bond and Domino from the water after they have ridden their horse off the parapet of a fortress, and also attacks some Arab tribesmen on the clifftop using a missile system mounted in the conning tower. The missiles were depicted by visual effects, but represented a real surface-to-air missile system known as the SLAM (Submarine Launched Air Flight Missile) which was derived from the Short Blowpipe man-portable SAM system. The original Blowpipe weapon was used by both sides in the 1982 Falklands War, and achieved two 'kills' in that conflict (an Argentine Macchi M.B. 339 and an RAF Harrier GR.3). The manufacturer, Short of Belfast, also produced a version holding six missiles which could be installed vertically in a submarine's conning tower, enabling a sub to shoot down aircraft targets while remaining at periscope depth.

As guidance was optical, using the submarine's periscope to aim, the system was unlikely to have been successful at bringing down a fast jet but would probably have had a good chance of a hit against a hovering or slow-moving anti-submarine helicopter. The system was trialled in HMS *Aeneas* (coincidentally the same vessel which depicted M's submarine in *You Only Live Twice*) and was fitted in some Israeli submarines, but was never used in action.

No real submarine was used in *Never Say Never Again*. Shots on the surface were achieved with a matte painting and stock footage, while underwater sequences re-used footage from *Ice Station Zebra* (1968). Some Navy SEALs are involved in the final attack on Largo's underground cavern, and these supposedly came from the US submarine.

Other films influenced by the war at sea

Another action genre which nearly took over from the James Bond series in cinemagoers' affections was the *Die Hard* series of films and its many imitations. The original *Die Hard* (1988) told the story of a New York cop, John McClane (Bruce Willis), who single-handedly defeats a gang of criminals who had taken over an office block in Los Angeles. The film proved hugely popular, and spawned a series of sequels and imitations which continues to this day.

One of the more successful clones of the *Die Hard* formula was the Steven Seagal movie *Under Siege* (1992), which was directed by Andrew Davies and may be regarded as a combination of an 80s-style action movie and a WW2 naval film.

The film opens with footage of the battleship USS *Missouri* about to be decommissioned after having served in the 1991 Gulf War. This is factually correct. During WW2, the Americans launched four *Iowa*-class battleships from 1943 onwards. These thickly-armoured monsters had 16-inch guns and were the most powerful warships ever built. (The Japanese constructed two huge battleships – the *Musashi* and the *Yamato* – with 18.1 inch guns, but these achieved little in WW2, largely due to oil shortages.)

The four *Iowa*-class ships (the *Missouri*, *Wisconsin*, *New Jersey* and *Iowa*) saw much service in WW2 and were then mothballed to save money, but were subsequently reconditioned for use in the Korean and Vietnam conflicts where they provided effective naval gunfire support. After the Vietnam War they were put back into storage, but they were refurbished again after Ronald Reagan became President in 1981 and received considerable modification. On this occasion the aft turret was removed to create a large flight deck capable of operating several helicopters. In addition, the vessels were fitted with Tomahawk cruise missiles which could carry either a conventional or nuclear warhead. The WW2-vintage 20mm Oerlikon and 40mm Bofors guns were removed and replaced with four 20mm Vulcan Phalanx automatic gun turrets, which could shoot down missiles and aircraft. Both these modern weapons systems played an important role in the plot of *Under Siege*.

After the initial scene-setting, the story opens with cook Casey Ryback (Steven Seagal) making preparations for the Captain's birthday celebrations. Ryback has a dark secret as he is really a former Navy SEAL (naval Special Forces soldier) who has won many medals, but who has been demoted for insubordination (a familiar Hollywood trope). Only a few people know about his past, including Captain Adams (Patrick O'Neal).

Ryback soon comes into conflict with his sociopathic, corrupt executive officer Krill (Gary Busey), who brings up a large grolly and spits it into a huge pot of Bouillabaisse which the cook has made. (After viewing this scene you will never want to eat Bouillabaisse again!) Ryback responds by punching Krill and is promptly locked in the freezer room, guarded by Private Nash (Tom Wood).

Meanwhile, a group of terrorists posing as a rock band and led by William 'Bill' Strannix (Tommy Lee Jones) arrive on the *Missouri* by helicopter to play at the Captain's birthday celebrations. (This is similar to the plot of the 1982 movie *Who Dares Wins*, in which the People's Lobby terrorists disguise themselves as a US Air Force Band in order to gain access to the US Ambassador's residence.)

After performing at the party, the terrorists produce weapons, kill some of the ship's crew and imprison the rest in a large compartment in the forecastle of the ship. Strannix attempts to drown the crew by flooding this compartment using the ship's sprinkler system. But Ryback has heard the shots and pleads with Nash to release him. When the Private refuses, he persuades him to check out what is happening and the young soldier 'phones the bridge for advice. By this time Strannix has taken over the vessel and sends two of his best men to deal with Ryback. But the former Navy SEAL easily outwits them. He hides above the door of the freezer room and then jumps down when the two terrorists enter, locking them in. The two soldiers soon shoot their way out, but Ryback quickly kills them, arms himself with their weapons and leaves a home-made time bomb in the microwave.

Meanwhile, the terrorists continue with their plan to steal the vessel's Tomahawk Cruise missiles and sell them to the highest bidder. In this plan they are assisted by North Korea, which has sent a submarine to offload the missiles. An F-14 Hornet fighter which is sent to investigate is shot down by one of the *Missouri*'s Phalanx guns (the first time this weapon has been depicted on screen).

However, Ryback is determined to thwart Strannix's plan and, helped by glamour model Jordan Tate (Erika Eleniak), he rescues the *Missouri*'s crew from drowning and deactivates the Phalanx system, allowing a team of Navy SEALs to approach the *Missouri* in a helicopter. Just as they are about to land, their helicopter is shot down by an AIM-92 Stinger missile by one of Strannix's men. It is now up to Ryback and his friends to save the day.

The North Korean sub moves away from the *Missouri* and prepares to dive. Ryback suggests using the battleship's secondary armament of 5-inch guns to sink the vessel but learns that there is no suitable ammunition left; starshells are all that remain. The only solution is to use the Missouri's main 16-inch guns. With the help of the crew, Ryback rotates one of the main gun turrets and fires a broadside, sinking the submarine.

Ryback then kills Strannix in a knife fight, but the villain has already fired off two Tomahawk missiles towards Honolulu. One is shot down by a US fighter jet, but the other continues towards its target and at the last minute is made to self-destruct using the correct computer code. The film ends with a funeral ceremony for Captain Adams on the deck of the *Missouri*. Ryback is now wearing a full-dress white uniform with all of his decorations on view.

Although some footage of the real *Missouri* appears in the film, most of it was shot on the USS *Alabama*, a preserved *South Dakota*-class battleship which is moored at Mobile in Alabama. The nearby WW2 US submarine USS *Drum* played the part of the North Korean submarine. The *Alabama* and *Drum* have both been used in a number of film and TV productions, including *War and Remembrance* (1988).

Under Siege premiered on 9 October 1992 and was hugely successful, making almost $160 million against a budget of $35 million. It was also widely praised by critics and generally considered to be Steven Seagal's best film. It is certainly one of the finest *Die Hard* clones, and had an impact on the original series of films as a proposed *Die Hard* sequel involving John McClane battling terrorists on a cruise ship was cancelled because of the success of *Under Siege*.

A sequel, *Under Siege 2: Dark Territory*, was released in 1995. This time the action took place on a train crossing the USA. The plot involved a group of terrorists taking over a train in order to further their plans to take control of a satellite-based laser weapons system (a plot idea which has some similarities with Blofeld's space laser in the 1971 Bond movie *Diamonds Are Forever*). No further *Under Siege* movies have been made, and though Steven Seagal has continued to star in action movies these have tended to be 'straight-to-DVD' releases.

Under Siege was an example of a movie which combined the elements of a WW2 naval film and a *Die Hard*-style action adventure. Another interesting Hollywood hybrid would be the 'science-fiction naval adventure', and the most recent example would be *Battleship* (2012) which also involved the USS *Missouri*, which is now preserved as a museum ship at Pearl Harbour. In this fictitious film, which starred Liam Neeson and was directed by Peter Berg, the *Missouri* is reactivated and used to defeat an alien invasion. The real *Missouri* was used in filming, although many scenes were created by CGI.

Another more successful attempt to combine a naval action film with science fiction was *The Final Countdown* (1980), which was directed by Don Taylor and starred Kirk Douglas, Martin Sheen, Katharine Ross, James Farentino and Charles Durning.

The screenplay was by Thomas Hunter, Peter Powell, David Ambrose and Gerry Davis. Davis was no stranger to science-fiction, as he was the script editor of *Doctor Who* from 1966-67, co-creator of the Cybermen, and co-writer of the first three Cybermen stories (though he wasn't always credited as such). He also created the BBC TV series *Doomwatch* (1970-72) with Kit Pedler before moving to the USA.

The plot of *The Final Countdown* could have come from an episode of *The Twilight Zone* TV series. A US aircraft carrier, the real-life USS *Nimitz*, is on exercises near Hawaii when it encounters rough weather. Captain Yelland (Kirk Douglas) orders the escorting destroyers to return to Pearl Harbour, leaving the *Nimitz* to face the storm alone.

It soon becomes clear that this is no ordinary storm, as the crew become engulfed by a multi-coloured mist and the *Nimitz* is silhouetted against a glowing, swirling pattern of lights. The sailors don't know it, but they have entered a naturally-occurring time vortex which takes them back in time to 6 December 1941: the eve of the Japanese attack on Pearl Harbour.

If you think the time storm sequence in the film looks a bit like the titles of a James Bond film, you would be right because they were created by the same person – Maurice Binder. The shot where the *Nimitz's* hull is silhouetted against a coloured background is very similar to many of Binder's Bond title sequences.

After a few minutes the 'time storm' subsides and the *Nimitz* resumes its patrol, but it is clear things aren't right. All VHF and UHF radio transmissions have stopped, and the radio operators on *Nimitz* can only pick up old-fashioned AM radio broadcasts. The crew can hear an old Jack Benny radio show which they assume to be an archive recording. They cannot contact Pearl Harbour using the normal frequencies.

Captain Yelland wonders if a nuclear war has broken out and orders an RF-8 Crusader reconnaissance aircraft to overfly Pearl Harbour and take some photos. It returns having taken photos of vintage US battleships lying at anchor, as they were just before the attack by the Japanese on 7 December 1941.

Meanwhile, a pair of Grumman F-14 Tomcat fighters has been sent aloft to investigate a surface radar contact which turns out to be a civilian motor yacht. As the two American pilots watch from high overhead, a pair of Japanese Mitsubishi A6M Zero fighters arrive and make repeated strafing runs, forcing its occupants – Senator Samuel Chapman (Charles Durning) and his personal assistant Laurel Scott (Katharine Ross) – to take to the water in lifejackets. The two Zeroes in this scene were replicas based on North American T-6 trainers which were originally built for the film *Tora, Tora, Tora* in 1968 and were subsequently acquired by the Confederate Air Force, based at Harlingen, Texas.

The American Tomcat pilots request permission to intervene, but Yelland will only give them authority to disrupt the Zeroes' attacks without opening fire. The two jets dive down and 'mix it' with the Zeroes, spoiling their attack. Yelland doesn't want to actually shoot down the planes, but one of his bridge officers points out that the Japanese planes are getting closer to the *Nimitz* which has fuelled planes on deck. Reluctantly, Yelland gives the pilots the order to 'splash the Zeroes'. One is speedily despatched with a Sidewinder heat-seeking missile, while the second is hit by a burst of 20mm Vulcan cannon fire and crashes into the ocean. The pilot stands on the wing of his downed plane and is rescued by a US Navy Sea King helicopter.

The two rescued American civilians and the Japanese pilot are taken back to the *Nimitz*. Commander Richard T. 'Dick' Owens (James Farentino), who is the Commander of the carrier's air wing, is an amateur historian who is writing a book on the Pearl Harbour attack and recognises Senator Chapman. He was going to be President Franklin D. Roosevelt's running mate (and possible successor), but had disappeared on 6 December 1941. By rescuing him, the crew of the *Nimitz* have changed history.

Captain Yelland had initially been sceptical about what has happened, but is now convinced that the *Nimitz* really has gone back in time to the eve of the attack on Pearl Harbour. Warren Lasky (Martin Sheen), a civilian contractor who works for Tideman Industries – who designed and built the carrier – points out that they have an opportunity to change history by thwarting the Japanese attack. Yelland realises that his duty is to serve the President of the USA, even if that is now Franklin D. Roosevelt.

Yelland makes plans for all *Nimitz's* aircraft to get airborne at dawn and attack the Japanese air group. He orders Owens to land Senator Chapman and Laurel Scott by helicopter on a nearby island where they will be safe. But they can only do this by tricking the Senator into believing he is being taken to Pearl Harbour. The Senator sees through the ruse and tries to take control of the Navy Sea King helicopter using a flare pistol. A fight breaks out, the helicopter is destroyed and Chapman killed, while Scott and Owens are left stranded on the island from where they can see the Japanese air fleet approaching.

By now the *Nimitz's* entire air group has got airborne and is heading directly for the approaching Japanese strike force. This is where I have issues with the plot, as a more effective way of blunting the Japanese attack would have been to hit the six carriers *before* they could launch their aircraft, in a devastating night attack. As depicted in the movie, the American plans involve shooting down as many of the Japanese planes as possible. But even if all the F-14s managed to fire off all their missiles and every one scored a hit, only a fraction of the attacking force would be shot down – especially as many of the American planes were Grumman A-6 intruders which had no air-to-air capability whatsoever, as they did not carry Sidewinder or Sparrow missiles or cannon.

The American planes are just about to fire their missiles when the time storm reappears near the *Nimitz*. Yelland makes a snap decision and recalls the planes. The time storm envelops the carrier and it returns to 1980. Soon afterwards, the air group reappears overhead and lands back on the carrier. Everything is as it was, although Commander Owens has been left back in 1941. And Laurel Scott's dog, Charlie, is now on board the *Nimitz*.

As Lasky leaves the carrier and walks along the quayside, followed by Charlie, the door of a limousine opens and a familiar voice calls out. Charlie runs up to the car where he is reunited with his former mistress. Rather perplexed, Lasky walks up to the limousine and discovers it contains 'Richard Tideman' who is none other than Commander Owens, plus Laurel Scott who is now 'Mrs Tideman'. 'Come in, Mr Lasky; we have a lot to talk about,' says Tideman.

The Final Countdown was well-received by critics, although some felt it looked like a Navy recruiting film as it featured many scenes of life aboard an aircraft carrier. One criticism of the plot, though, was that the audience was expecting a big air battle with modern jets downing Japanese propeller-driven aircraft, but (apart from the brief dogfight involving four aircraft) it never happened. Instead, things were put back to the way they were, giving the film a *coitus interruptus* feel! Personally, I feel a more satisfying ending would have depicted the climactic air battle and then have the time storm return and 'wind time back' so that things returned to the way they were. Obviously this would have been more spectacular, but also more expensive to produce.

Some years ago it was announced that a new version of *The Final Countdown* was to be made, again featuring the USS *Nimitz* and set in the waters off Japan, but to date it has not yet appeared.

Another science-fiction film which involved time travel and the US Navy was *The Philadelphia Experiment* (1984), which was supposedly based on a real incident on 28 October 1943 when the US Navy destroyer USS *Eldridge* vanished from its moorings at Philadelphia Navy Yard and reappeared in New York. This allegedly happened because of a scientific experiment to make the vessel radar invisible (or even optically invisible) using a high-frequency current, which inadvertently caused a warp in the space-time continuum in accordance with Einstein's Unified Field Theory.

It must be said at this point that there is no real evidence that the incident actually happened. Also, the physical effects of this alleged experiment don't conform to what we know about physics. Nonetheless, it has been the basis of many fascinating books, articles, documentaries and two feature films.

The first mention of this incident came in 1955 when astronomer and UFO buff Morris K. Jessup, author of the book *The Case for the UFO*, received two letters from Carlos Miguel Allende (aka Carl M. Allen) who claimed to have witnessed a secret WW2 experiment at Philadelphia Navy Yard in 1943 in which the USS *Eldridge* was rendered invisible, teleported to New York and then to another dimension, where the crew encountered aliens and were then transported through time, resulting in the deaths of several sailors, some of whom ended up fused with the ship's hull.

This rather unbelievable story subsequently appeared in a 1963 book, *Invisible Horizons: True Mysteries of the Sea* by Vincent Gaddis. It also formed the basis for a 1978 novel *Thin Air* by George E. Simpson and Neal R. Burger in which a Naval Officer investigates wartime experiments in matter transmission, and technology to create invisibility.

The 'Philadelphia Experiment' became widely known through the publication of a 1979 book by author Charles Berlitz, who had previously written a book about the Bermuda Triangle. *The Philadelphia Experiment: Project Invisibility* purported to be a factual account, quoted Einstein's Unified Field Theory, and alleged there had been a government cover-up.

This book formed the basis of a film *The Philadelphia Experiment* (1984), which starred Michael Pare and Nancy Allen and was directed by Stewart Raffill.

The film begins in 1943. Two US Navy sailors, David Herdeg (Michael Pare) and Jim Parker (Bobby De Cicco), are assigned to the destroyer USS *Eldridge* which is involved in a project to make it invisible to radar. Unfortunately the experiment goes wrong and the two men find themselves in the middle of the desert in the year 1984.

David and Jim eventually meet a lady called Allison (Nancy Allen). The time travel process is badly affecting Jim, who starts having frequent seizures and eventually disappears from his hospital bed in a corona of energy.

David subsequently discovers that Jim is still alive in 1984, but as an old man as he had gone back to 1943 after he vanished from his hospital bed. He also finds out that a Dr Longstreet, who was involved in the original experiments in

1943, is still around and using the same technologies to create a shield against ICBM attack. Unfortunately the original 1943 experiment has created a time vortex which is sucking matter into it. The only solution is to enter the vortex, go back to 1943 and shut down the generator on the USS *Eldridge*. David volunteers to do this and, having completed the task and saved the world, he jumps over the side of the ship and is catapulted back to 1984.

In 1993 a sequel to this film, *The Philadelphia Experiment II* was made with a completely different cast. This time David Herdog was played by Brad Johnson, and the plot involved a scientist sending an American Lockheed F-117 stealth fighter back in time to 1943 Nazi Germany. As a result the Nazis bomb Washington with nuclear weapons in 1943 and win the Second World War in a new timeline.

With his ability to travel through time and space, David Herdeg finds himself in this parallel world in which the Nazis have conquered the USA. In this respect the film is a bit like the BBC production *S.S. GB* (2017) or Amazon Studios' *The Man in the High Castle* (2015-present). David realises that the solution is to travel through the time vortex and destroy the captured stealth fighter before it can carry out the mission. He achieves his goal and returns back through the time vortex to his original world, where he is reunited with his son.

Alternative histories of WW2 are a common genre in fiction, although they have rarely been turned into films because of the likely high cost. Science fiction author Harry Turtledove has written a whole series of books which present an alternative WW2 which started a year early in 1938. He has also written two books about an alternative Pacific War in which the Japanese carried out a third airstrike on Pearl Harbour and then invaded Hawaii.

There have even been a few books about further wars in the Falkland Islands and alternative histories of the Falklands Conflict. One book I particularly enjoyed reading was *The Fireflies of Port Stanley* (2014) by Marc Jones. In this alternative recounting of history, three Sherman Fireflies – upgraded versions of the Sherman tank with powerful British 17-pounder guns – plus ammunition supplies are dispatched to the Falkland Islands in the early fifties due to a clerical error. They are carefully maintained and serviced for the next three decades and then, in April 1982, these three tanks prove crucial in repelling the Argentine invasion, sinking an Argentine Type 42 destroyer, a tank landing craft and several Amtracks. This buys time for the British, who send SAS reinforcements to the islands by Hercules transport plane. The Royal Navy submarine HMS *Conqueror* also manages to sink the Argentine aircraft carrier ARA *Veinticinco de Mayo* (instead of the cruiser *Belgrano*), and Argentina eventually has to sue for peace. As I said, though, it is unlikely that any of these alternative history books will ever be filmed due to the cost.

REFERENCES

GENERAL REFERENCES

Wikipedia (www.wikipedia.org) and the Internet Movie Database (www.imdb.com) were used as a basic reference source for all films and TV series covered in this book. The book *When Eagles Dared* by Howard Hughes (I.B. Tauris, 2012) was also used as a reference source for all the WW2 movies in the book. For information about aircraft used in various British films, *Flying Film Stars* by Mark Ashley (Red Kite Books, 2014) was consulted. Another very useful tome was *The Aircraft Spotter's Film and Television Companion* by Simon D. Beck (McFarland, 2016). Two websites which were consulted about most of the films mentioned in this book were www.nzpetesmatteshot.blogspot.com (about pre-CGI special effects) and www.modelshipsinthecinema.com

Other books and publications consulted for specific chapters were as follows:

INTRODUCTION

Who Won the Battle of Britain? by Wing Commander H.R. 'Dizzy' Allen, DFC.
ISBN 978-0586042816
Harper Collins, 1976.

BATTLESHIPS: WARSHIPS IN ACTION

Battles on Screen: World War II Action Movies by Colin M. Barron
ISBN 978-0-9955897-0-4
Extremis Publishing, 2017
Chapter on *Sink the Bismarck!*

All My Flashbacks by Lewis Gilbert
ISBN 978-1904674245
Reynolds and Hearn, 2010

Cinema Retro
Vol. 10, Issue 30, 2014
Article by Howard Hughes on making of *Hell Boats*.

RAIDS FROM THE SEA

Cinema Retro
Vol. 9, Issue 25, 2013
Article on making of *Attack on the Iron Coast* by Howard Hughes.

Britain at War
Key Publishing
Issue 124, August 2017
Articles on Dieppe Raid.

OPERATION DYNAMO

Britain at War
Issue 123, July 2017
Article on Operation Dynamo and new film.

Aeroplane Magazine
Vol. 45, No. 9, September 2017
Article on *Dunkirk* film.

Aeroplane Magazine
Vol. 45, No. 10, October 2017
Article on *Dunkirk* film.

The Making of Dunkirk by James Mottram; Foreword by Christopher Nolan
ISBN: 978-1-68383-107-5
Insight Editions, 2017.

UNDERWATER SABOTAGE

Cinema Retro
Vol. 9, Issue 27, 2013
Article by Howard Hughes on making of *Submarine X-1*.

CARRIER ACTIONS

Carrier Combat by David Wragg
ISBN 978-1-84015-113-7
Sutton Publishing, 2007

Planes on Film: Ten Favourite Aviation Films by Colin M. Barron
ISBN 978-0-9934932-6-3
Extremis Publishing, 2016
Chapter on *Tora, Tora, Tora.*

Pearl Harbor: The Movie and the Moment
ISBN 978-0-7868-6780-9
Hyperion Books, 2001

B-25 Mitchell
ISBN: 9781912205073
Key Publishing Special, 2017
Article on 1942 Doolittle Raid.

Air Classics
November 1988
Article by James H. Farmer on making of aerial scenes for *War and Remembrance.*

AMPHIBIOUS OPERATIONS

Battles on Screen: World War II Action Movies by Colin M. Barron
ISBN 978-0-9955897-0-4
Extremis Publishing, 2017
Chapters on *The Longest Day* and *Saving Private Ryan.*

Movie Classics: WW2 Movies on the Sixties
Cine Retro Special Edition
Special Edition No 6, 2017

Article on Making of *Anzio*

The Hollywood Hall of Shame: The Most Expensive Flops in Movie History by Harry Medved and Michael Medved
ISBN 978-0-207-14929-1
Angus & Robertson Publishers, 1984
Chapter on *Inchon*.

ACTION IN THE SOUTH ATLANTIC

Falklands: Untold Stories of the War in The South Atlantic
Multiple authors
Key Publishing, 2012

Four Weeks in May: The Loss of HMS Coventry, a Captain's Story by David Hart-Dyke
ISBN 978-1-84354-590-3
Atlantic Books, 2007

Air War South Atlantic by Jeffrey Ethell and Alfred Price
ISBN 978-0-283-99035-X
Sidgwick and Jackson, 1983

The Royal Navy and the Falklands War by David Brown
ISBN 978-0-09-957390-3
Arrow Books, 1989

Hostile Skies by Dave Morgan
ISBN 978-0753821992
Weidenfeld & Nicholson, 2012

Watching Men Burn by Tony McNally
ISBN: 978-0955285455
Monday Books, 2007

Aircraft Magazine
May 2010
Article on 'The Man Who Sank the Coventry'.

Battle of the Falklands by Max Hastings and Simon Jenkins
ISBN 978-0393017618
WW Norton & Co Inc., 1983

OTHER GENRES

The Bond Film Informant: Bond and the Navy
www.mjnewton.demon.co.uk
Website about naval vessels in the Bond films.

APPENDIX 1

List of aircraft used in *Midway* (aka *Battle of Midway*), 1976.

Type	Civil Registration	Owner
Consolidated PBY-6A Catalina	N16KL	American Air Museum Society of San Francisco
Douglas A-24 Banshee	N15749	Naval Air Station, Pensacola, FL [Non-airworthy. Used in cockpit shots.]
Grumman FM-2 Wildcat	N6290C	Rudy Frasca, Frasca Air Museum IL
Grumman FM-2 Wildcat	N90541	Junior Burchninal, Texas Flying Legends Museum
Grumman J2F-6 Duck	N1214N	John C. Seidel, Sugar Grove IL

APPENDIX 2

List of aircraft used in *War and Remembrance* (1988)

Type	Civil Registration	Owner
Douglas SBD-5 Dauntless	N670AM	Planes of Fame
Douglas A-24B Banshee	N54532	Confederate Air Force
Grumman FM-2 Wildcat	N47201	Bob Pond, Palm Springs Air Museum
Grumman FM-2 Wildcat	N5HP	Howard Pardue, Breckinridge, Texas
'Kate' Replica	N7062C	Hugh and Mike Conley, College Park, CA
'Kate' Replica	?	?
'Zero' Replica	?	?
North American T6/SNJ	?	Ed Bowlin
North American T6/SNJ	N2996Q	Billy and Scott Birch
North American T6/SNJ	?	Chuck Clapper
North American T6/SNJ	N3406	Tom Crevasse
North American T6/SNJ	?	Dick Foote
North American T6/SNJ	N246AT	Ray Goodrich
North American T6/SNJ	?	Roy Hammett
North American T6/SNJ	N3267G	Alan Henley
North American T6/SNJ	?	Bob James

Type	Civil Registration	Owner
North American T6/SNJ	?	Dennis Marcotte
North American T6/SNJ	?	Tom Reilly
North American T6/SNJ	?	Bob Tinsley
T6/SBD Replica	?	Bruce Orriss
T6/SBD Replica	?	Bruce Orriss
T6/SBD Replica	?	Bruce Orriss
Beech T-34C Mentor (16 used)	?	US Navy
North American T-28 camera plane	?	?
Bell Jet Ranger camera plane	?	?

Notes

1) Kate replicas were originally built for *Tora, Tora, Tora* (1970) using converted Vultee BT-13 and BT-15 Valiants. They were painted to represent US Navy Douglas TBD Devastators.

2) 12 North American T6 and SNJ trainers were modified to represent Douglas SBD Dauntlesses with 1942 colours and US Navy markings and twin Browning 0.30 in machine guns in rear cockpit.

3) Three Douglas SBD Dauntless replicas based on T-6 airframes were originally constructed for the 1984 movie *Swing Shift* starring Goldie Hawn and were used in carrier deck scenes. They were built originally by Aero Associates/Aircraft mock-ups, and were supplied by Bruce Orriss.

4) 16 US Navy Beech T34C trainers were used to increase number of aircraft in formation.

INDEX

#

20,000 Leagues Under the Sea (novel) 125
2001: A Space Odyssey 58
20th Century Fox 182, 187
24 (TV series) 220
25 Days in May (book) 253
49th Parallel (1941 film) 88
633 Squadron 25, 26, 31, 37, 42, 49, 55, 57, 79, 156, 158, 161, 163, 167, 225, 262

A

'Allo! 'Allo! (TV series) 89
Abbott, L.B. 16, 269
ABC (American Broadcasting Company) 162
Above Us the Waves (1955 film) 136, 137
Above Us the Waves (book) 137
Academy Awards.27, 28, 35, 151, 156, 167, 187, 194, 195, 198, 234
Aces High (company) 212
Action in the North Atlantic 121
Acton 273
Adam, Ken 281
Adams, Jonathan 127
Admiral Schneer (ship) 120
Aeronautica Macchi (company) 250, 285
Aerospatiale (company) 225
Affleck, Ben 148, 234
Africa Shell (ship) 12
Aichi Kokuki (company) 147
Air War South Atlantic (book) 248, 250
Airbus (company) 80
Aircraft Restoration Company 80
Airline (1969 film) 206
Airline (TV series) 128, 212
Airplane! 57
Akagi (ship) 142, 147, 157
Alabama 289
Alameda Naval Air Station .. 156
Alameda Naval Base 153
Alamo, The 187
Albert, Edward 161
Aleutian Islands 92
Alexander, Harold 181
Alexandria 24, 25, 28, 129, 130
Algeciras 132, 135
All Quiet on the Western Front 38
Allen, Carl M. .... See: Allende, Carlos Miguel
Allen, Irving 47
Allen, Irwin ....
.... 16, 98, 265, 266, 268

Allen, Nancy 296
Allen, Paul................................79
Allen, Ronald............................41
Allende, Carlos Miguel.........295
Allied 263
Allied Intelligence Bureau........ 61
Allison (company) 197
Almirante Cochrane (ship) ...142
Alvis (company) 191
Amazon Studios.....................297
Ambler, Eric............................101
Ambrose, David.....................290
American Air Museum Society
 160
American Volunteer Group
 (AVG) 171
American War of Independence
125
Amiens...............................46, 137
Anderson, Gerry............ 126, 220
Anderson, Michael... 27, 68, 182, 215
Andrews, Dana........................ 91
Anka, Paul.........................75, 185
Annakin, Ken 183
Anthropoid............................... 32
Anzio (1968 film)... 178, 179, 181, 207
Anzio (book) 179
Anzio (city) 177-181
Appointment in London........163
ARA *Guerrico*.......................240
ARA *Hercules*....................... 245
ARA *Santisima Trinidad*..... 245

ARA *Veinticinco de Mayo*. 298
Arana, Tomas 233
Argentina 240, 298
Argentine Air Force 251
Argentine Navy...................... 244
Armstrong Whitworth Aircraft
 ....46, 49
Arne, Peter.................................51
Arnhem 46
Arnold, Henry H. 'Hap' 151
Arnold, Malcolm......................69
Arthur (ship)...........................136
Ascension Island 260
Ashlea (ship)..............................12
Ashley, Mark................... 73, 299
Asquith, Anthony................... 89
Associated British Picture
 Corporation 182
Atlantic Conveyor (ship) 242, 248, 251
Atonement.......................... 73, 76
Attack on the Iron Coast ..54-56, 58, 137, 158
Attenborough, Richard ....
 .... 27, 35, 55, 68
Aumack, Bob.................. 164, 165
Australia. 61-63, 117, 155, 237, 243
Avengers, The (TV series)....14, 42, 220
Avro (company) 49, 131, 135, 260

B

Bach, Barbara 282
Bacon, Lloyd............................121

Bahamas, The 280, 282
Baja Film Studios 150, 283
Baker, George 35, 36
Baker, Stanley 101
Balcon, Michael 143
Baldwin, Adam 237
Baldwin, Alec 231, 232, 234
Ballinesker 189
Balme, David 115
Band of Brothers (TV series) 198
Banks, Will 81
Bar Yotam, Reuven 40
Barnard, Aneurin 75
Baron, The (TV series) 57
Barry, John 14, 111, 139, 280
Basehart, Richard 268
Bataan 34
Battle of Britain (1969 film) ... 26, 49, 56, 70, 72, 73, 76, 81, 114, 159, 163, 177, 191, 194, 212, 258, 260
Battle of Britain (proposed remake) 86
Battle of Britain (conflict) 3, 4, 148, 203
Battle of Cisterna 180
Battle of El Alamein 5
Battle of Inchon 203
Battle of Midway 161-163, 165, 166
Battle of Midway (1976 film) .... See: *Midway* (1976 film)
Battle of Midway (conflict) .. 3, 5, 155-159, 162, 195

Battle of Midway, The (documentary) 33
Battle of San Carlos Water 251
Battle of Santa Cruz 22
Battle of Stalingrad 5
Battle of the Atlantic 6, 101, 104, 120
Battle of the Bulge ... 71, 179, 218, 260
Battle of the Denmark Strait 15, 18
Battle of the Falklands .... See: *Task Force South* (unproduced film)
Battle of the River Plate (conflict) 12
Battle of the River Plate, The (1956 film) 13
Battle of Trafalgar 203
Battle of Waterloo 203
Battle Squadron .... See: *Eagles Over London*
Battles on Screen (book) 3, 92, 191, 300
Battleship 290
Bavaria Studios 113
Baxter, Anne 91
Baxter, Jane 143
Bay of Biscay 113
Bay, Michael 148
BBC (British Broadcasting Corporation) .6, 55, 57, 58, 66, 68, 69, 84, 103, 126-128, 138,

224, 228, 229, 256, 257, 261, 269-272, 274, 275, 291, 297
BBC World Service 257
Beach, Adam 200
Beach, Edward L., Jr 95
Beatles, The (music band) 58
Beatty, Warren 37
Beckinsale, Kate 148, 157
Bedford Incident, The ... 218, 220
Beechcraft (company) 65
Beeson, Paul 42
BEF (British Expeditionary Force) 4, 68, 71, 76
Belfast 247, 250, 285
Belgian Army 260
Belgrano (ship) .... See: *General Belgrano* (ship)
Bell (company) 165, 197
Bell, Frederick 14
Belmondo, Jean-Paul 70
Belushi, James 117
Beneath the Planet of the Apes 41
Ben-Hur 196
Benn, Anthony 'Tony' Wedgwood 241
Benny, Jack 291
Benson, James 137
Berg, Peter 290
Bergen 145
Berlin 210, 211
Berlin Airlift 212
Berlitz, Charles 296
Bermuda 52

Bermuda Triangle 296
Bernstein, Elmer 75
Big Pick-Up, The (book) 68
Big Picture, The: Who Killed Hollywood? (book) 195
Bigelow, Kathryn 236
Biggin Hill Heritage Hangar ... 80
Bikel, Theodore 98
Binder, Maurice 291
Bishop, Ed 220
Bismarck (ship) ....
.... 12, 15, 17, 18, 146, 275
Bisset, Jacqueline 205, 206, 207
Black Hawk Down 187
Black, Ian Stuart 269
Blackburn Aircraft (company)
.... 145, 242
Blair, Anthony 'Tony' Charles Linton 119, 239
Blake, Robert 38
Blue Angels (flight team) 164
Blue Max, The .. 74, 163, 186, 189
Boat, The .... See: *Das Boot*
Boddey, Martin 277
Boeing (company) 28, 88, 123, 214, 285
Bofors (company) 11, 20, 22, 33, 103, 162, 248, 278, 287
Bogarde, Dirk 45
Bogart, Humphrey 92, 121
Bonaparte, Napoleon 126, 127
Bond, Ward 93
Bonzo, Hector 244
Bordeaux 50, 61

Borehamwood 56, 57, 79, 138, 221
Borgnine, Ernest 99, 220
Borneo 64
Boston Boatyard 190
Bourne Identity, The 193
Bovington 191
Bowie Organisation, The 58
Bowie, Les 58, 139
Bowler, Norman 138
Bowmanville Break, The (book) 104
Bradford, J.S. 68
Bradford, Jesse 200
Bradley, James 200
Branagh, Kenneth 75, 138
Brandauer, Klaus Maria 231
Brando, Marlon 262
Brass Target 211
Bratt, Benjamin 65
Braveheart 107, 189
Brazil 259, 260
Breen, Robert L. 37
Brewster (company) 20
Bricusse, Leslie 14
Bridge Too Far, A (1976 film) .. 45, 46, 76, 139, 182, 190, 191, 194, 195, 258-260, 262
Bridge Too Far, A (book) 182
Bridges at Toko-Ri, The (1954 film) 166, 167
Bridges at Toko-Ri, The (book) 166, 167
Bridges, Lloyd 56, 58, 173

Bristol (city) 92
Bristol (company) . 5, 80, 145, 275
British Aerospace 131, 193, 242
British Army 69, 71, 105, 210, 229, 270-274
British Rail 65
Broccoli, Albert R. ... 47, 135, 284
Brody, Adrien 198
Brooks, Clive 119
Brown, Jim 220
Brown, Peter 37
Browning (company) 5, 33, 45, 145, 153, 163, 192, 197, 214
Browning, Frederick 45
Brubaker, Donald S. 167
Bruckheimer, Jerry ... 148, 170, 235
Bruneval 44-49
Bruneval Raid 44
Bryce, Ivor 134
Buchheim, Lothar-Gunther 113
Bulganin, Nikolai 133
Bulgaria 210
Bulkeley, John D. 34
Bullitt 108, 206
Bungo Straits 95, 96
Burger, Neal R. 296
Burma 188
Burnett, W.R. 91
Burns, Edward 193
Burton, Donald 229
Burton, Richard 185
Busey, Gary 287
Bushell, David 125
Bushido (warrior code) ... 92, 199

Byrnes, Edd 37

C

Caan, James 138, 139
Cabanatuan 65
Cage, Nicolas............................. 30
Caio Dullo (ship) 146
Calabria....................................177
California 31, 83, 84, 147, 149, 153, 155, 156, 161, 188, 200, 201
California (magazine) 170
Callaghan, James 230
Calvert, James F......................266
Camber Sands.................... 69, 70
Cambridge 78
Cameron, David......................137
Cameron, James...............150, 283
Canada 48, 69, 89, 104, 236
Canberra (ship)...............241, 259
Cannon for Cordoba................ 58
Captain Horatio Hornblower.....
....15
Captain Scarlet and the Mysterons (TV series)... 126, 220
Carey, Walter............................64
Carite (submarine) 111
Carve Her Name with Pride. 16, 48
Casablanca........................28, 121
Case for the UFO, The (book) 295
Cash, Jim................................. 170
Casino Royale (1967 film) 284

Castellari, Enzo G. 71, 73
Castor (ship) 78
Catto, Max......................108, 109
Cawdron, Robert....................127
Cerwin-Vega (company) 162
Chadwick, Roy 131, 135
Chakiris, George 262
Chamberlain, Neville 89
Champion, John C. 57, 137
Chandon, John 36
Chapman, Edward..................120
Chatham 77
Chechnya................................ 235
Chevrolet (company) 282
Chicago 81, 201
Chichester............................... 133
Chile....................................243, 259
China..152, 154, 202, 203, 212-214, 217
Chindits (Long Range Penetration Groups) 258
Chinese Air Force 152, 214
Chino 149
Choctaw Field.................165, 166
Choiseul....................................38
Chomat, Gilbert......................186
Christ, Jesus........................... 204
Churchill, Winston.. 4, 18, 43, 52, 59, 60, 144, 178, 181, 209, 210
CIA (Central Intelligence Agency)........ 99, 127, 231, 232
Cinemascope..........17, 51, 99, 196
Clancy, Tom.............168, 230, 231
Clark, Mark W....... 179, 180, 181

Clarke, Malcolm 278
Clarkson, Jeremy 58
Clear and Present Danger 234
Clement (ship) 12
Clements, John 120, 143
Cleopatra 187
Clinton, Bill (William Jefferson) 30
Clooney, George 198
CND (Campaign for Nuclear Disarmament) 261
Coburn, Anthony 228
Cockleshell Heroes, The ... 50, 61
Cold War 3, 168, 208-214, 220, 228, 230-235, 265, 268
Coletti, Duilio 94, 179
Collins, Joan 14
Collins, Leon 227
Collins, Lewis 230, 252, 253
Columbia Pictures 92
Columbo (TV series) 180
Comanche Fighters 78
Commemorative Air Force 82
Communist Peoples Liberation Army (PLA) 215-217
Computer Generated Imagery (CGI) .. 31, 32, 74, 86, 149, 173, 198, 201, 208, 232, 260, 290, 299
Confederate Air Force (CAF) 164, 292
Connery, Sean .. 47, 123, 185, 224, 228-232, 284

Consolidated Aviation (company) 31, 119, 131, 160
Conte di Cavour (ship) 146
Convair (company) 217
Convoy (1941 film) 119
Convoy (TV series) 123
Coonts, Stephen 168, 169
Cooper, Gary 98
Cordell, Frank 42
Cornell, Ivan 74
Cornwall 190
Coronation Street (TV series) 24
Corpus Christi 157
Corregidor 34
Corsica 183, 186
Courtney, Nicholas 271
Covent Garden 271
Coward, Noel 23-28, 67
Crabb, Lionel 'Buster' 129-136
Craig, H.A.L. 179
Crash Dive 90
Crete 23-25, 175
Crewdson, John 225
Crimson Tide 235
Crombie, Donald 63
Crossroads (TV series) 41
Cruel Sea, The (1952 film) .. 6, 35, 100, 104, 120, 275
Cruel Sea, The (book) 101
Cruickshank, Andrew 103
Cruise, Tom 150, 170-173
Csokas, Marton 65
Cuba 172

Culver City..................................156
Cumbria 104
Curteis, Ian............................... 256
Curtiss (company) ...26, 148, 159, 161
Curtiz, Michael....................... 121
Cushing, Peter............................41
Czechoslovakia 192, 210

D

D'Arcy, James 75
Dad's Army (TV series)..........41
Dafoe, Willem 168
Dahl, John................................. 65
Daimler-Benz (company)..........80
Dale, James Badge 198
Daleks: Invasion Earth 2150AD 41
Daley, Ray 196
Dalyell, Thomas 'Tam'.. 241, 244
Dambusters (proposed remake) 86
Dambusters, The... 27, 37, 49, 57, 74, 215
Damon, Matt 193
Dane, Eric 237
Danger Man (TV series)..... 120, 221
Danger Route........................... 58
Danish Navy 160
Dark Blue World...................... 91
Darren, James 58, 262
Das Boot (1980 film)........ 112, 113
Das Boot (book) 113

Davenport, Dean..................... 155
Davies, Andrew...................... 286
Davies, Jeremy........................193
Davies, Robin 190
Davies, Rupert 138
Davis, Gerry 269, 290
Davis, Robert 130
Dawson, Anthony 206
Day of the Triffids, The (1963 film) 236
Day the Earth Stood Still, The 95
D-Day Landings ...21, 78, 91, 176, 182, 184, 187, 195
D-Day: Sixth of June (1956 film) 60, 182
De Cicco, Bobby 296
De Laurentiis, Dino 115, 179
De Laurentiis, Martha 115
Dearden, Basil 35
Deep, The...............................206
Delgado, Roger 126, 276
Delon, Nathalie...................... 227
Denham Studios....................... 26
Denmark Strait................... 12, 18
Denver 168
Derbyshire 276
Dern, Bruce 167
Destination Tokyo.................. 92
Destroyer (unproduced film).86, 253, 255, 256
Devon...25
Diamonds Are Forever.123, 220, 228, 290

Die Hard..
.... 168, 230, 266, 286, 289, 290
Dieppe 56, 58, 60
Dieppe Raid.............................177
Diesel, Vin................................193
Dion, Celine.............................150
Dirty Dozen, The............. 57, 220
Dirty Harry film series 167
Dive Bomber....................159, 160
Dixon, Jeane............................204
Dmytryk, Edward.................. 179
Doctor Who (TV series). 27, 41, 42, 55, 84, 120, 126-128, 138, 215, 229, 269-275, 290
Doctor Zhivago...................27, 70
Dogfights (documentary series) 201
Donald, James............................55
Donovan Robert J.................... 37
Donovan, Jason 63
Doohan, James.........................123
Doolittle Raid..... 92, 93, 148, 154, 157
Doolittle, James 92, 149-157
Doomwatch (TV series)........ 291
Doppelganger 225
Doric Star (ship) 12
Dornier Flugzeugwerke (company) 180
Dorset...191
Douglas Aviation (company) 152, 160-165, 169, 170, 197, 206, 212
Douglas, Kirk..................290, 291

Dove, Patrick.............................13
Dover 43, 274
Dr Finlay's Casebook (TV series)................................... 103
Dr No........................47, 204, 206
Dr Strangelove, or How I Learned to Stop Worrying and Love the Bomb..........217
Dracula......................................51
Drewitch, Edmund...................38
Dubai................................... 259
Dudley-Smith, Trevor 68
Duffy, Patrick............................31
Dullea, Keir 196
Duncan, Donald D. 151, 152
Dunkirk....4, 27, 43, 67, 69-71, 73-78, 81-86, 175, 202
Dunkirk (1958 film) 68, 74, 76
Dunkirk (2017 film) 70, 73, 74, 84, 85, 138
Dunkirk (play) 68
Durante, Jimmy...................... 205
Durning, Charles 290, 292
Dutch Army........................... 260
Duxford................. 25, 78, 80, 84
Dwan, Allan............................ 199
Dyce, Hamilton.......................127
Dye, Dale 193
Dying Harder: Action Movies of the 1980s (book)... 134, 252, 284
Dynasty (TV series) 162
Dysart, William.......................138

E

Eagle Has Landed, The 78
Eagles Over London 71, 73, 81
Ealing Studios 35, 119, 143
Earthquake 162
EastEnders (TV series) 272
Eastwood, Clint 200, 201, 223
Edge of Darkness (TV series)
 256
Edwards, Anthony 171
Edwards, R.A.B. 17
Eglin 152, 153
Eglin Field 156
Einstein, Albert 295, 296
Eisenhower, Dwight D ... 179, 210
Elco (company) 33, 35, 38
Eleniak, Erika 288
Ellis, Bruce 165
Elmes, Guy 138
Elstree Studios 134, 182
Embalse De Santillana 196
Enemy Below, The (1957 film)
 .... 97, 98, 121
Enemy Below, The (book) 97
Enigma (code system) ....
 .... 40, 60, 115, 116, 119
Enola Gay (aircraft) 31
Enola Gay: The Men and the Mission 31
Eon Productions 47, 278, 284
Epps, Jack, Jr. 170
Escape to Nowhere 188
Escher, M.C. 84
Ethell, Jeffrey 248, 250

Everett, Chad 37
Exmouth Gulf 61, 62

F

Fabian (singer) 75, 185
Fail Safe 217
Fairchild (company) 80
Fairey Aviation Company .. 5, 16, 18, 109, 143, 144, 146, 242
Falk, Peter 180
Falkland Island Defence Forces (FIDF) 240
Falkland Islands 3, 7, 13, 20, 65, 66, 86, 143, 230, 239, 240-263, 282-285, 298
Falklands Play, The (TV drama) 256, 257
Falklands War ....
 ...... 3, 7, 11, 20, 65, 66, 86, 176, 239-263, 282-285, 298
Fallon 172
Falls Lake 83
Falmouth 53
Fareham 284
Farentino, James 290, 292
Faslane 281
Fearnley, Edward 217
Felixstowe 217
Fell, Norman 38
Ferguson, Larry 231
Ferguson, Michael 127, 270
Ferrer, José 50
Ferzetti, Gabrielle 206
Few, The (unproduced film) . 171

Fiat (company) 117
Fields, W.C. 205
Fiennes, Joseph 65
Fighter Squadron 188
Fighting Lady, The
  (documentary) 159
Fighting Sullivans, The ....
  .... See: *The Sullivans* (1944
  film)
Film Flight Ltd. 225, 227
Final Countdown, The ... 290-295
Final Flight, The (book) 168
Finch, Peter 14
Find, Fix and Strike
  (documentary) 143
Fireflies of Port Stanley, The
  (book) 298
Firefox 223
Firth, Colin 255, 256
Firth, Peter 232
Fisz, Benjamin 258
Fitzgerald, Walter 51
Fitzroy 251
Flags of Our Fathers (2006 film)
  .... 84, 197, 200, 201
Flags of Our Fathers (book) . 200
Fleischer, Richard 147
Fleming, Ian ....
  40, 60, 134, 278, 279, 284, 285
Flight of the Intruder (1991
  film) 168
Flight of the Intruder (book) 168
Flight of the Phoenix (1965 film)
  .... 68, 110

Flight of the Phoenix (2004 film)
  68
Flight of the Phoenix (book) .. 68
Florida 35, 38, 152, 156, 161, 165,
  176
Florida Keys 35, 38
Flying Film Stars (book) 73
Flying Heritage Collection ....
  .... 80, 82
Flying Leathernecks, The 159
Flynn, Errol 160
FMA (Fabrica Militar de
  Aviones) 65
Foch (ship) 236
Focke-Wulf (company) 59, 117,
  122
Folland Aircraft (company) .. 173
Follett, James 252
Fonda, Henry 33, 160, 217
Fontaine, Joan 267
For Your Eyes Only 283
Forbidden Planet 267
Ford, Glenn 99, 160
Ford, Harrison .. 193, 231, 234, 236
Ford, John 33, 35, 158, 159
Forester, C.S. 15
Formosa .... See Taiwan
Forsyth, Frederick 66
Fort Lauderdale 35
Fort Manoel 42
Fort St Rocco 42
Foster, Barry 14

France... 4, 5, 9, 36, 59, 60, 67-70, 76, 106, 112, 122, 125, 127, 142, 149, 178, 183, 186, 187, 277
Francen, Victor............... 122, 213
Franciscus, James.................39, 41
Franco, James............................ 65
French Army.....................183, 185
French Connection, The.......204
French Navy..................... 70, 236
Frend, Charles................100, 120
Freyburg, Bernard.................... 23
Friedkin, Dan............................78
Friedkin, Tom.........................165
From Here to Eternity 147
From Russia with Love.. 47, 204, 225
Frost, John 46, 49
Fuchida, Mitsuo.......................147
Fugitive, The (TV series).....206
Fukasaku, Kinji........................147
Full Metal Jacket 170
Fuller, Samuel..........................212
Fulton, Robert.................. 125-128

G

Gable, Clark............................. 95
Gaddis, Vincent 296
Gallipoli..................................... 43
Gallison, Joseph 39
Galtieri, Leopoldo 240, 262
Garden Island 63
Gardner, Arthur......................105
Gardner, Ava 237
Garner, James 100

Gary, Romain.......................... 183
Gavin, James............................185
Gavin, John.............................. 123
Gazzara, Ben 205
GB Helicopters (company) 81
General Belgrano (ship) .243-245, 298
Geneva Convention................. 50
Genn, Leo 49
Germany .. 9, 12, 13, 23, 32, 51, 67, 87, 94, 122, 141, 142, 178, 183, 209-213, 258, 297
Gestapo (*Geheime Staatspolizei*)
.... 51
Gibraltar 130-132, 136, 244, 280
Gibson, Mel.....................189, 193
Gidget film series 58
Gift Horse............................ 54, 55
Gilbert, Lewis.............. 15, 16, 300
Glamorgan 127, 259
Glasgow 56, 101
Glenn, Scott..................... 232, 233
Glory Boys, The (TV drama)
....128, 262
Gloster Aircraft Company.....144
Glover, Danny....................... 169
Godfrey, Derek.......................229
Godzilla (1955 film)................ 266
Goldberg, Adam 193
Golden Gate Bridge 155
Golden Raspberry Awards.... 151
Goldeneye................................191
Goldfinger (1964 film).....14, 107, 194

Goldfinger (song) 14
Goldman, William...................195
Goldsmith, Jerry......................206
Good Life (TV network)......204
Goodwin, Ron....................57, 139
Goose Green 250, 257
Gorbachev, Mikhail............... 232
Gordon, Mark 188
Gotell, Walter 57, 90
Grade, Michael....................... 256
Graf Spee (book).......................13
Graf Spee (ship) 12, 13, 14
Graf Zeppelin (ship)................142
Graham, Walter 137
Grand Prix (1966 film) 100
Grant, Cary 92
Gray Lady Down................... 223
Great Escape, The........................
..........................55, 75, 100, 158
Great Raid, The....................... 65
Great Train Robbery, The ... 108
Great White ....
................See: *Last Shark, The*
Greatest Raid of All Time, The
  (documentary) 58
Greatorex, Wilfrid 212
Greece................................ 23, 175
Green Berets, The.................. 204
Greening, Ross 154
Greenland 218
Greenstreet, Sydney........ 121, 122
Gregory, James 38
Gregory, Tom..........................165
Gregson, John..........................14

Griem, Helmut 105
Griffon Merlin (blog)...............85
Grist, Paul...............................127
Gruffudd, Ioan 15
Grumman (company) 31, 108-110,
  158-163, 167-170, 292, 294
Guadalcanal ....
 .... 38, 155, 188, 195, 198, 199
Guam..................................29, 199
Guiry, Tom..............................119
Guns of Navarone, The....37, 57,
  58, 107, 192, 262
Guns of the Magnificent Seven
....58

H

Hackman, Gene....................... 235
Haig, Alexander..................... 205
Haisman, Mervyn.................. 270
Halifax (Canadian city)..........236
Hallam, John........................... 109
Halsey, William, Jr..................161
Hamburg...................................113
Hamilton, Guy 73
Hammer Films.........................58
Hampshire 51, 284
Hancock, Prentis.................... 224
Hanks, Tom.............................193
Hanover Street........................ 26
Hardin, Ty................................38
Hardy, Laurence 50
Hardy, Tom...............................75
Hari Karier (aircraft)..............154
Harlingen................................292

Harris, Charles 'Bucky' 38
Hart-Dyke, David 253-256
Hartnell, William 27, 215, 269
Hartnett, Josh 148
Harwood, Henry 14
Hashimoto, Mochitsura 29
Haskin, Byron 121
Hasler, Herbert G. 'Blondie' .. 50, 51
Hatfield 193
Havers, Nigel 258
Hawaii 97, 146-149, 169, 200, 291, 298
Hawker Aircraft Ltd 210
Hawkins, Jack 101
Hawn, Goldie 165
Healey, Denis 241
Heatherden Hall ....
.... See: Pinewood House
Hedison, Al ....
.... See: Hedison, David
Hedison, David 98, 99, 268
Hei Ho (ship) 64
Heinkel (company) ... 81, 114, 121, 145, 177
Hell and High Water 212, 213
Hell Boats 39, 158, 300
Heller, John G. 41
Henderson Field 195, 197
Hendon 81
Hendry, Ian 105
Herbert, Percy 51
Heroes 2: The Return (TV series) 63, 64

Heroes of Telemark, The 69, 191
Heroes, The (TV series) .. 63, 64
Hershey, Barbara 41
Heston (town) 25
Heston, Charlton 161, 162
Heydrich, Reinhard 32
High Noon 221
Hill, Faith 150
Hillary, Richard 258
Hines, Frazer 270
Hinton, Steve 78, 164, 165
Hiroshima 6, 28, 266
Hiryu (ship) 142, 157
Hispano (company) 72, 78, 80, 149
Hitler, Adolf ....
.... 36, 50, 59, 87, 94, 178
HMAS *Derwent* 229
HMAS *Nepal* 26
HMCS *Leamington* 55
HMCS *Terra Nova* 236
HMCSO *Jibwa* 236
HMNZS *Achilles* 13
HMS *Achilles* 14
HMS *Aeneas* 281, 285
HMS *Ajax* 13, 14
HMS *Amethyst* 215, 216
HMS *Andrew* 230
HMS *Antelope* 251, 259
HMS *Antrim* 247, 259
HMS *Ardent* 242, 251, 259
HMS *Argus* 141
HMS *Ark Royal.* 15, 18, 129, 143, 230, 241, 242, 279

HMS *Aubretia* 115
HMS *Barham* 129
HMS *Basilisk* 78
HMS *Bedouin* 44
HMS *Belfast* 15, 84
HMS *Berkeley* 59
HMS *Blake* 230
HMS *Brilliant* 246, 255, 259
HMS *Britomart* 77
HMS *Broadsword* . 246, 253, 254, 259
HMS *Bulldog* 115
HMS *Bulwark* 230, 243
HMS *Campbeltown* 52-55
HMS *Cavalier* 77
HMS *Concord* 216, 217
HMS *Conqueror* ... 243, 244, 298
HMS *Consort* 216, 217
HMS *Coreopsis* 103
HMS *Coventry* 86, 251-255
HMS *Coventry* Association .. 255
HMS *Cumberland* 14
HMS *Daedalus* 278
HMS *Danae* 229
HMS *Dido* 229
HMS *Diomede* 229
HMS *Dryad* 284
HMS *Eagle* 142
HMS *Edinburgh* 255, 259
HMS *Endurance* 240, 243
HMS *Engadine* 141
HMS *Eskimo* 44
HMS *Essex* 216
HMS *Exeter* 13, 14

HMS *Express* 141
HMS *Fearless* 247, 259, 282
HMS *Furious* 10, 141
HMS *Ganges* 217
HMS *Glamorgan* 247
HMS *Glasgow* 255
HMS *Glorious* 11
HMS *Graph* 111
HMS *Havant* 77
HMS *Hermes* ... 65, 142, 241, 242, 247, 259, 260
HMS *Hermione* 229
HMS *Hood* 12, 14, 18, 275
HMS *Illustrious* 146, 241
HMS *Indomitable* 19
HMS *Intrepid* 247, 248, 259, 282
HMS *Invincible* 143, 242, 243, 259, 279
HMS *Jaguar* 77
HMS *Jamaica* 14
HMS *Juno* 229
HMS *Jupiter* 229
HMS *Kelly* 23, 24, 26
HMS *King George V* 18
HMS *Leamington* 55
HMS *Legion* 44
HMS *Magpie* 216
HMS *Medusa* 78
HMS *Nelson* 10, 11
HMS *Phoebe* 229, 230
HMS *Plymouth* 247
HMS *Porpoise* 63
HMS *Prince of Wales*. 10, 14, 18, 19, 20, 26, 210

HMS *Princess Beatrix*............. 44
HMS *Queen Elizabeth*.... 10, 129
HMS *Queen Emma*................. 44
HMS *Reclaim* 276
HMS *Repulse*............. 19, 20, 210
HMS *Riviera*........................... 141
HMS *Rodney*...........10, 11, 19, 21
HMS *Rothesay* 280
HMS *Salisbury*........................ 243
HMS *Sheffield*.. 14, 245, 246, 251
HMS *Somali*............................ 44
HMS *Somerset*........................ 283
HMS *Sultan* 230
HMS *Tartar*............................. 44
HMS *Teazer* 217
HMS *Tenby*........................... 280
HMS *Thetis*.................... 221, 222
HMS *Trourbridge*.................. 219
HMS *Tuna*.......................... 50, 51
HMS Ulysses (book).................. 6
HMS *Valiant*......................... 129
HMS *Vanguard*..................11, 15
HMS *Vanquisher*.................... 77
HMS *Victorious*................. 15, 18
HMS *Vivacious*....................... 77
HMS *Wakeful*....................... 219
HMS *Westminster* 283
HMS *Yarmouth*............. 245, 247
HNLMS *Naaldwijk* 77
HNLMS *Sittard* 77
Hodge, Patricia....................... 256
Hodgson, Brian........................ 84
Holden, William............. 166, 167
Holgate, Frank....................... 164

Holland, James 85
Holliman, Earl................. 167, 181
Hollywood Hall of Shame, The: The Most Expensive Flops in Movie History (book) 207
Holy Loch 252
Hong Kong 229, 280
Hopkins, Anthony... 46, 223, 224
Horch (company)................... 190
Hornblower (novel cycle)........ 15
Hornblower (TV series)........... 15
Hosho (ship)............................142
Hosking, Craig 81, 165
Hot Shots.................................173
Hotchkiss (company).............. 183
Howard, John.........................185
Howard, Trevor 51, 54
Hudson, Rock........................ 220
Huelva Beach 71
Hulke, Malcolm 276
Hungary..................................210
Hunt for Red October, The (1990 film)........... 168, 230-234
Hunt for Red October, The (book) 168, 231
Hunt, Rex............................... 256
Hunter, Ewan 68
Hunter, Jeffrey 37
Hunter, Thomas 290
Huntsman (ship)......................12
Hutton, Robert 93

I

I Bombed Pearl Harbour........159

I Was Graf Spee's Prisoner (book) 13
I-58 (submarine) 29, 30
Ice Station Zebra (1968 film) 220-222, 267, 286
Ice Station Zebra (book) 220, 267
Iceland 201
Ijsselmeer Lake 83
Ile De Re 186
IMAX (film format) .. 73, 78, 79, 82
Imperial War Museum..... 15, 184
In Which We Serve 23-25, 28, 67, 89
Inchon (1981 film) 203-208
Inchon (town) 202, 207, 208
India 61, 188
Indian Navy...................... 14, 259
Indian Ocean 12
Indiana Jones film series 162
INS *Delhi* (ship) 14
Interservice Hovercraft Trials Unit................................... 278
Inverness........................... 78, 138
Invisible Horizons: True Mysteries of the Sea (book) 296
Ipcress File, The..................41, 57
Ireland 104-107, 186, 189, 203
Irish Army.............................. 189
Iron Eagle film series.............. 170
Isaacs, Anthony 229
Ishii, Mitsuharu 204
Isle of Bute..............................120
Isle of Wight...........................276
Italian Navy 129
Italy 9, 21, 32, 94, 115, 142, 177-180, 203
ITC (Incorporated Television Company) 41, 57, 111
ITV (Independent Television) 15, 41, 49, 85
Iwo Jima............................199-201

J

Jack Ryan film series....... 231, 234
Jack Ryan: Shadow Recruit...234
Jackson, Gordon 120
Jackson, Pat 120
Jackson, Peter 86
James Bond film series .14, 16, 47, 57-60, 94, 99, 123, 134, 187, 191, 220-224, 228, 267, 278-280, 284-286, 291
James, Robert 126
Janson, Horst...........................108
Janssen, David 205, 206
Japan.... 6, 9, 88, 94, 142, 147, 151-157, 199, 201, 202, 213, 214, 295
Japanese Air Force 154
Japanese Navy........................... 11
Jarre, Jean Michel..................... 70
Jarre, Maurice 70
Jason Bourne film series..........193
Jason King (TV series) 277
Jaws......................................30, 73

Jayston, Michael 68, 224
Jendrich, Johnny 185
Jessup, Morris K. 295
Johnson, Brad 168, 297
Johnson, Lamont 104
Johnson, Van 72, 155
Jonathan Livingston Seagull
   (1973 film) 41
Jones, James 183
Jones, James Earl 232
Jones, Marc 298
Jones, R.V. 45, 50
Jones, Tommy Lee 287
Journey to the Stars 24
Judd, Edward 111, 112
Junkers (company) ... 23-25, 35, 81,
   117, 139, 142-145
Jurgens, Curt 97
Justice, James Robertson 111

K

K-19 (submarine) 236
K-19: The Widowmaker 236
K-77 (submarine) 236
Kafjord 136
Kahn, Karen 205
Kai-shek, Chiang 215
Kalkara 42
Kastner, Elliott 224, 228
Keach, Stacy 30
Keeghan, Barry 75
Keir, Andrew 57
Keith, Brian 105
Kelly, Grace 166

Kelly, Robert 34
Kelly's Heroes .. 42, 191, 192, 196,
   260
Kennedy, Arthur 179
Kennedy, John F. 36-39
Kennedy, Joseph 37
Kent 49, 69
Kerans, John 215-217
Kesselring, Albert 180
Ketapang 64
Key Biscayne 35
Key West 35, 38
Keyes, Sir Roger 43
KGB (Komitet Gosudarstvennoy
   Bezopasnosti) 57, 213
Kiel Canal 90
Kilmer, Val 172
King, Ernest J. 151
Kjellin, Alf 223
Klimov (aircraft engine design
   bureau) 211
Kobe 154
Kofuku Maru (ship) 61
Kokubo, Christina 161
Konigsberg (ship) 145
Korea 214
Korean War ....
   .... 161, 166-180, 201, 211
Kosinski, Joseph 173
Krait (ship) 61, 62
Kriegsmarine (German Navy) ....
   .... 4, 53, 78, 88, 104
Kriezis (ship) 103
Kruschev, Nikita 133

Kubrick, Stanley......................217
Kuribayashi, Tadamichi........ 201

L

La Ferte Alais......................... 106
La Rochelle........................112-114
La Spezia 114
Ladd, Alan............................... 48
Laker Airways 212
Laker, Freddie 212
Lamonby, Steve............... 189-192
Lancaster, Burt.......................... 95
Land of the Giants (TV series)
.... 265
Lane Victory (ship). 84, 197, 201
Langsdorff, Hans.............12, 13, 14
Larch, John 123
Las Vegas................................ 166
Last Enemy, The (book) 258
Last Escape, The......................158
Last Nine Days of the Bismarck, The (book) 15
Last Shark, The....................... 73
Last Ship, The (TV series)... 236
Lawrence of Arabia............27, 70
Lawrence, Robert 256
Lawson, Ted............................ 155
Le Havre................................... 44
Le Mesurier, John......................14
Lean, David 27
Lee, Bernard 55, 68
Lee, Christopher 51
Leech, Richard 215
Lee-on-Solent.................... 81, 278

Lelystad......................................81
Letters from Iwo Jima 201
Letts, Barry......................120, 275
Levy, Jules V............................105
Levy, Raoul 182
Leyton, Johnny.........................75
Libeccio (ship)........................146
Licence to Kill.....................48, 99
Lincoln, Henry 270
Lipstick...................................105
Little Palm Island......................38
Littorio (ship) 146
Live and Let Die.............. 99, 123
Liverpool.................................221
Lloyd, Euan 252, 261
Lloyd, Innes............................269
Lloyd, Sue............................ 41, 57
Loch Fyne................................. 46
Lockheed (company) 29, 89, 152, 159, 272, 297
Lofoten Islands......................... 44
Loire 77
Lombok Strait 62
London 15, 56, 69, 72, 84, 91, 137, 184, 212, 220, 252, 266, 269-273
London Underground 270
Long Beach 161
Longest Day, The (1962 film) ....
... 37, 75, 182, 185-187, 196, 207
Longest Day, The (book).......182
Longitude 78 West (screenplay)
...............................134, 136, 284
Lorre, Peter 267

Los Angeles .48, 83, 156, 161, 201, 286
Lost in Space (TV series) 16, 265, 268
Lotus Cars (company) 282
Low, Francis 151
Lowden, Jack 75
Lucas, John P. 179
Lucas, Leighton 215
Luftwaffe (German Air Force) .. .3-5, 24, 25, 72, 75, 90, 121, 148
Luna Cinema 69
Luzon 65
LWT (London Weekend Television) 65, 230, 258
Lydecker, Howard 16, 269
Lydecker, Theodore 16
Lyon, Ivan 61, 63, 64

M

MacArthur, Douglas 34, 202-208
MacArthur, James 218
MacGreevey, Oliver 225
Mackintosh, Ian 228
MacLean, Alistair 6, 220, 222, 223, 228, 267
MacNee, Patrick 14
Maddern, Victor 51
Madoc, Philip 41
Madrid 196
Magnum Force 167
Mahaddie, Hamish 49
Maibaum, Richard 48

Maigret (TV series) 138
Maille-Breze (ship) 77
Majon-ni 166
Major, John 189
Malaya 19, 210
Maleme 23, 24
Malick, Terrence 196
Maloney, John 164, 165
Malta ... 5, 14, 39, 42, 48, 115, 212, 255
Malta Film Facilities.. 42, 111, 255
Malta Story, The 48
Malvern 249
Man From UNCLE, The (TV series) 56
Man From UNCLE, The (2015 film) 260
Man in the High Castle, The (TV series) 297
Man Who Hunted Himself, The (TV series) 42, 229
Manchuria 214
Mandela, Nelson 261
Manhattan Project 213
Manning, Katy 278
Manoel Island 42
Mantz, Paul 110
Manzanares El Real 196
March, Frederic 166
Marianas Islands 199
Marianas Trench 267
Marines Let's Go 37
Markstein, George 252
Marooned 41

Marsden, Roy 212, 228
Marshall, Bryan 229
Martin (company) 152
Martin, Andrea 100
Martin, Derek 272
Martinson, Leslie H 38
Marton, Andrew 183, 196
Massey, Raymond 89, 121
Masuda, Toshio 147
Matter of Life and Death, A ... 13
Matthews, Francis 126
Maverick (TV series) 100
Maxwell, Lois 94
Mayo, Archie 91
Mazzello, Joe 198
McCallum, David 56
McClory, Kevin 134, 135, 284
McConaughey, Matthew 116
McDonnell (company) ... 167, 170
McDonnell-Douglas (company)
 242
McGillis, Kelly 171
McGoohan, Patrick 220, 221
McKenzie Break, The ... 104, 189, 260
McKenzie, Compton 54
McLellan Field 153
McNally, Tony 249, 250
McQueen, Steve 108, 266
McRae, John 127
McTiernan, John 168, 230
McVay, Charles B 29, 30
Meddings, Derek 282
Medley, Ralph 14

Medved, Harry 207
Medved, Michael 207
Memphis Belle ... 76, 170, 171, 191
Merapas 63, 64
Merville 81
Message to Marseille ....
 ...... See: *Passage to Marseilles*
Messerschmitt (company) 70, 72, 79, 80, 138, 142, 149, 184, 198
Metrocolor 99
Mexico .. 82, 150, 156, 161-165, 283
MGM (Metro-Goldwyn-
 Meyer) 56, 57, 79, 138, 155, 156, 221, 267
MGM Studios 56, 57, 138, 221
MI6 (UK Secret Intelligence
 Service) 132, 133, 279
Miami 35
Michener, James 166, 167
Microsoft (company) 79
Middlesbrough 73
Middlesex 57
Midway (1976 film) . 33, 148, 158-163
Midway Island 155, 159
Mifune, Toshiro 205
Mighty Eighth, The (TV series)
 199
Mikell, George 57
Mikumu (ship) 157
Milestone, Lewis 37
Milius, John 168, 232
Millar, Ronald 90
Mills, Hayley 70

Mills, John. 27, 68-71, 74, 89, 90, 129, 136
Mills, Keith............................. 240
Mines Field.............................. 156
Minogue, Kylie........................ 63
Mirimar 171
Mirisch Corporation 39, 55-58, 158, 162
Mirisch, Marvin 55
Mirisch, Walter 55, 158
Mirish, Harold 55
Mission of the Shark: The Saga of the USS Indianapolis 30
Mitchum, Robert 97, 161, 180
Mitra, Rhona 237
Mitscher, Mark 154
Mitsubishi (company) 19, 292
Mobile (city) 289
Moby Dick (book) 95, 218
Modine, Matthew 170
Molotov-Ribbentrop Pact 209
Monsarrat, Nicholas 35, 101
Montevideo 13, 14
Montgomery, Robert 33, 35
Moon, Sun Myung 204
Moore, Robin 204
Moore, Roger 41, 57, 99, 123, 228, 267
More, Kenneth 17, 37
Morgan, Dave 254
Morley, Angela 228
Morley, Robert 227
Morris, Philip 272
Morton, Clive 276

Moscow 217
Mosquito Squadron ... 25, 42, 46, 56, 91, 137, 138, 158, 161, 163, 182
Mostow, Jonathan 115
Mount Suribachi 200
Mountbatten, Louis 23-26, 45, 59
Mrs Miniver 67, 89
Mucci, Henry 65
Murika (ship) 64
Murmansk 121
Murphy, Cillian 75
Murphy's War (1971 film) ... 107, 108, 111
Murphy's War (book) ... 108, 109
Musashi (ship) 11, 286
Museum of Science and Industry (Chicago) 81
Mustika (ship) 64
Muszala, John 165, 166
Mutiny on The Bounty 262
My Heart Will Go On 150
Mystery Submarine 111

N

Nagasaki 6, 266
Nagato (ship) 148
Nagoya 154
Naismith, Laurence 17
Nakajima (company) 147
Nanking 215
Nantes 77
Nassau 135

NATO (North Atlantic Treaty Organisation) 218
Nautilus (submarine) 125, 126
Naval Institute Arm 168
Naval Intelligence Division 60
Navarre Beach Pier 166
Navy Lark, The (radio series) 275
Neeson, Liam 208, 236, 290
Neighbours (TV series) 63
Neill, Sam 233
Nelson, Horatio 126, 127
Netherlands, The 81, 83
Neufeld, Mace 168, 231
Nevada 172
Never Say Never Again 135, 223, 231, 284, 285
Nevertheless: A Memoir (book) 231
Neville, Paul 229
New South Island 61
New York City 181, 217, 267, 286, 295
New York Times, The (newspaper) 181
New Zealand 23, 200
Newhaven 44
Newley, Anthony 14, 51
Newman, Paul 266
Newton Beach (ship) 12
Nielsen, Connie 65
Nigeria 272
Night Bombers (documentary) 49

Niland Brothers, The 188
Nimitz, Chester W 33, 160
Nitto Maru (ship) 153
Niven, David 13, 37
Nixon, Richard 169
NKVD (Narodnyy Komissariat Vnutrennikh Del) 213
Nobody Does It Better (book) 226
Noiret, Phillipe 109
Nolan, Christopher 70, 74/79, 85, 86
Nolbandov, Sergei 143
Nolte, Nick 198
Nord (company) 70, 184
Nordholz 141
Norman, Barry 68
Norman, Leslie 68, 74, 100
Norman, Mike 256
Normandie (ship) 51
Normandy 182, 187, 188
North American Aviation (company) 38, 72, 114, 147, 152, 155, 160, 163, 170, 188, 199, 206, 292
North Korea ... 166, 202, 203, 288
North River Steamboat of Clermonts (ship) 126
North Weald 212
North, Edmund H. 15, 17, 138
Norton, William V 104
Norway 27, 44, 136, 138
Norwegian Navy 44

Nothing Lasts Forever (book) 266
Nott, John 242, 243
NTSC (National Television System Committee) 268

O

O'Brien, Edmond 100
O'Keefe, David 60
O'Neal, Patrick 287
O'Toole, Peter 108, 109
Oakland 156
Oakmont Productions .39, 42, 55, 56, 57, 137, 158, 161, 207
Objective Burma 195
Oerlikon Contraves (company) 11, 21, 22, 26, 53, 120, 162, 248, 287
Olivier, Laurence 89, 205
Omaha Beach 21, 183, 186, 187, 188, 189, 190, 193, 194, 195
On Her Majesty's Secret Service 206, 225, 228
On the Beach (1959 film) 237
On the Beach (book) 237
On, Ley 89
One Direction (band) 75
One Man's Falklands (book) 244
One Million Years BC 58
One-Way Productions 203
Ontario 104
Opel (company) 190
Operation Algeciras 244
Operation Avalanche 177

Operation Baytown 177
Operation Biting 44, 45
Operation Chariot 51
Operation Chromite (2015 film) 207, 208
Operation Claymore 44
Operation Collar 43, 44
Operation Crossbow (1965 film) 27, 41, 48, 76, 262
Operation Daybreak (1975 film) 32
Operation Dynamo 43, 67, 68, 70-78
Operation for Special Services (OSS) 62
Operation Frankton 50, 61
Operation Hornball 63
Operation Husky 176, 177
Operation Jaywick 61-64
Operation Jericho 46, 137
Operation Jubilee 56-61, 177
Operation Judgement 146
Operation Market Garden 45, 262
Operation Mercury 23
Operation Overlord 182, 187
Operation Pacific (1951 film) .. 93
Operation Pedestal 5
Operation Rimau 63
Operation Rosario 240
Operation Roundup 59
Operation Ruthless 40
Operation Rutter 59
Operation Sealion 4, 177

Operation Slapstick 177
Operation Source.............136, 137
Operation Title.......................136
Operation Torch...... 132, 133, 177
Operation Victory...................94
Orange Beach 31
Ordzhonikidze (ship)............... 133
Oreston 190
Orinoco River 108-111
Orkney Islands 145
Orriss, Bruce................ 1, 165, 166
OSS 117: Double Agent..........123
Ostend.....................................184
Oswald, Gerd 183
Ouistreham.............................. 186
Owen, Bill...................................35
Owen, Philip 99

P

Pacific, The (TV series) 198
Pakistan....................82, 259, 260
Palm Springs................... 190, 307
Palos Verdes............................. 83
Panavision................................. 39
Paramount Pictures 231, 232
Paratrooper....................................
...............See: *Red Beret, The*
Pardue, Howard..............164, 165
Pare, Michael 296
Parker, Nathaniel..................... 65
Parker, Sir Peter....................... 65
Pas-De-Calais........................... 43
Passage to Marseilles....... 121, 122
Pathfinders (TV series)..........49

Patriot Games.........................234
Patton (1970 film).....81, 195, 260
Patton, George S....179, 205, 210, 211
Paul Temple (TV series).......126
Paula Bintan 64
Paxton, Bill 116
Payne, Laurence.......................111
Pearl...148
Pearl Harbor (2001 film).91, 148-151, 156, 182, 187
Pearl Harbour (location)...34, 50, 92-100, 146-151, 290-293, 298
Pearl Harbour Raid........ 146, 148
Pebble Island 65, 66, 253, 254
Pebble Island Raid................... 66
Peck, Bob 256
Peck, Gregory...... 15, 37, 237, 262
Pedjantan Island...................... 64
Pedler, Kit............... 269, 272, 291
Peel, David 90
Pegasus (TV series) 128
Pegasus Bridge........................185
Penn, Sean 198
Pensacola....................161-166, 305
Peppard, George 262
Pepper, Barry 193
Percival (company)................ 106
Perfect Hero (TV series).......258
Perier, Etienne 224
Perkins, Anthony 262
Perry, Joyce 138
Persuaders, The (TV series)..111
Pertwee, Jon.... 126, 127, 274, 275

Pessagno (ship) 146
Petersen, Wolfgang 112
Pevney, Joseph 99
Philadelphia Experiment II, The 297
Philadelphia Experiment, The 295, 296
Philadelphia Experiment, The: Project Invisibility (book) 296
Philadelphia Navy Yard 295
Philby, Kim 132
Philippines 32-34, 65, 94, 99
Phillipe, Ryan 200
Phillips, Sian 109
Phoenix (city) 188
Pickard, Percy Charles 'Pick' .. 46
Picture Letters from Commander in Chief (book) 201
Pidgeon, Walter 266
Piece of Cake, A 65
Pilsey Island 133
Pine, Chris 234
Pinewood House 224
Pinewood Studios .14, 17, 49, 111, 224, 225, 282
Pinter, Harold 68
Piper (company) 81
Pistilli, Luigi 72
Pitt, Brad 263
Pitts (company) 173
Planes of Fame Museum 149, 164

Planes on Film (book) 3, 148
Planet Hollywood (company) 166
Plummer, Christopher 73
Plus Film Services (company) 189
Plymouth 27, 190, 283
Poitier, Sidney 218
Poland 209, 210
Polish Free Army 131
Port Rashid 259
Port San Carlos 246
Port Stanley 240, 251, 255, 256
Port-en-Bessin 186
Portman, Eric 89, 90, 218
Portsmouth 15, 51, 133, 276
Portugal 51
Poseidon Adventure, The 265
Post Office Tower 270
Potsdam Conference 212
Pound, Dudley 17
Powell, Dick 97
Powell, Michael 13, 88
Powell, Peter 290
Power, Tyrone 91
Powers, Ron 200
Prague 32
Pratt & Whitney (company) 149
Predator 168, 230
Presley, Elvis 204
Pressburger, Emeric 13, 88
Price, Alfred 248, 250
Prince Eugen (ship) 18
Prince, William 93

Princess O'Rourke 28
Prisoner, The (TV series) ... 120, 221
Professionals, The (TV series) 230
Psycho 123
PT Raiders ....
.... See: *Ship That Died of Shame, The*
PT-109: John F. Kennedy in World War II (book) 36
PT-109 (1963 film) 36, 37
PT-109 (ship) 38, 39
PT-59 (ship) 39
Puttnam, David 170
Pyle, Ernie 180

Q

Quaid, Dennis 68
Quatermass (TV series) 274
Quayle, Anthony 14, 37
Queen Elizabeth II (QE2) (ship) 241, 259
Quiller (TV series) 68, 224
Quiller Memorandum, The 68
Quiller novel cycle 68
Quinn, Anthony 37, 262

R

Rachmil, Lewis J. 42
Radar Research Institute 249
RAF (Royal Air Force) ... 3-5, 20, 23-26, 43, 46-49, 52, 53, 57, 60, 65, 72, 81, 85, 88, 131-133, 144, 145, 148, 149, 173, 184, 198, 210, 217, 225, 242, 244, 258-260, 272, 275, 285
RAF Abingdon 48
RAF Bomber Command 5, 52
RAF Bovingdon 225
RAF Chivenor 25
RAF Enemy Aircraft Flight ... 25
RAF Fairford 272
RAF Gibraltar 244
RAF Museum 81
RAF Waddington 49
Raffill, Stewart 296
Raiders of the Last Ark 113
Raikes, Dick 50
Rains, Claude 121
Rambo: First Blood Part II 42
Ramsgate 43
Rattigan, Terence 24
Rayner, Denys 97
Reach for the Sky 16, 37, 74
Reagan, Ronald 261, 262, 287
Red Beret, The 47, 48, 50
Red Dawn 168
Redcar 73
Redgrave, Corin 225
Reed, Donna 33, 34
Reese, Sammy 39
Reisner, Dean 113
Relph, Michael 35
Republic Pictures 16, 200
Revell (company) 39
Revlis (ship) 78
Reynolds, Bill 61

Rhine Crossings 176
Rhys, Paul................................. 63
Ribisi, Giovanni......................193
Richards, C.M. Pennington... 111
Richardson, Ian 256
Richfield, Edwin 278
Ridgely, John............................92
Rigg, Diana 42
Rio De Janeiro........................ 244
Ritchie, C.R............................... 38
River Clyde 101, 120
River Elbe 210
River Orwell 217
River Plate.................................13
River Solent............................ 133
River Stour..............................217
RKO Studios 37
RMS *Queen Mary*....................51
RN......... See: Royal Navy (RN)
RNAS Hatston........................145
RNVR (Royal Naval Volunteer Reserve)....40, 136, 279
Robbery 108
Robertson, Cliff 37, 262
Robinson, Patrick....................231
Robson, Mark 166
Rodat, Robert 188
Roddenberry, Gene.................98
Roeves, Maurice 226
Rogaland (ship)........................78
Rolls-Royce (company) 4, 80, 81, 131, 144, 184, 211
Rome 178-181

Rommel, Erwin...........5, 178, 179
Rooney, Mickey..............166, 167
Roosevelt, Franklin D. 37, 52, 59, 151, 155, 188, 210, 293
Rose, Pat.................................. 133
Rose, Reginald 252
Ross, Katharine..............290, 292
Rothesay...................................120
Rouen.......................................125
Rouen, Reed De......................126
Roundtree, Richard....... 205, 206
Royal Air Force..See: Royal Air Force (RAF)
Royal Australian Navy.197, 229
Royal Canadian Air Force......89
Royal Canadian Navy...... 55, 104
Royal Marines 50, 190, 229, 240, 256, 274
Royal Navy (RN) 4, 5, 10-28, 40, 45, 50-59, 67, 69, 76, 77, 82, 85, 91, 94, 97, 101, 103, 106-111, 116, 120, 125, 126, 129-138, 141-146, 175, 215-221, 224-231, 240-249, 253, 259, 260, 275-283, 298
Run Silent, Run Deep............. 95
Ruptured Duck (aircraft) 155
Russell, William 55, 126
Russia.... 6, 47, 67, 204, 209, 210, 212, 235
Ryan, Cornelius 182
Ryan, Robert................... 180, 185
Ryan's Daughter...................... 27
Rylance, Mark 75

S

S.S. GB (TV series)...............297
S-270 (ship).............................236
Sacramento 153
Sagona (ship)...........................129
Sahara (1943 film)............92, 187
Sahara (1995 film)....................117
Saint, The (TV series)..............41
Saipan...199
Salerno 177
Saltzman, Harry........47, 135, 284
Salvation Army....................... 237
Samdong-ni 166
San Carlos......................... 251, 253
San Demetrio (ship) 120
San Demetrio London 120, 275
San Diego.................148, 170, 237
San Francisco. 28, 92, 93, 153-156, 160, 167, 305
Sand Pebbles, The.................... 95
Sandbaggers, The (TV series)
....................................128, 228
Sanders, Tom........................... 189
Sands of Iwo Jima, The.........199
Sanford, Donald 138, 161
Santoni, Reni............................181
SAS (Special Air Service) ....
................65, 66, 252, 280, 298
Savile, David.....................42, 229
Saving Private Ryan....................
................82, 187, 192-198, 201
SBS (Special Boat Service)....253, 280
Scapa Flow..................................9

Scharnhorst (ship).....................51
Schindler's List........................186
Scholl, Art................................173
Schumann, Gerard....................57
Schwartzman, Jack................. 284
Schwarzenegger, Arnold........144
Scotland ...105, 107, 138, 190, 224, 252, 253, 281
Scott, Ridley...................... 86, 170
Scott, Tony.......150, 170, 172, 235
Scully, Terry.............................127
Sea Around Us, The.............. 265
Seagal, Steven...................286-290
Seda, Jon 198
Segal, George............................ 68
Sellers, Peter.............................217
Sensurround 162
Seoul... 202
Shaw, Robert 30
Shawcraft Models (company).16
Sheen, Charlie..........................173
Sheen, Martin................290, 293
Shell Oil Company 152
Shepherd, Elizabeth................. 42
Shepperton Studios.................218
Sherwin, Derrick.................... 272
Ship That Died of Shame, The
....35, 36
Shipley, Ed................................. 78
Ships with Wings............143, 146
Short (company)....217, 247, 250, 285
Shotley Gate 217
Shute, Nevil 237

Sicily 40, 176-179
Sikorski, Wladyslaw 131, 132
Sikorsky (company) 167, 169, 219, 227
Silent Enemy, The 129, 134-136
Silent Running 167
Silliphant, Stirling 108
Simmons, Bob 47, 224, 226
Simon & Schuster (company) 182
Simpson, Don 170, 235
Simpson, Dudley 128
Simpson, George E. 296
Sinden, Donald 101
Singapore 20, 61-64, 210, 217, 229
Sink the Bismarck! 14-17, 109, 138, 300
Sir Galahad (ship) 250, 251
Sir Percival (ship) 250
Sir Tristram (ship) 251
Sizemore, Tom 193
Skarsgard, Stellan 233
Skoda (company) 189, 192
Sky Harbor Airport 188
Smight, Jack 158
Softly, Softly (TV series) 138
Softly, Softly: Task Force (TV series) 57
Soldiers (documentary) 66
Soryu (ship) 157
Sound of Music, The 95
South Africa 20, 261
South Georgia (island) 240

South Korea 202-208
Southsea 51
Soviet Air Force 210
Soviet Navy 134, 278
Spain 196
Spanish Air Force 81
Spanish Army 71
Sparks, Bill 50, 51
Spartacus 123
Special Operations Executive (SOE) 62
Spectre 187
Spielberg, Arnold 188
Spielberg, Steven 162, 188-192
Spooks (TV series) 228
Spruance, Raymond A. 160
Spy Who Loved Me, The ... 229, 267, 279, 281
Square Sail (company) 190
St Austell 190
St Martin's Plains 275
St Nazaire 51-58
St Nazaire Raid 137
Stafford, Frederick 71
Stagecoach (1939 film) 33
Stalin, Josef .. 59, 131, 152, 209-214
Stalingrad 6
Stallone, Sylvester 144
Standard, Robert 204
Star Trek (TV series) 98, 123
Star Trek: The Motion Picture 95
Star Wars 17
Star Wars film series 162

Stears, John 16
Steiner, Max 121
Sterling, Robert 267
Stewart, Donald 231
Stewart, James 68
Stock, Nigel 221
Stockwell, John 171
Stokes Bay 133
Stott, Walter .... See Morley, Angela
Straits of Gibraltar 114
Stratton, John 101
Strauss, Robert 166
Streonshalh (ship) 12
Sturges, John 220
Styles, Harry 75
Submarine Attack 94
Submarine Raider 179
Submarine X-1 .... 137-139, 158
Sud-Aviation (company) 186
Suez Operation 216
Sullivans, The (1944 film) 188
Sum of All Fears, The 234
Superman (1978 film) 58
Superman film series 162
Supermarine (company) 184
Survivors (TV series) 236
Sutherland, Donald 220
Sutherland, Kiefer 220
Swanage 83
Sweden 136
Swerling, Jo 91
Swing Shift 165, 166

T

Tablada 72
Tairoa (ship) 12
Taiwan 215
Tallman, Frank 109, 110
Tallmantz Aviation 110
Tamiroff, Akim 216
Tank Museum (company) 191
Tanner, Peter 101
Tarantino, Quentin 73
Taranto 146, 177
Tarantula 266
Tarawa 200
Target for Tonight 46
Task Force (1949 film) 158
Task Force South (unproduced film) 252, 253
Taylor, Robert 60, 182
Technicolor 90, 120, 194
Teddington Lock 69
Temora Aviation Museum .. 197
Tennyson, Pen 119
Terminal Island Naval Air Base 161
Texas 157, 201, 292
Thatcher, Margaret 239, 243, 244, 256, 260
Them (1954 film) 266
There You'll Be 150
They Were Expendable 33
Thin Air (book) 296
Thin Red Line, The (1964 film) 196

Thin Red Line, The (1998 film) 84, 196, 198, 201
Thin Red Line, The (book) .. 196
Thirty Seconds Over Tokyo.. 92, 155, 158
Thirty Seconds Over Tokyo (book) 155
Thom, Leonard G. 38
Thomas Jefferson (ship) 190
Thomas, Emma 74, 79
Thompson (company) 192
Thorne, Ken 111
Thorpe, Roderick 266
Thousand Plane Raid, The 158
Thunderball (1965 film) .... .47, 134-136, 204, 223-227, 280, 284
Thunderball (book) 134, 285
Thursday Island 61
Tibbs, Paul 31
Tidepool (ship) 243
Time Tunnel, The (TV series) 265
Times, The (newspaper) 278
Tinian 28, 199
Tiomkin, Dimitri 221
Tiptoe Boys, The (book) 252
Tirpitz (ship) 12, 51, 136, 137
Titanic 150, 283
Todd, Richard 37, 60, 182, 185, 215, 216
Tokyo 92, 93, 99, 154, 156, 213, 266
Tokyo Rose (announcer) 96

Tomkins, Alan 191
Tomorrow Never Dies..150, 279, 283
Tomorrow People, The (TV series) 85
Tondern 141
Top Gun 150, 170-173, 231, 235
Top Gun: Maverick 173
Tora, Tora, Tora 16, 32, 147-150, 159-166, 292
Torbay 226
Torpedo Run 99
Tower Bridge 15, 69
Towering Inferno, The 266
Tracy, Spencer 155
Trento (ship) 146
Trevanion (ship) 12
Trevor, Elleston .... *See* Dudley-Smith, Trevor
Triton (TV series) 126-128
Troughton, Patrick 269, 270, 275
Truman, Harry S. 203, 212, 213
Trumbull, Douglas 167
Tucker, Rex 126
Tumbledown (TV series) 256
Tung, Mao Tse 215
Tupolev (company) 214, 222
Turkey 104, 107
Turkish Navy 107, 260
Turtledove, Harry 297
Twickenham Studios 111
Twilight Zone, The (TV series) 291

U

U-110 (submarine) 115
U-570 (submarine) 111
U-571 (2000 film) 88, 98, 111, 115-119, 179
UFO (TV series) 220
Uganda (ship) 241
Under Siege 31, 286-290
Under Siege 2: Dark Territory 290
Ungentlemanly Act, An (TV drama) 256
Unification Church 204
Unified Field Theory 295, 296
Union of Soviet Socialist Republics (USSR) 152, 154, 198, 203, 209, 213, 218, 234, 236
United Artists (company) 139
United Nations (UN) .. 201, 202, 267, 272
Universal Studios 73, 83, 162
Up Periscope (1959 film) 100
Up Periscope (book) 100
Urquhart, Robert 217
Uruguay 13
US Air Force Band 288
US Army .. 148-152, 184, 185, 205, 232
US Army Air Force (USAAF) 195
US Army Rangers 59, 180, 185
US Marine Corps 91, 164, 183, 193-199, 220-222, 232

US Navy ... 5, 11, 14, 21, 22, 29-31, 35, 38, 50-55, 88, 91-95, 98, 100, 102, 107, 115-119, 123, 135, 142, 146, 148-152, 155, 157, 161-169, 172, 173, 184, 195-199, 219, 231-235, 252, 285, 292-296
US Navy SEALs 135, 285-288
USAAF (United States Army Air Force) 38, 149, 152, 155, 188, 199, 214
USS *Alabama* 30, 235, 236, 289
USS *Antietam* 158
USS *Arizona* 147, 150
USS *Barbel* 236
USS *Buchanan* 52
USS *Constellation* 157
USS *Dallas* 231-233
USS *Decatur* 236
USS *Drum* 30, 289
USS *Eldridge* 295-297
USS *England* 102
USS *Enterprise* 153, 171, 172
USS *Essex* 167
USS *Florida* 235
USS *Hammann* 157
USS *Hornet* 152-156
USS *Houston* 231
USS *Independence* 169
USS *Indianapolis* 28-30
USS Indianapolis: Men of Courage 30
USS *Iowa* 286
USS *Juneau* 188
USS *Jupiter* 142

USS *Langley* 142
USS *Lexington* 157-164
USS *Louisville* 231
USS *Missouri* 286-290
USS *Nashville* 153
USS *Nautilus* 266
USS *New Jersey* 286
USS *Nimitz* 291-295
USS *Northampton* 165
USS *Oklahoma* 147
USS *Oriskany* 167
USS *Redfish* 96
USS *Salem* 14
USS *Saufley* 38
USS *Savo Island* 166
USS *Skate* 266
USS *South Dakota* 22
USS *Stark* 246
USS *Tilefish* 111
USS *Twiggs* 55
USS *Utah* 147
USS *Valley Forge* 167
USS *Whitehurst* 97
USS *Wisconsin* 286
USS *Yorktown* 148, 157-161

V

Valetta 14, 42
Valiant, The 129
Valley of Gwangi, The 41
Vandervoort, Benjamin 185
Vaughan-Thomas, Wynford 179
Veevers, Wally 129, 132
Venezuela 108, 111

Venezuelan Navy 111
Ventnor 81
Verne, Jules 125, 265
Verneuil, Henri 70
Versailles 9
Versailles Treaty 9, 12
Vickers (company) 26, 48
Vietnam War 111, 168-170, 287
Vikrant (ship) 259
Vintage by Hemingway
    (company) 70
VistaVision 14
Vladivostok 154
Von Ryan's Express 75
Vought (company) 160, 170
*Voyage to the Bottom of the
    Sea* (1961 film) 265, 266
*Voyage to the Bottom of the
    Sea* (TV series) ... 16, 98, 265,
    268
Vultee Aircraft (company) ..147,
    160, 163

W

Wakefield, James 190
Wales 127
Walking Dead, The (TV series)
    236
Wallace, William 107
Wallenstein, Jake 180
Walsh, Raoul 37, 121
Walsh, Terry 271

War and Remembrance (TV series)......1, 3, 31, 160-162, 289, 307
War in the Air, The (TV documentary)......................69
War Lover, The......................220
Warden, Jack........................... 196
Warhead (unproduced film). 284
Warner Brothers (company). 83, 92
Warren, C.E.T.........................137
Warriors Inc. (company).........193
Warship (TV series)...... 42, 228, 229
Warwick Films................... 47, 50
Washington DC........ 91, 147, 193
Washington Treaty........... 9, 142
Washington, Denzel................235
Washington, George................ 10
Watching Men Burn (book).249
Watling, Deborah 270
Watling, Jack...........................270
Watson, Harold........................154
Watson, Jack...............................14
Way Ahead, The...................... 24
Wayne, John.. 33, 34, 93, 144, 185, 199, 200
We Dive at Dawn.....................89
Weekend at Dunkirk................70
Wehrmacht (German Army) 76, 192
Wendkos, Paul 39, 55, 58
Wentworth, Chuck 165, 166
West Malling............................49

West Side Story....................... 95
West, Alan.............................. 242
Western Approaches..............120
Westland (company)....... 65, 219, 225-229, 281-283
Weston, Simon........................251
Weybridge...............................206
Weymouth.................................83
When Eight Bells Toll....223, 224
When Time Ran Out............ 265
Where Eagles Dare.... 41, 76, 224
Whicker, Alan 181
Whicker's War (book) 181
Whirling Dervish (aircraft)...154
White, Robb........................... 100
White, William L...................... 33
Whitehead, Fionn.....................75
Whiting, John............................35
Whittingham, Jack...........134, 284
Who Dares Wins.........................
.... 48, 56, 225, 252, 261, 288
Wicki, Bernhard...................... 183
Widmark, Richard...212, 213, 218
Wild Geese, The.............. 48, 261
Williams, John................. 161, 192
Willis (company) 190
Willis, Bruce........................... 286
Wilson, Harold....................... 282
Wilton, Robb 90
Win, Lose or Die (book).......279
Winds of War, The (TV series)
....162
Wing and a Prayer..................158
Wingate, Orde Charles..........258

Winkast Productions 223
Wise, Robert 95
Wood, Tom 287
Woodason Aircraft Models.... 25
Woodward, John Forster
 'Sandy' 251
World Backgrounds (company)
71
Wouk, Herman 162
Wright, Joe 73
Wyler, William 67
Wynter, Dana..............18, 60, 182

Y

Yakolev (company).................. 79
Yalu River 202
Yamamoto, Isoroku................. 155
Yamato (ship)....................11, 286
Yangtse Incident, The.....27, 215, 216
Yangtse River................. 215, 217
Yates, Peter 107
Yellow Submarine.................... 58
Yeovilton 109, 145
Yokohama................................154
Yokosuka 154
Yonay, Ehud............................170
Yordan, Merlyn..................... 196
York, Susannah 73
Yorkshire Television (company)
 ....128, 212, 228
You Only Live Twice (1967
 film) ..186, 194, 220, 279, 280, 281, 285
You Only Live Twice (radio
 adaptation)........................ 224
Young, Terence........ 47, 204, 207
YouTube...........................66, 204

Z

Zanuck, Darryl F. 182, 183
Z-Cars (TV series)....57, 128, 138
Zedong, Mao..... See Tung, Mao Tse
Zeebrugge...................................43
Zeppelin..................................186
Zero Hour..................................57
Zguchik (ship)...........................55
Zimmer, Hans 74, 84
Zuiderzee 83

ILLUSTRATIONS

(From the private photographic collection of Colin M. Barron.)

The *Town*-class cruiser HMS *Belfast* was used in the filming of *Sink the Bismarck!* in 1959. It is now preserved as a tourist attraction by the Imperial War Museum, near Tower Bridge on the Thames.

(Image Credit: Pixabay.)

Alternative view of the *Town*-class light cruiser HMS *Belfast*, commissioned by the Royal Navy on 5 August 1939 and now permanently moored as a museum ship on London's River Thames.

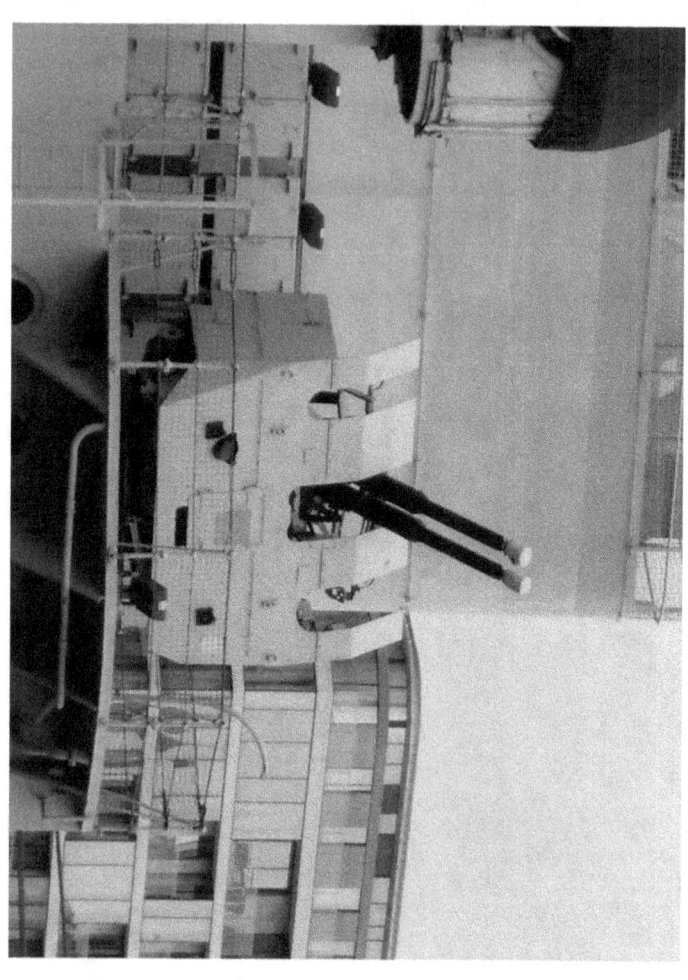

(From the private photographic collection of Colin M. Barron.)

A powered twin Bofors 40mm gun mounting on HMS *Belfast*. This Swedish-designed weapon was built under licence in the UK and USA.

(Image Credit: Pixabay.)

Armaments on the deck of the USS *Missouri* (BB-63), a United States Navy *Iowa*-class battleship. *Missouri* was the last battleship to be commissioned by the United States (on 11 June 1944), and found its place in history as the site of the surrender of the Empire of Japan which brought an end to World War II.

(Image Credit: Pixabay.)

The Fairey Swordfish, a biplane torpedo bomber designed by the Fairey Aviation Company. Operated by the Royal Navy and Royal Air Force, the Swordfish was introduced in 1936 and retired in 1945. This particular aircraft, LS326, was used in the filming of *Sink the Bismarck!* in 1959.

(Image Credit: Pixabay.)

The bombing of the USS *Arizona* (BB-39) during the Japanese attack on Pearl Harbor on 7 December 1941. The battleship exploded violently and sank, irreparably damaged, with the loss of 1,177 officers and crewmen. A memorial was dedicated to the *Arizona* on 30 May 1962, located above the site of the wreck of the ship's hull.

(Image Credit: Pixabay.)

The engine room of the United States battleship USS *North Carolina* (BB-55), launched on 13 June 1940 and decommissioned on 27 June 1947. The most decorated American battleship of World War II, the *North Carolina* is now a museum ship and memorial situated in Wilmington, North Carolina.

(Image Credit: Pixabay.)

A modern re-enactment of a ship's infirmary, or sickbay, aboard a World War II-era United States aircraft carrier.

(Image Credit: Pixabay.)

The torpedo room of a World War II-era American submarine, including a view of the torpedo tubes, as preserved in a US Fleet Museum at Pearl Harbour, Hawaii.

(Reproduced by kind courtesy of the Simon Beck Collection.)

Douglas SBD-5 Dauntless Bu No 28536, which was used for studio cockpit filming in *The Battle of Midway* (aka *Midway*) which premiered in 1976. It was then restored to airworthy condition as N670AM and flew for the carrier sequences in *War and Remembrance* (1988).

(Image Credit: Pixabay.)

The World War II-era German U-boat (*Unterseeboot*) *U-434*, a Type VII submarine which was launched in 1941, sunk later that year on her first patrol, and subsequently recovered. The *U-434* is now a museum vessel permanently berthed at Hamburg's *U-Bootmuseum*.

(Image Credit: Pixabay.)

The conning tower of a United States Navy submarine, shown penetrating an Arctic ice sheet. This manoeuvre has been popularised by films such as John Sturges's *Ice Station Zebra* (1968).

(Image Credit: Pixabay.)

The Mark 46 torpedo, shown here being used in a naval exercise by the *Arleigh Burke*-class guided missile destroyer USS *Mustin* (DDG-89). The Mark 46 is an aerial torpedo, designed to attack high-performance submarines, and was designed in 1960.

(Image Credit: Pixabay.)

The Convair C-131 Samaritan, an American twin-engined military transport. Produced by Convair from 1954 to 1956, it was the United States Navy and United States Air Force version of the Convair CV-240 family of airliners.

(Image Credit: Pixabay.)

The Grumman C-2A Greyhound and C-2C Hawkeye, twin-engine, high-wing cargo aircraft which were designed to transport supplies, documents and passengers to and from United States Navy aircraft carriers. The C-2A was introduced in 1966.

(Image Credit: Pixabay.)

The USS *Nimitz* (CVN-68), lead ship of her class of supercarriers. A nuclear-powered aircraft carrier in service with the United States Navy, the ship was commissioned on 3 May 1975 and is named after the World War II United States Pacific Fleet Commander, Fleet Admiral Chester W. Nimitz (1885–1966).

(Image Credit: Pixabay.)

The *Nimitz*-class nuclear-powered supercarrier USS *John C. Stennis* (CVN-74). Named in honour of United States Senator John C. Stennis of Mississippi (1901-1995), the ship was commissioned by the United States Navy on 9 December 1995.

(Image Credit: Pixabay.)

The United States Navy's Flight Demonstration Squadron, the Blue Angels, flying McDonnell Douglas F/A-18 Hornets in formation. The F/A-18 was designed by McDonnell Douglas (now Boeing) and Northrop for use by the US Navy and Marine Corps.

(Image Credit: Pixabay.)

The USS *Tennessee* (SSBN-734), a United States Navy *Ohio*-class ballistic missile submarine that was commissioned on 17 December 1988.

(Image Credit: Pixabay.)

The Sikorsky SH-60/MH-60 Seahawk, a twin turboshaft engine, multi-mission helicopter introduced by the United States Navy in 1984.

(From the private photographic collection of Colin M. Barron.)

The Short Seacat (upper) and British Aerospace Seawolf (lower) ship-launched surface-to-air missiles, which were used in the 1982 Falklands War. Argentine forces used the land-based version of the Seacat, the Tigercat, to defend Port Stanley airfield. Photo taken by the author at the Imperial War Museum, Duxford in September 2008.

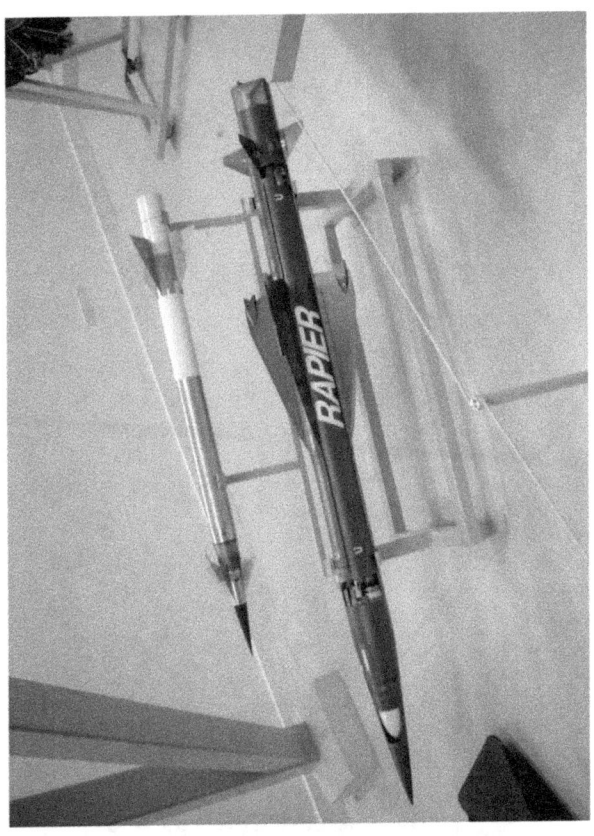

(From the private photographic collection of Colin M. Barron.)

The Blowpipe and Rapier surface-to-air (SAM) missiles, which were used by the British Army in the 1982 Falklands War. Blowpipe was also used by Argentine forces in this conflict and was employed in the SLAM submarine-launched SAM system, which was never used in combat but was featured in *Never Say Never Again* (1983). Photo taken by the author at the Imperial War Museum, Duxford in September 2008.

(From the private photographic collection of Colin M. Barron.)

A 20mm Oerlikon cannon mounted on the *Leander*-class frigate HMS *Danae* (F47). The 20mm Oerlikon gun saw widespread service with the US Navy and the Royal Navy in WW2, and featured in many films in this book including *In Which We Serve* (1942). It was also used in the 1982 Falklands War.

(From the private photographic collection of Colin M. Barron.)

The 20mm Vulcan Phalanx Close-in Weapons System (CIWS) as fitted to HMS *Edinburgh* (D97), a Type 42 destroyer, following the 1982 Falklands War. One of the main lessons of this conflict was that warships needed to have fast-firing computer-controlled guns to shoot down incoming aircraft and missiles.

About the Author

Dr Colin M. Barron was born in Greenock, Scotland in 1956, and was educated at Greenock Academy (1961-74) and Glasgow University (1974-79) where he graduated in Medicine (M.B. Ch.B.) in 1979. He worked for the next five years in hospital medicine, eventually becoming a Registrar in Ophthalmology at Gartnavel General Hospital and Glasgow Eye Infirmary.

In December 1984 he left the National Health Service to set up Ashlea Nursing Home in Callander, which he established with his first wife Sandra and ran until 1999. He was the chairman of the Scottish branch of the British Federation of Care Home Proprietors (BFCHP) from 1985 to 1991, and then a founding member and chairman of the Scottish Association of Care Home Owners (SACHO) from 1991 to 1999.

Colin has a special interest in writing – his first non-fiction book *Running Your Own Private Residential and Nursing Home* was published by Jessica Kingsley Publishers in 1990. He has also written around 150 articles for various publications including *This Caring Business, The Glasgow Herald, Caring Times, Care Weekly, The British Medical Journal, The Hypnotherapist, The Thought Field* and many others. He was a regular columnist for *This Caring Business* between 1991 and 1999.

Colin has always had a special interest in hypnosis and alternative medicine. In 1999 he completed a one-year Diploma course in hypnotherapy and neuro-linguistic programming with the British Society of Clinical and Medical Ericksonian Hypnosis (BSCMEH), an organisation created by Stephen Brooks who was the first person in the UK to teach Ericksonian Hypnosis. He has also trained with the British Society of Medical and Dental Hypnosis (BSMDH) and with Valerie Austin, who is a top Harley Street hypnotherapist. Colin is also a licensed NLP practitioner. In 1992 he was made a Fellow of the Royal Society of Health (FRSH). He is a former member of various societies including the British Society of Medical and Dental Hypnosis - Scotland (BSMDH), the British Thought Field Therapy Association (BTFTA), the Association for Thought Field Therapy (ATFT), the British Complementary Medicine Association (BCMA), and the Hypnotherapy Association.

Colin has been using TFT since early in 2000, and in November 2001 he became the first British person to qualify as a Voice Technology TFT practitioner. He used to work from home in Dunblane and at the Glasgow Nuffield Hospital.

Colin has also had 40 years of experience in public speaking, and did some training with the John May School of Public Speaking in London in January 1990.

In May 2011 his wife Vivien, then 55, collapsed at home due to a massive stroke. Colin then became his wife's carer but continued to see a few hypnotherapy and TFT clients. In late July 2015 Colin suffered a very severe heart attack and was rushed to hospital. Investigation showed that he had suffered a rare and very serious complication of myocardial infarction known as a ventricular septal defect (VSD) - effectively a large hole between the two main pumping chambers of the heart.

Colin had open heart surgery to repair the defect in August 2015, but this first operation was unsuccessful and a second procedure had to be carried out three months later. On 30th November he was finally discharged home after spending four months in hospital.

As a result of his wife's care needs and his own health problems Colin closed down his hypnotherapy and TFT business in April 2016 to concentrate on writing books and looking after his wife.

Colin's books for Extremis Publishing include *The Craft of Public Speaking* (2016), *Planes on Film: Ten Favourite Aviation Films* (2016), *Dying Harder: Action Movies of the 1980s* (2017), and *Battles on Screen: World War II Action Movies* (2017).

His interests include walking, cycling, military history, aviation, plastic modelling, and reading.

For more details about Colin and his work, please visit his website at: **www.colinbarron.co.uk**

Also Available from Extremis Publishing

Battles on Screen
World War II Action Movies

By Colin M. Barron

The Second World War was one of the defining historical events of the Twentieth Century. This global conflict was responsible for enormous trials and great heroism, and the horrors and gallantry that it inspired has formed the basis of some of the most striking movies ever committed to celluloid.

From the author of *Planes on Film*, *Battles on Screen* offers both an analysis and celebration of cinema's engagement with World War II, discussing the actors, the locations, the vehicles and the production teams responsible for bringing these epics to life. Reaching across the decades, the impact and effectiveness of many classic war films are examined in detail, complete with full listings of their cast and crew.

Ranging from the real-life figures and historical events which lay behind many of these features to the behind-the-scenes challenges which confronted the film crews at the time of their production, *Battles on Screen* contains facts, statistics and critical commentary to satisfy even the most stalwart fan of the war movie genre.

Also Available from Extremis Publishing

Planes on Film
Ten Favourite Aviation Films

By Colin M. Barron

One of the most durable genres in cinema, the aviation film has captivated audiences for decades with tales of heroism, bravery and overcoming seemingly insurmountable odds. Some of these movies have become national icons, achieving critical and commercial success when first released in cinemas and still attracting new audiences today.

In *Planes on Film: Ten Favourite Aviation Films*, Colin M. Barron reveals many little-known facts about the making of several aviation epics. Every movie is discussed in comprehensive detail, including a thorough analysis of the action and a complete listing of all the aircraft involved. With information about where the various planes were obtained from and their current location, the book also explores the subject of aviation films which were proposed but ultimately never saw the light of day.

With illustrations and meticulous factual commentary, *Planes on Film* is a book which will appeal to aviation enthusiasts, military historians and anyone who has an interest in cinema. Written by an author with a lifelong passion for aircraft and their depiction on the silver screen, *Planes on Film* presents a lively and thought-provoking discourse on a carefully-chosen selection of movies which have been drawn from right across the history of this fascinating cinematic genre.

Also Available from Extremis Publishing

Dying Harder
Action Movies of the 1980s

By Colin M. Barron

The 1980s were a golden age for action movies, with the genre proving popular at the box-office as never before. Across the world, stars such as Sylvester Stallone, Arnold Schwarzenegger and Bruce Willis were becoming household names as a result of their appearances in some of the best-known films of the decade.

But what were the stories which lay behind the making of these movies? Why were the eighties to bear witness to so many truly iconic action features? And who were the people who brought these legends of action cinema to life?

In *Dying Harder: Action Movies of the 1980s*, Colin M. Barron considers some of the most unforgettable movies of the decade, exploring the reasons behind their success and assessing the extent of their enduring acclaim amongst audiences which continues into the present day.

Also Available from Extremis Publishing

The Craft of Public Speaking

By Colin M. Barron

Public speaking is one of the most important skills in personal and professional life. Yet too often this key ability is neglected, leading to presentations which are dull, uninspired and poorly delivered.

The Craft of Public Speaking examines some of the crucial aptitudes which are fundamental to delivering an effective presentation for listeners. These include preparation, structure and rehearsal, in addition to some of the more overlooked aspects of oration such as the use of visual aids, adding humour, and dressing for success. As well as discussing how to deliver effective live addresses in public settings, the book also covers interview techniques for TV and radio along with how to organise seminars and conferences.

Dr Colin M. Barron has delivered hundreds of lectures and presentations to audiences during a long career, giving speeches on a wide variety of different subjects over many years. In *The Craft of Public Speaking*, he shares the essential knowledge that you will need to become a truly successful public speaker.

Also Available from Extremis Publishing

Tales from the Western Front

By Ed Dixon

Tales from the Western Front is a collection of stories about the people and places encountered by the author during more than three decades of visiting the battlefields, graveyards, towns and villages of France and Belgium.

Characters tragic and comic, famous and humble live within these pages, each connected by the common thread of the Great War. Meet Harry Lauder, the great Scottish entertainer and first international superstar; Tommy Armour, golf champion and war hero; "Hoodoo" Kinross, VC, the Pride of Lougheed; the Winslow Boy; Albert Ball, and Jackie the Soldier Baboon among many others.

Each chapter is a story in itself and fully illustrated with photos past and present.

For details of new and forthcoming books
from Extremis Publishing,
please visit our official website at:

www.extremispublishing.com

or follow us on social media at:

www.facebook.com/extremispublishing

www.linkedin.com/company/extremis-publishing-ltd-/

www.ingramcontent.com/pod-product-compliance
Lightning Source LLC
Chambersburg PA
CBHW070526010526
44118CB00012B/1066